INDUSTRIAL DEVELOPMENT IN INDIA

INDUSTRIAL DEVELOPMENT IN INDIA

(With Special Reference to FDI)

Dr. S. Narasimha Chary

ANMOL PUBLICATIONS PVT. LTD.

NEW DELHI - 110 002 (INDIA)

ANMOL PUBLICATIONS PVT. LTD.
H.O.: 4374/4B, Ansari Road, Darya Ganj
New Delhi-110 002 (India)
Ph.: 23278000, 23261597
B.O.: 1015, Ist Main Road, BSK IIIrd Stage
IIIrd Phase, IIIrd Block
Bangalore - 560 085 (Karnataka)
Ph: 080-41723429, Tel/Fax: 080-2672 3604
Visit us at: www.anmolpublications.com

Industrial Development in India

First Published, 2007

ISBN 978-81-261-3380-2

PRINTED IN INDIA

Printed at Mehra Offset Press, Delhi.

Contents

Forword vi
Preface viii
Acknowledgements x
List of Abbreviations xii
List of Tables xiv
List of Figures and Graphs xvii
1. Overview of Foreign Direct Investment 1
2. Foreign Collaborations in India 92
3. Foreign Direct Investment–Global Perspective 110
4. Aggregate Analysis of FDI in India 173
5. State and Industry-wise Analysis of FDI 214
6. Prospects and Opportunities of FDI 245
7. Impact of FDI on Industrial Development 276
8. Summary of Findings and Suggestions 305
Annexures 321
Bibliography 324
Index 330

Foreword

International financial markets in recent years have been witnessing greater degree of integration in the era of globalization and liberalization. The restrictions on cross-border capital flows have been eased in most of the economies including developing countries. In fact with globalization of markets, International Financial Flows have been outpacing the flow of goods and services among trading countries. A significant development has been the emergence of developing countries as recipients of funds from the international financial markets. In fact timely availability of external finance, particularly by way of foreign direct investment (FDI) in adequate amounts has become indispensable for their sustained economic development.

Since the opening up of the economy in 1991 by the economic reform process, the Government of India recognized the role of foreign capital, more so foreign direct investment in the process of its industrial development. Foreign Direct Investment brings manifold advantages like new capital technology, managerial expertise and access to foreign markets. Sometimes it is also on the negative side; certain aspects which have to be looked into seriously by the Government in having an open door policy for unlimited foreign investments. May be it is here the Government has to bring a policy framework where the negative impact is minimized and the positive impact is broadened.

It is in this context an exhaustive scientific study done by Dr. S. Narasimha Chary on "Industrial Development in India with reference to FDI" is a significant research contribution that analyses the extent of impact of foreign investment on various facets of Indian Industry. This book covers recent changes, developments, trends in FDI at global vis-a-vis Indian context along with its impact on industrial development in India.

Dr. Narasimha Chary has made fact finding study in the context of LPG (Liberalisation, Privatisation and globalization) and succeeded in establishing the status of India. He has shown evidence of critical analysis and logical interpretation of facts and figures. The findings of the study are interesting and the suggestions are useful to all concerned especially to the policy makers. The book, I am sure will provide a right direction to policy makers, Industrialists, and Researchers. The students of MBA, M.Com., MCA, CA, ICWA, and various other University Programmes would find the book highly useful.

I wish the author all the best.

Place: Warangal **(Prof. V. Gopal Reddy)**

Vice-Chancellor

Kakatiya University

Warangal-506009 (A.P.)

Preface

The process of Economic Reforms initiated by the Government in June 1991 has completed 15 years. The reforms have involved opening up the economy, making it more competitive, getting the Government out of the huge morass of regulation, empowering the States to take more responsibility for economic management and thereby creating a kind of competition among them for foreign investment.

The Industrial Policy of 1991 abolished licensing and freed the private corporate sector to undertake investments in a much more congenial environment. The Government has been overbending to woo foreign capital by granting a large number of concessions. Although the official policy spoke of permitting a higher doze of foreign capital in hi-tech and priority areas like power, telecommunications, petroleum refining, etc, in practice the government has been permitting foreign collaborations in industries ranging from strategic and high-tech categories to items of frivolous and luxurious consumption.

In the backdrop of the East Asian crisis, growth did slow down, but India has kept growing and has avoided the worst of the crisis. The two factors that India adopted were quite helpful. Firstly, to keep some limit on the short-term capital inflows and did not go overboard in borrowing short-term funds from abroad. This helped India to avoid the financial crisis of some of its neighbours. Secondly, to maintain the rupee flexibility and the depreciation helped the economy more competitive and growing.

India's neighbours that are relying heavily on FDI, such as China, Indonesia, Malaysia, and Thailand, have been pulling far ahead in economic growth, income levels, and productivity, while also increasing their security and geopolitical influence.

India went through a near disaster in 1991 and implemented the liberalized economic policies. There are number of international investors who would flock to India, especially for them India has become safe heaven for investment. Further, FDI brings huge advantages (new capital, technology, managerial expertise, and access to foreign markets) with little or no negative effect, accordingly, the Government has set an ambitious target of achieving $ 10 billion in actual FDI inflows per year through undertaking new dimensions in FDI policies. For this target to be met, and to invite the foreign investment to India, there is a need for well developed infrastructure. Therefore, an attempt has been made to assess the impact of reforms in FDI on the Indian Economy.

The present study has been carried out by taking into account the various aspects of the flows of FDI at global context, country-wise, state-wise and sector-wise analysis of FDI by considering its Government policy.

Necessary data and information of the sample companies for this study have been collected from the Government Officials, Reports at national and international levels, and websites. Various statistical techniques namely Regression Analysis, Co-efficient Correlation, t-test, F-test, Trend Analysis (Second Degree Parabola), Chi-Square Test have been used in this study to analyse and interpret the data. The entire work has been presented in eight chapters including the summary of findings and suggestions.

(NARASIMHA CHARY. S)

Acknowledgements

I extend my deep sense of gratitude to my teacher and Research Supervisor, Professor V. Gangadhar for the scholarly guidance, meticulous care, discreet care, constructive suggestions, and above all his warm, tender, personal affection, without which this thesis would not have seen the light of the day. I am fortunate to have begun and completed this thesis while Prof. Gangadhar has been the Convener of ICET – 2005. He has been kindly and readily continued to evince keen interest in my research even after his busy schedule. Words will not measure to express my heartfelt gratitude to him.

I am grateful to Prof. V. Gopal Reddy, Vice-Chancellor, Kakatiya University, Warangal for writing the foreword inspite of his busy administrative programmes. I thank Prof. R. Sudarshan, Controller of Examinations, Prof. B. Venkat Ratnam, Head of the Department, Prof. K. Krishna Reddy, Dean, Prof. P. Krishnama Chary, Chairman, Board of Studies (Commerce & Business Mgt.), for their moral support and encouragement.

I express my sincere thanks to Prof. G. Srinivasa Reddy, Principal, University Arts & Science College (Accredited with "A" Grade by the NAAC), Dr. D. Sakriya, Vice-Principal for their continuous encouragement.

I also thank Prof. O. Ghanshyam Das, Incharge Department, Prof. S. Ravi Prakash, Prof. M.S. Sarma, Dr. K. Sayulu, Dr. Ch. Bhagawan Rao, Dr. K. Raji Reddy, Dr. T. Balaraju, Dr. P. Amaraveni, Dr. K. Rajender, Mr. G. Naresh, and other friends Dr. P. Karunakar Rao, Dr. Peddi Venkataiah,

A. Maheshwar Rao, Sriman, Rahaman for their kind cooperation and help during the course of the study.

I am thankful to the Kakatiya University authorities for providing the research facilities.

I am extremely indebted to my beloved wife Mrs. Kavitha and my children Nitish Chandra and Nikitha, my brother Udaya Shankar my uncle Sri N. Vishwanatham, co-brother Jyothy Raju, Pavan and my parents for their patience and cooperation throughout the research period.

Narasimha Chary S.

List of Abbreviations

ADRs	:	American Depository Receipts
ADS	:	American Depository Shares
ASSOCHAM	:	Associated Chamber of Commerce and Industry of India
CEE	:	Central and Eastern European
CCEA	:	Cabinet Committee on Economic Affairs
CCFI	:	Cabinet Committee on Foreign Investment
EOUs	:	Export Oriented Units
EPZ	:	Export Processing Zone
ECBs	:	External Commercial Borrowings
FERA	:	Foreign Exchange Regulation Act
FTCs	:	Foreign Technology Cases
FTZ	:	Free Trade Zone
FCCBs	:	Foreign Currency Convertible Bonds
FII	:	Foreign Institutional Investment
FIPL	:	Foreign Investment Promotion Law
FDI	:	Foreign Direct Investment
FC	:	Foreign Collaboration
FTCs	:	Foreign Technology Collaborations
FIPB	:	Foreign Investment Promotion Board
FIIA	:	Foreign investment Implementation Authority
GDRs	:	Global Depository Receipts
GDP	:	Gross Domestic Product
GFCF	:	Gross Fixed Capital Formation
LAC	:	Latin America and the Caribbean

MNCs	:	Multi National Corporations
M&As	:	Mergers and Acquisitions
MIGA	:	Multilateral Investment Guarantee Agency
NBFCs	:	Non Banking Financial Companies
NRIs	:	Non Resident Indians
NIBM	:	National Institute of Bank Management
ODA	:	Official Development Assistance
OECD	:	Organisation for Economic Co-operation and Development
RBI	:	Reserve Bank of India
SIA	:	Secretariat for Industrial Assistance
SEZs	:	Special Economic Zones
TPS	:	Technology Policy Statement
UNCTAD	:	United Nations Conference on Trade and Development
WBES	:	World Business Environment Survey

List of Tables

1.1	Component-wise Revised FDI	48
1.2	Foreign Direct Investment outflows	49
2.1	Foreign Collaborations in India during 1991-2004	98
2.2	Component-wise number of Foreign Collaboration Approvals	100
2.3	Industry-wise Distribution of Foreign Collaboration Approvals	102
3.1	Selected Indicators of FDI and International Production 1982-2003	112
3.2	Global Inflows of FDI by Host Region 1991-2003	114
3.2a	Empirical Results – Global Inflows of FDI	118
3.3	Global Outflows of FDI – by Host Region 1991-2003	120
3.4	Number of Countries with Declines in FDI Inflows – 2002	131
3.4a	FDI Inflows to Major Economies 2001 and 2002	135
3.4b	World FDI Inflows – top 5 Countries	136
3.5	Inward FDI Performance Index by Region 1988-2003	141
3.6	Ranking by Inward FDI Performance Index 2001-2003	143
3.7	Inward FDI Potential Index, by Group of Economies 1998-2002	145
3.8	Top 25 Rankings by the Inward FDI Potential Index 1988-2002	146
3.9	Outward FDI Performance Index for the 20 leading Investor Economies 1998-2003	148
3.10	Developed Countries: FDI Inflows – top 10 Countries 2002-2003	151

3.11	Developed Countries: FDI Outflows – top 10 2002 and 2003	152
3.12	Africa: Top 10 recipients of FDI Inflows 2002 and 2003	155
3.13	Asia and The Pacific: top 10 recipients of FDI inflows 2002 and 2003	157
3.14	FDI Outflows as a percentage of GFCF in selected Developing Economies 2001-03	161
3.15	LAC: top 10 recipients of FDI Inflows 2002 and 2003	163
3.16	CEE: top 10 recipients of FDI Inflows 2002-03	167
4.1	Component-wise Amount of Foreign Direct Investment Approvals 1991-2004	183
4.2	Chi-Square Test results	185
4.3	Approvals of Country-wise FDI During 1991-2004	186
4.4	Trend Values of year-wise Approvals of FDI	195
4.5	Country-wise FDI & (FTCs) Approved January-August 2004	196
4.6	FDI in India: Approvals and Actual Inflows 1991-2004	199
4.7	Year-wise Inflows of Foreign Direct Investment 1991-2004	203
4.8	FDI Inflows in Selected Asian Countries	211
5.1	State-wise Foreign Direct Investment Approved during Aug. 1991-Aug. 2004	216
5.2	Sector-wise Foreign Direct Investment & FTCs Approved 1991-2004	221
5.3	Sector-wise Total Inflows of FDI during Jan. 1991-March 2004	242
7.1	Gross Domestic Product at Factor Cost by Industry Origin	283
7.2	Correlation Result of FDI and the GDP at factor Cost by Industry of Origin	284
7.3	Foreign Capital Inflows and Exports during 1991-2004	287

7.4	Relationship between Foreign Capital and Exports of Indian Industry	288
7.5	ANOVA – Foreign Capital Vs. Exports	289
7.6	Sources of Accretion to Foreign Exchange Reserves 1991-2004	290
7.7	Foreign Investment Inflows and Foreign Exchange Reserves 1991-2004	291
7.8	Relation between FDI and FOREX Reserves	292
7.9	ANOVA – FDI Vs. FOREX Reserves	293
7.10	Foreign Investment Inflows and Balance of Payments in India 1996-2003	297
7.11	Relation between FDI and BOP	298
7.12	ANOVA – FDI and BoP	299
7.13	Employment Elasticities in Major Sectors in India	301
7.14	Employment by Sectors	302

List of Figures and Graphs

3.1 Top 20 recipients of FDI Inflows 2002 and 2003 117

3.1a Trend of Global Inflows of FDI (Second Degree Parabola) 119

3.2 Top 20 Economies for Outward FDI 2002 and 2003 121

3.3 Percentage Distribution of World FDI Inflows 1992-2003 127

3.4 Total Resource Flows to Developing Countries, by type of Flow, 1990-2002 129

3.5 FDI Inflows, Private Domestic Investment and Public Investment in Developing Countries and Central and Eastern Europe, 1990-2000 130

3.6 The 30 Economies Most Affected by the Downturn, 2002 133

3.7 World's top 30 FDI Recipients, 2002 134

3.8 Inward FDI Flows, by Sector, 1999-2000 and 2001 137

3.9 Type-wise FDI Inflows, 1990-2002 138

3.10 FDI Inflows in Developed Countries: 2002 and 2003 151

3.11 FDI Outflows in Developed Countries: 2002 and 2003 152

3.12 FDI Inflows in Africa : 2002and 2003 155

3.13 FDI Inflows in Asia and The Pacific: 2002 and 2003 157

3.14 FDI Inflows in LAC – 2002 and 2003 163

3.15 FDI Inflows in CEE: 1998-2003 166

3.16 CEE: top 10 Recipients of FDI Inflows 2002 and 2003 167

4.1 Foreign Direct Investment Approved 1991-2004 (top 10 Investors in India) 192

4.2 Country-wise share in Approvals 1991-2004 193

4.3 Linear Trend by the Method of Least Square 195

5.1 State-wise Approvals of FDI: 1991-2004 217

5.2 Sector-wise share in Approvals of FDI during 1991-2004 225

1

Overview of Foreign Direct Investment

1.1 Introduction

Economic development necessitates availability of natural resources like land, water, adequate levels of savings and its transformation into investments; skilled labour force and entrepreneurship; technical knowledge, etc. A developing economy may have a relatively low level of savings, an unskilled labour force, limited entrepreneurship and lack of technical knowledge to exploit its natural resources for economic development. Most of the underdeveloped countries suffer from low level of income and low level of capital accumulation. In such circumstances, it might seek assistance of countries which are economically better developed in terms of technology, labour skills, entrepreneurship, savings and investments. Assistance from other countries might flow in the form of investment. It may be from foreign Governments, foreign private companies or international financial institutions. However, despite the shortage of capital, the countries have developed a strong urge for industrialization and economic development.

In India, private foreign investment has been predominant. Though Government of India has always welcomed foreign investment with certain restrictions, the Government policy towards Foreign Investment has undergone remarkable changes, since independence, from time to time. Economic policy reforms have played a critical role in the performance of the Indian Economy since 1991. Among other things, the reforms have involved opening up the economy, making it more competitive, empowering the states to take more responsibility for economic management and thereby creating a kind of competition among them for foreign investment.

For accelerating the pace of growth and development of a developing country, capital flows have become a necessity and, therefore, almost all the developing countries, have been trying hard to attract more capital flows. Further, these countries have rightly realised that assigning great role to private sector has become the need of the hour. Since the beginning of 1980s', capital flows to the developing countries have started gaining momentum and by the end of 1980s', there had been an enormous increase in the volume of capital flows to such countries.

1.2 Need for Foreign Investment

If backward and underdeveloped countries interested in rapid economic development, it will have to import machinery, technical know-how, entrepreneurship, and foreign investment. One of the methods of paying for the imports is to set up exports or second alternative of getting foreign technology and equipment, and it also depends upon foreign assistance in some forms or the other. Most countries of the world, which embarked on the road to economic development, had to depend on foreign capital to some extent. The fact cannot be denied that the foreign capital contributed in many important ways to the process of economic growth and industrialization. The need for foreign capital for a developing country like India can arise on account of the following reasons:

(a) Domestic capital is inadequate for purposes of

economic growth and it is necessary to invite foreign capital.

(b) Since the underdeveloped countries want to industrialize themselves within a short period of time, it becomes necessary to raise the level of investment substantially. This requires, in turn, a high level of savings. However, because of general poverty of masses, the savings are often very low. Hence, emerges a resource gap between investment and savings. This gap has to be filled up through foreign capital.

(c) The underdeveloped countries have very low level of technology as compared to the advanced countries. This raises the necessity for importing technology from the developed countries. Such technology usually comes with foreign capital when it assumes the form of private foreign investment or foreign collaboration.

(d) Foreign capital brings with it other scarce productive factors, such as technical know-how, business experience and knowledge, which are equally essential for economic development.

(e) The underdeveloped countries need much larger imports than the exports in the initial phase of economic development in the balance of payments position. As a result, the balance of payments generally turns adverse. This creates a gap between the earnings and expenditure of foreign exchange. Foreign capital presents a short-run solution to the problem.

Supporters of private foreign investment argue that the foreign investment brings with it new technology, better management and organization, superior marketing and sometimes cheaper finance. The arguments in favour of private foreign investment are the following:

(a) Foreign investment constitutes a net addition to

investible resources in host countries, and as such raises their rates of growth;

(b) Foreign investment results in a pattern of growth which is desirable from the point of view of underdeveloped countries since new products are introduced and marketed, new tastes are created, and specific needs of the host country are met; and

(c) Free flow of capital is conductive for the welfare of both total world and each individual country. The operations of foreign firms, especially of modern multinational firms, especially of modern multinational firms, knit countries together and closer into the web of international commerce, both by (vertical and horizontal) economic integration and by the transmission of tastes, designs, ideas and technology.[1]

1.3 Concepts of FDI

The Foreign Investment in India may be classified broadly into two types, namely Foreign Direct Investment (FDI) and Foreign Portfolio Investment (FPI).

Foreign Direct Investment—Definitions

Foreign Direct Investment (FDI) contributes directly and indirectly in building national capabilities. FDI is considered the best complement to domestic investment to bridge the gap between the investment needs of the country and its savings. FDI has long term and substantial developmental impact on the country's economy. FDI helps transfer and upgrade technology, improves skills and managerial capabilities; provides competitive edge to country's exports; improves efficiency and quality of services and goods; and helps create additional jobs.

Foreign Direct Investment (FDI) is the outcome of the mutual interests of multinational firms and host countries.

FDI is generally defined as a form of long-term international capital movement, made for the purpose of productive activity and accompanied by the intention of managerial control or participation in the management of a foreign firm.

- According to the International Monetary Fund, FDI is defined as "Investment that is made to acquire a lasting interest in an enterprise operating in an economy other than that of the investor. The investor's purpose is being to have an effective voice in the management of the enterprise".[2] It should not be confused with portfolio investment, which does not seek management control, but is motivated by profit. Portfolio Investment occurs when individual investors invest, mostly through stockbrokers, in stocks of foreign companies in foreign land in search of profit opportunities.
- The essence of Foreign Direct Investment is the transmission to the host country of a package of capital, managerial, skill and technical knowledge. It is an investment made to acquire a lasting interest in foreign enterprise with the purpose of having an effective voice in its management. FDI may take the form of purchase of securities in a foreign corporation, existing or formed, for the purpose, but its essence is control. Control is sought for the purpose of squeezing all the rent, in a Ricardian sense, out of a given advantage, often one technology, sometimes is the capacity of a vertically integrated company, stretching across national boundaries, to coordinate separate stages of production and distribution more efficiently than the automatic competitive market can.
- FDI refers to investment in a foreign country where the investor retains control over the investment. It typically takes the form of starting a subsidiary,

acquiring a stake in an existing firm or starting a joint venture in the foreign country.

- Foreign Direct Investment (FDI) is defined as an investment involving a long-term relationship and reflecting a lasting interest and control of a resident entity in one economy (foreign direct investor or parent enterprise) in an enterprise resident in an economy other than that of the foreign direct investor (FDI enterprise or affiliate enterprise or foreign affiliate).[3] Foreign Direct Investment implies that the investor exerts a significant degree of influence on the management of the enterprise resident in the other economy. Such investment involves both the initial transactions between the two entities and all subsequent transactions between them and among foreign affiliates, both incorporated and unincorporated. Individuals as well as business entities may undertake foreign Direct Investment.

  Foreign-direct-investment inflows and outflows comprise capital provided (either directly or through other related enterprises) by a foreign direct investor to a FDI enterprise, or capital received from a FDI enterprise by a foreign direct investor. Flows of FDI comprise capital provided by a foreign direct investor to an FDI enterprise, or capital received from an FDI enterprise by a foreign direct investor.

- United Nations Conference on Trade and Development (UNCTAD)'s World Investment Report[4] defined Foreign Direct Investment (FDI) as "International Investment that reflects the objective of a resident entity in one economy (Foreign Direct Investor or Parent enterprise) obtaining a 'Lasting Interest' and control in an enterprise resident in an economy other than that of the foreign direct investor. 'Lasting Interest' implies the existence of a long-term relationship between a direct investor and the enterprise and a significant degree of influence on the management of the enterprise.[5]

- According to IMF guidelines, FDI is defined as "a source of capital funds from host country's point of view as it need not necessarily imply immediate addition to plant and machinery or stock.[6]

1.4 Characteristics of FDI

The following are the positive characteristics of Foreign Direct Investment (FDI):

1. Foreign investment can fill the gap between desired investment and locally mobilized savings. Local capital markets are often not well developed. Thus, they cannot meet the capital requirements for large investment projects. Besides, access to the hard currency needed to purchase investment goods not available locally can be difficult. FDI solves both these problems at once, as it is a direct source of external capital. It can fill desired foreign exchange requirements and those derived from net export earnings.
2. Foreign investment can supply a package of needed resources such as management experience, entrepreneurial abilities, organizational and technological skills. Foreign investment brings with it technological knowledge while transferring machinery and equipment to developing countries. Production units in developing countries use outdated equipment and techniques that can reduce the productivity of workers and lead to the production of goods of a lower standard. The ability of domestic producers to compete abroad for export markets are

reduced which, in turn, contributes to the difficulties of the developing countries to earn hard currencies. FDI can solve this problem because investment goods generally embody advanced technology.

3. Foreign investment can create employment in the modern sectors of developing countries.
4. It can benefit consumers in Low-developed Countries (LDCs) through lower prices/improved quality of goods and through new products.
5. Foreign investment can stimulate domestic investment through forward and backward linkages. For example, output of a foreign firm can be an input of domestic industries. Similarly, output of the domestic industries can be inputs for the foreign firms. If this is so, foreign firms create demand for industries producing goods purchased by them.

Some of the negative characteristics are:

- Foreign Investment contributed to guide under development of India by concentrating on the production and export of raw materials and foodstuffs.
- It went into sectors, which catered to foreign markets and not Indians home market.
- The multiplier effects in terms of income, employment, capital; technical knowledge and growth of external economies of these investments were largely exported backs to developed countries.

1.5 Significance of Foreign Direct Investment

Foreign Investment is playing an increasing role in economic development. Economic reforms and policy changes encouraging foreign investment in many countries – both the developed and developing (including the erstwhile communist and socialist) – in the 1980s favoured a surge in international investment flows.

As countries began to welcome foreign direct investment and transacting business over long distances grew easier, companies were motivated to reorganize their activities, and they sliced up the value-added chain and established production facilities in different markets. This proliferation of production networks has allowed firms to specialise, focus their research efforts, and leverage their core managerial and marketing skills; it has also reinforced the openness, resulting from trade liberalization and the removal of barriers to capital mobility.[7]

Even with these changes, globalization might not have taken of were it not for seismic shift in attitudes. Countries worldwide have moved to market based economies and democratic forms of government. This broadening of political participation is feeding centrifugal pressure within nation.[8]

Foreign investment has assisted and is assisting the economic growth of many countries. As the World Development Report, 1991, points out, for the developing countries FDI has several advantages over the official development assistance (ODA).[9]

- FDI shifts the burden of risk of an investment from domestic to foreign investors.
- Repayments are linked to profitability of the underlying investment, whereas under debt financing the borrowed funds must be served regardless of the project costs.
- Further, it has also been observed that FDI is the only capital inflow that has been strongly associated with higher GDP growth since 1970.

The fact that the ratio of FDI flow to domestic investment

(gross capital formation) rose for most developed and developing countries highlight the contribution of FDI to economic growth in the past. Although the bulk of the FDI goes to developed countries, its share in their gross fixed capital formation (GFCF) is only about half of that in developing countries because of the massiveness of their GFCF.

Apart from potential gains though technology transfer, FDI has generated large employment opportunities in a number of countries, accounting for as much as 60 percent of manufacturing employment in some countries such as Singapore.[10]

Addressing a session on infrastructure at the seminar on 'moving to the market: sustaining reforms in India and Asia,' organized by the Confederation of Indian Industry (CII) and Asian Society in New Delhi on March 9, 1997, Gordon Wu has observed that foreign investment brings four 'E's – efficiency, equity, experience and expertise. In return, there is a fifth 'E'—expatriation of profits.

Another contribution of FDI is that it provides the much-needed foreign exchange to help bridge the balance of trade deficit. Indeed, in the wake of the debt crisis, FDI has come to be viewed as an increasingly important source of external finance for developing countries.

A much more important contribution of FDI lies in raising the technological standards and levels of efficiency and competitiveness of the host country. This can occur in several ways. FDI brings with it complementary assets such as technology, management and organizational competence and there are spillover effects of these assets on the rest of the economy. As the foreign-owned enterprise comes into competition with the local firms, the latter categories of enterprises are forced to improve their technology and standards of product quality. Further, the foreign-owned enterprises pressurizes and assists the local related and support industries to improve the quality of their products and ensure greater reliability of delivery, both of which make it necessary for the related and support industries to upgrade their technology.

Another benefit of FDI is that it helps the host country improve its export performance. By raising the level of efficiency and the standards of product quality, FDI makes a positive impact on the host country's export competitiveness. Further, because of the international linkages of transnational corporations (TNCs), FDI provides to the host country better access to foreign markets. Also, where the foreign investment has been made with the specific intention of sourcing parts/components (or even final products) from the host country to take advantage of low cost conditions there (e.g. low wages), FDI contributes to exports directly.

It is needless to add here that enhanced export possibility contributes to the growth of the host economies by relaxing demand side constraints on growth. This is especially important for those countries, which have a small domestic market and must increase exports vigorously to maintain their tempo of economic growth.

In judging the significance of FDI, especially from the viewpoint of developing countries, it is useful to make a distinction between macro-economic and micro-economic effects. The former is connected with issues of domestic capital formation, balance of payments, and taking advantage of external markets for achieving faster growth, while the latter is connected with the issues of cost reduction, product quality improvement, making changes in industrial structure and developing global inter-firm linkages.

In this context, it needs to be recognized that FDI is an aggregate entity, the sum total of the investments made by many diverse multinationals, each with its own corporate strategy. The micro-economic effects of the investment made by one multinational may be quite different from that of another multinational even if the investments are made in the same industry. Also, what benefits the local economy will be able to reap from the investments depends among other factors on the capabilities of the host country in regard to technology transfer and industrial restructuring.

1.6 Components of Foreign Direct Investment

There are three components of FDI, namely, equity capital, reinvested earnings and intra-company loans.

1. Equity capital is the foreign direct investor's purchase of shares of an enterprise in a country other than his own country.
2. Reinvested earnings comprise the direct investor's share (in proportion to direct equity participation) of earnings not distributed as dividends by affiliated or earnings not remitted to the direct investor. Such retained profits by affiliates are re-invested.
3. Intra-company loans or intra-company debt transactions refer to short- or long-term borrowing and lending of funds between direct investors (parent enterprises) and affiliate enterprises.

It may be noted that Government of India used to exclude reinvested earnings from the estimation of FDI in India. Government sources have, however, indicated that Government would redefine FDI including reinvested earnings also. If the investor has only a sort of property interest in investing the capital in buying equities, bonds, or other securities abroad, it is referred to as "Portfolio Investment". In the portfolio investments the investor uses his capital in order to get a return on it, but has no much control over the use of the capital. Portfolio investment is "the investment by individuals, firms, or public bodies (like governments or government organizations) in financial instruments (such as stocks and government bonds)". FDI are governed by long-term considerations because these investments cannot be easily liquidated. Hence, factors like long-term political stability, government policy; industrial and economic prospects etc. influence the FDI decision.

Revised Coverage of FDI

In the recent past, there have been discussions in various foray regarding the coverage of foreign direct investment (FDI) statistics in India, which mainly include equity capital, *vis-à-vis* the data published by some other countries which include equity capital, reinvested earnings (retained earnings of FDI companies) and other capital (inter-corporate debt transaction between related entities).

In an effort to bring the reporting system of FDI data in India into alignment with international best practices, the Department of Industrial Policy and Promotion (DIPP), Ministry of Commerce and Industry, Government of India (GoI), in consultation with RBI, constituted a committee in May 2002 comprising officials from RBI and DIPP to study this issue. The Committee studied the relevant conceptual and methodological issues and identified the data gaps involved in order to make necessary recommendations for strengthening the collection, compilation and reporting of FDI data. The Committee submitted its Report in October 2002 recommending that the FDI statistics should include, besides equity capital, 'reinvested earnings' (retained earnings of FDI companies) and 'other direct capital' (inter-corporate debt transactions between related entities) in accordance with the international best practices. The Committee also recommended that the steps be taken jointly by RBI and DIPP to expand the coverage of FDI statistics in India.

As a follow-up action to the submission of FDI Compilation Report, a Technical Monitoring Group (TMG) with representatives from RBI, DIPP, Department of Economic Affairs (DEA), Department of Company Affairs (DCA) and National Informatics Centre (NIC) was constituted by DIPP in November 2002, for speedy implementation of the recommendations made by the above Committee. The main focus of the TMG was to identify various components of FDI, which are operationally feasible and capture these components in a specified institutional framework and within a specified time period. TMG submitted its first Action Taken Report on June 27, 2003.[11]

Proposed Coverage of FDI to India

After reviewing the international best practices as also some select country experiences, the TMG concluded that inclusion of the following *fourteen* items in Indian FDI data under three major heads would, by and large, comply with the reporting system in line with international best practices.

A. Equity Capital

1. Equity capital of unincorporated entities;
2. Non-cash acquisition against technology transfer, plant and machinery, goodwill, business development and similar considerations;
3. Control premium;
4. Non-competition fees.

B. Reinvested Earnings

1. Reinvested earnings of incorporated entities;
2. Reinvested earnings of unincorporated entities;
3. Reinvested earnings of indirectly held direct investment enterprises.

C. 'Other Capital'

1. Short-term and long-term inter-corporate borrowings;
2. Trade credit;
3. Suppliers credit;
4. Financial leasing;
5. Financial derivatives;
6. Debt securities; and
7. Land and buildings.

Against this background, RBI and DIPP jointly decided to expand the coverage of data on FDI, both inflow and outflow for 2000-01 and 2001-02. The revised data on FDI include all items indicated under *equity capital* (except non-cash acquisitions). The equity capital of unincorporated entities (Item no. 1 above) includes the equity capital of foreign banks' branches in India. All items under the *reinvested earnings* have been included except reinvested earnings of indirectly held direct investment enterprises. Data under 'Other Capital' relate to short-term and long-term borrowing, trade credit (more than 180 days), suppliers' credit (more than 180 days), and financial leasing. Thus, in this exercise, out of fourteen items stated above, the FDI data do not include the following *six* items *viz;* (i) non-cash acquisitions, (ii) reinvested earnings of indirectly held direct investment enterprises, (iii) short-term trade credit, (iv) financial derivatives, (v) debt securities and (vi) land & buildings. The TMG is exploring the feasibility of including these items in future.

The flow of direct foreign investment to India has been comparatively limited because of the type of industrial development strategy and the very cautious foreign investment policy followed by the nation.

Foreign Direct Investment in India was adversely affected by the following factors:

- The public sector was assigned a monopoly or dominant position in the most important industries and, therefore, the scope of private investment, both domestic and foreign, was limited.
- When the public sector enterprises needed foreign technology or investment, there was a marked preference for the foreign government sources.
- Government policy towards foreign capital was very selective. Foreign investment was normally permitted only in high technology industries in priority areas and in export oriented industries.
- Foreign equity participation was normally subject to a ceiling of 40 per cent, although exceptions were allowed on merit.
- Payments of dividends abroad, repatriation of capital, etc., as well as inward remittances were subject to stringent laws like the Foreign Exchange Regulation Act (FERA), 1973. These discouraged foreign investment.
- Corporate taxation was high and tax laws and procedures were complex.

All these factors either restricted the scope of or discouraged the foreign investment in India.

1.7 Theories of Foreign Investment

The theories of foreign investment seek to explain the reasons for foreign investment. A brief account of the important theories, which attempt to explain the foreign investment, is given below.

1.7.1 Theory of Capital Movements (Hymer-Kindleberger Theory)

The earliest theoreticians, who assumed, in the classical tradition the existence of a perfectly competitive market, considered foreign investments as a form of factor movement to take advantage of the differential profit.

According to the Hymer-Kindleberger[12] theory (Kindleberger, 1969), the foreign-owned firm would make an investment in the host country only if it possesses some compensating advantage which allows it to compete on equal terms with indigenous firms. This is, however, not a sufficient condition for FDI since the firm has the option of licensing the advantage (technology) tan indigenous producer or exporting the product to the host country. Clearly, certain other conditions have to be satisfied for FDI to arise. Three such conditions are: (a) the advantage is internally transferable (it can be exploited by a subsidiary of the parent firm without any additional cost to the parent firm or to the subsidiaries already exploiting it), (b) it is more profitable for the foreign-owned firm to exploit the advantage itself than to license it to an indigenous producer (because of imperfections in the market for knowledge and heavy firm to firm transfer costs of the advantage), and (c) exporting the product to the host country is not possible or unprofitable due to tariff or transport cost barriers.

1.7.2. Market Imperfections Theory

One of the important market imperfection approaches to the explanation of the foreign investments is the "Monopolistic Advantage Theory", propounded by Stephen in 1960. According to this theory, foreign direct investment occurred largely in oligopolistic industries rather than in industries operating under near perfect competition. Hymer suggested that the decision of a firm to invest in foreign markets was based on certain advantages the firm possessed over the local firms (in the foreign country) such as economies of scale, superior technology or skills in the fields of management, production, marketing and finance.

Kindleberger also argued that market imperfections were the basis of foreign investment.

The Market Imperfections Theory does not answer several questions related to foreign investment. For example, why does a firm prefer foreign investment to other alternative market entry modes like exporting, licensing, franchising, etc.?

1.7.3. Internalization Theory

According to the Internalization Theory, which is an extension of the Market Imperfections Theory, foreign investment results from the decision of a firm to internalize a superior knowledge (i.e., keeping the knowledge within the firm to maintain the competitive edge)? For example, if a firm decides to externalize its know how by licensing a foreign firm, the firm (the licensor) does not make any foreign investment in this respect but, on the other hand, if the firm decides to internalize it may invest abroad in production facilities.

Methods of internalization include formal ways like patents and copyrights and informal ways like secrecy and family networks.

A more general theory of TNCs traces their emergence to internalization of markets (Buckley and Casson, 1991). The theory is based on three simple postulates:

- Firms maximize profits in a world of imperfect markets;
- When markets in intermediate products are imperfect there is an incentive to bypass them by creating internal markets (within the firm); and
- Internationalization of markets across national boundaries generates MNEs.

It is argued that the location strategy of a vertically

integrated firm is determined mainly by the interplay of comparative advantage, barriers to trade and regional incentives to internalize; the firm will be multinational whenever these factors make it optimal to locate different stages of production in different countries.

Another prediction of this theory is that unless transport costs are very low, returns to scale at the plant level are high, or the comparative advantage of one location is very significant. the international acquisition and exploitation of knowledge will normally involve international production through a world-wide network of basically similar plants. Following this theory, one can see an important difference between the MNEs operating in the early part of this century and those, which emerged in the later part of the century. It is argued that prior to the Second World War multinational was a by-product of the internalization of intermediate product markets in multi-stage production process, and in the post-war period it is a by-product of internalization of markets in knowledge.

1.7.4. Appropriability Theory

According to the Appropriability Theory, a firm should be able to appropriate (to keep for its exclusive use) the benefits resulting from a technology it has generated. If this condition were not satisfied, the firm would not be able to bear research and development. MNCs tend to specialise in developing new technologies, which are transmitted efficiently through their internal channels.

It is obvious that the Appropriability Theory is similar to the internalization theory in terms of creating an internal market (internal channels) for exploiting the firm's specific advantages.

1.7.5. Location Specific Advantage Theory

The Location Specific Advantage Theory suggests that foreign investment be pulled by certain location specific advantages. According to Hood and Young, there are four factors, which are pertinent to the Location Specific Theory. They are:

- Labour costs
- Marketing factors (like market size, market growth, and stage of development and local competition)
- Trade barriers
- Government policy

The above factors have, of course, very important bearing on foreign investment. However, there are also other factors like cultural factors, which influence foreign investment. Further, it is the total cost, and not labour cost alone that is important.

1.7.6. International Product Life Cycle Theory

According to the Product Life Cycle Theory developed by Raymound Vernon and Lewis T. Wells, the production of a product shifts to different categories of countries through the different stages of the product life cycle.

According to this theory a new product is first manufactured and marketed in a developed country like the U.S. (because of favourable factors like large domestic market, entrepreneurship and ease of organizing production). It is then exported to other developed markets. As a competition increases in these markets, manufacturing facilities are established there to cater to these markets and also to export to the developing countries. As the product becomes standardized and competition further intensifies, manufacturing facilities are established in developing countries to lower production costs and due to other reasons. The developed country markets may also be serviced by exports from the production units in the developing countries.

1.7.7. Eclectic Theory

Dunning's eclectic theory of international production (Dunning, 1988) explains both the ways in which overseas markets are served by enterprises of different nationalities and the industrial and geographical composition of such activities. According to this theory, a firm will make a direct investment in a foreign country if the following three conditions are satisfied:

- it possesses some ownership advantages vis-à-vis firms of other nationality in serving particular markets;
- it is more beneficial for the firm to use the advantages itself than to sell or lease them to foreign firms, and
- It is profitable for the enterprise to utilise these advantages in conjunction with at least some factor inputs outside the home country.

The greater the ownership advantage of the enterprise, the more the incentive to exploit these them. The more the economies of production and marketing favour a foreign location, the greater is the inducement for FDI.

The eclectic theory suggests that all forms of international production can be explained by reference to the above conditions. Location specific or country specific advantages have an important bearing on FDI; such advantages of particular host countries make FDI in them preferable to not only other potential host countries, but also domestic investment. It needs to be recognized further that an important determinant of FDI is the ability of the firm to generate ownership advantages, which are best, exploited by the firm in a foreign rather than in a domestic location. In this way, the eclectic theory is able to provide an explanation for differences in the industrial pattern of outward FDI of different industrialized countries.

While the eclectic theory provides a good explanation for the decisions of firms to invest abroad, it seems to us that the theory does not cover the competitive FDI induced by trade restrictions. When a country imposes restrictions on imports of a particular industrial product, there is obviously inducement to multinational firms of the industry to invest in that country. If one or two firms invest, the others must also do so to counter competition and ensure their market share even if the returns to investment are negligible or negative, particularly for late entrants. Some FDI in the US and Europe are of this variety. Also, multinationals may enter a market today even if it is not profitable to do so, because they foresee the future growth and want to have the first entrant's advantage.

1.8 Factors affecting Foreign Investment

The theories of foreign investment described above have indicated several possible reasons for foreign investment. This section is a further extension of the important factors affecting foreign investment.

1. *Rate of Interest*: One of the most important stimuli to foreign capital movements is the difference in the rate of interest prevailing at different places. Other things i.e. interest rates or foreign exchange rates being equal, capital has a tendency to move from a country with a low rate of interest to a country where it is higher.

2. *Speculation*: Short-term capital movements may be influenced by speculation pertaining to anticipated changes in the interest rates or foreign exchanges rates.

3. *Profitability*: Private foreign capital movement is influenced by the profit motive. Hence, other things being equal, private capital will be attracted to countries where the return on investment is comparatively higher.

4. *Costs of Production*: Private capital movements are encouraged by lower costs of production in foreign countries. As Kreinin[13] points out, we may distinguish between two types of cost reducing investment. The first arises from the need to obtain raw materials from abroad. Such materials may be either unavailable at home or obtainable only at extremely high costs, but they are essential for the production and sale of final products at home or abroad. Without them profit opportunities would remain unexploded. Indeed, vast investments in the extractive industries are motivated by the fact that the capital must go where the resources are. The second type of cost-reducing investment pertains to costs of commodities other than materials, primarily labour.

5. *Economic Conditions*: Economic conditions, particularly the market potential and infrastructural facilities, influence private foreign investment. The size of the population and the income level of a country have an important bearing on the market opportunities.

6. *Government Policies*: Government Policies, particularly towards foreign investment, foreign collaboration, remittances, profits, taxation, foreign exchange control, tariffs and monetary, fiscal and other incentives, are important factors that may influence foreign investment in a country.

7. *Political Factors*: Political factors like political stability, nature of important political parties and relations with other countries also influence capital movements.

The United Nations Commission for Asia and the Far East has drawn up the following list of conditions that have to be met if foreign capital is to be attracted to underdeveloped countries.

- Political stability and freedom from external aggression.

- Security of life and property.
- Reasonable opportunities for earning profit.
- Prompt payment of fair and transferable compensation in case of nationalization of a foreign owned enterprise.
- Guarantee of the possibility of remittance of profits, dividends and interest, as well as of a reasonable depreciation allowance on the capital invested.
- Facilities for immigration and employment of foreign technical and administrative personnel/
- A system of taxation that does not impose a crushing burdens on private enterprise.
- Freedom from double taxation.
- Non-discriminatory treatment of foreigners in the administration of existing controls.
- Absence of competition between State-owned enterprises and private foreign capital.
- A general spirit of friendliness toward foreign investors.

1.9 The Government of Indias Policy Towards Foreign Capital

The predominance of capital over other factors in the production process has been ever increasing due to fast technological changes during the second half of twentieth century. There are many countries in the world, which are capital surplus, while there are many others, which are facing the shortage of capital to exploit the resources available in the country. To remove this constraint, the need for foreign investment is very strongly felt by the capital starved countries. By inviting foreign investment, the capital from capital surplus countries can be deployed to exploit the so far unexploited resources of the deficit countries. The 'Two Gap Model' [14]has been used to focus on the specific role of foreign investment in relieving the foreign exchange requirements for economic growth. Growth needs investment and this may have import content. The two gap means: the gap between savings and investments and gap between foreign exchange availability and import needs.

Foreign investment apart from fulfilling investment gaps also improves competitive strengths and core competencies in the overseas market. Through transfer of technology foreign investment also helps developing countries to compete in the global markets. FDI also brings with it the management and organizational competence and there is spill over effects of these on the rest of the economy. Another contribution of FDI is that it provides the much-needed foreign exchange[15] to help bridge the balance of trade deficit. Indeed, in the wake of the debt crisis, FDI has come to be viewed as an increasingly important source of external finance for developing countries. The competition of foreign-owned enterprises with the local firms forces the latter category to improve the technology and quality of their product.

It may be argued that the Indian economy was on the brink of collapse. Foreign investment was a critical necessity, but the foreign investor's confidence in the Indian economy was at its lowest ebb. The gravity of situation was described by the then Finance Minister in 1991. He pointed out that the foreign reserves had dwindled to Rs. 2,600 crore, barely sufficient for two week's imports. International commercial banks were refusing to extend new credits. Large outflows were taking place from NRI deposits. Industrial growth rate had turned negative. Therefore, the Central Government has already made certain efforts towards inviting foreign investment into India. The Industrial Policy, 1948 and the subsequent policy adjustments have liberalized the industrial policy regime in the country, especially, as it applies to foreign investment policy, beyond recognition. Export development, access to foreign technology, transfer of skills to the locals, development of supporting local enterprises, etc. were some of the benefits, which were sought to be attained from the foreign investment policy.

The Government of India's policy regarding foreign capital was enunciated in the Industrial Policy Resolution of April 6, 1948. At the time of Independence, the attitude towards foreign capital was one of fear and suspicion. This was natural on account of the previous exploitative role-played by it in 'draining away' resources from this country. The suspicion and hostility found expression in the Industrial Policy of 1948 which, though recognizing the role of private foreign investment in the country, emphasized that its regulation was necessary in the national interest. Because of this attitude expressed in the 1948 Resolution, foreign capitalists got dissatisfied and as a result, the flow of imports of capital goods got obstructed. As a result, the Prime Minister had to give following assurances to the foreign capitalists in 1949:

The Government of India will not differentiate between the foreign and India capital. The implication was that the government would not place any restrictions or impose any conditions on foreign enterprise, which were not applicable to similar Indian enterprise.

The foreign interests operating in India would be permitted to earn profits without subjecting them to undo controls. Only such restrictions would be imposed which also apply to the Indian enterprise. If and when foreign enterprises are compulsorily acquired, compensation will be paid on a fair and equitable basis as already announced in government's statement of policy.

Though the Prime Minister stated that the major interest in ownership and effective control of an undertaking should be in Indian hands, he gave assurance that there would be "no hard and fast rule in this matter".

By a declaration issued on June 2, 1950, the government assured the foreign capitalists that they could remit the foreign investments made by them in the country after January 1, 1950. In addition, they were also allowed to remit whatever reinvestment of profit had taken place.

Despite the above assurances, foreign capital in the requisite quantity did now flow into India during the period of the First Plan. The atmosphere of suspicion had not changed substantially. However, the policy statement of the Prime Minister issued in 1949 and continued practically unchanged. The Industrial Policy Resolution, 1956 had opened up immense fields to foreign participation. The Resolution (1956), made it clear, "that as a rule, the major interest in ownership and effective control, should always be in Indian hands. In all cases, however, the training of suitable Indian personnel for the purpose of eventually replacing foreign experts will be insisted upon." Thus, while recognizing the need for foreign capital in the industrialization of the economy, the government insisted upon the progressive Indianisation of foreign concerns.

The Industrial Policy statement of 1973, inter-alia, identified high-priority industries where investment from large industrial houses and foreign companies would be permitted.

The Industrial Policy Statement of 1977 restricted foreign equity participation to 40 per cent. The participation of foreign investment and foreign companies was made strictly in accordance with Foreign Exchange Regulation Act (FERA). It was also laid down that the Government would issue a list of industries where no foreign collaboration was deemed necessary.

The Industrial Policy Statement of 1980 laid regarding

participation of foreign investment and foreign companies in India's industrial development, the Government made it clear that the provisions of the FERA would be strictly enforced on the existing foreign countries. But a higher percentage of foreign equity was considered in priority industries if the technology was sophisticated and not available in the country, or if the venture was largely export-oriented. In addition, the trends towards liberalization grew slowly and gradually more strong and the role of foreign investment grew more and more important. The government relaxed its policy concerning majority ownership in several cases and granted several tax concessions for foreign personnel. Substantial liberalization was announced in the New Industrial Policy declared by the government in July 1991 and doors of several industries have been opened up for foreign investment.

While freeing Indian industry from official controls, opportunities for promoting foreign investment in India should also be fully exploited. This is particularly necessary in the changing global scenario of industrial and economic cooperation marked by mobility of capital. The government will, therefore, welcome foreign investment, which is in the interest of the country's industrial development.

In order to invite foreign investment in high priority industries requiring large investments and advanced technology, it has been decided to provide approval for direct foreign investment up to 51 per cent of foreign equity in such industries. There shall be no bottlenecks of any kind in this process. This group of industries has generally been known as the "appendix industries" and are areas in which FERA companies have already been allowed to invest on a discretionary basis.

This change will go a long way in making Indian policy on foreign investment transparent. Such a framework will make it attractive for companies' abroad to invest in India.

1.9.1 Policy Regarding Routes for FDI Flow

FDI can be approved either through the Automatic Route or by the Government.

1. Automatic Route

Companies proposing foreign investment under the automatic route do not require any government approval, provided the proposed foreign equity is within the specified ceiling and the requisite documents are filed with the Reserve Bank of India (RBI) within 30 days of receipt of funds. The automatic route encompasses all proposals:

(a) where the foreign investment in the equity capital of the Indian Company is up to 50/51/74/100 per cent as the case may be as applicable to the list of high priority industries/items given in Annexure III, and

(b) Where the proposed items of manufacture/activity do not require an Industrial License and is not reserved for the Small Scale Sector.

The above is also applicable for existing companies wishing to raise foreign equity up to 50/51/74/100 per cent, as the case may be. If the equity is proposed as part of an expansion programme, the expansion programme must be in the high priority industries listed in Annexure III. When the increase in equity is not proposed for purposes of an expansion, the company must be pre-dominantly engaged in the high priority industries listed in Annexure III.

The automatic route for FDI and/or technology collaboration would not be available to those who have on hand any previous joint venture on technology transfer/trade mark agreement in the same or allied field in India.

2. Government Approval

For the following categories, government approval for FDI through the FIPB would be necessary:

(a) Proposals attracting compulsory licensing.

(b) Items of manufacture reserved for the small-scale sector.

(c) Acquisition of existing shares.

(d) Foreign investment proposals where the parameters for automatic approval are not met and the company has to notify the same to SIA (Secretariat for Industrial Assistance) within 30 days of receipt of funds as also allotment of shares.

(e) In case of infusion of foreign equity by a company without changing the percentage of equity that has already been approved by the Government and where the original project cost was up to Rs.600 crore, no prior approval of FIPB/Government is required. The company has to notify the same to SIA within 30 days of receipt of funds as also allotment of shares.

1.9.2 Post-Liberalization Reforms in Foreign Direct Investment

The important measures announced in July, 1991 and afterwards are as follows:

1. In 1991, the government announced a specified list of high technology and high-investment priority industries (listed in Annexure III) wherein automatic permission was granted for foreign direct investment (FDI) up to 51 per cent foreign equity. The industries in which automatic approval has been granted include a wide range of industrial activities in the capital goods and metallurgical industries, entertainment electronics, food processing, and the service sectors having significant export potential. Besides, these include a number of other industries, which are important for the rapid growth of the economy.

2. Prior to 1991 the government generally discouraged foreign equity holding in service sector except for hotels. The 1991 policy invited foreign equity holding up to 51 per cent by international trading companies. In addition to hotels, 51 per cent of equity was also allowed in other tourist- related areas.
3. A special empowered board has been constituted to negotiate with a number of large international firms and approve direct foreign investment in select areas. There would be a special programme to attract substantial investment that would provide access to high technology and world markets. The investment programmes of such firms would be considered in totality, free from pre-determined parameters or procedures.
4. Hiring of foreign technicians and testing of indigenously developed technology abroad earlier required case-by-case approval by the government. This involved unavoidable delay. This requirement has been waived and thus no permission is now required for these purposes.
5. Hastening the progress in the ailing power sector, the government in a policy decision announced on July 31, 1991 to allow 100 per cent foreign equity participation for setting up power plants in the country. Hundred per cent foreign equity participation allows free repatriation of profits and other incentives. Besides, it will help foreign parties to set up power plants without delay, which considerably escalate the cost. Such equity participation will also enable foreign terms to meet the total costs, including the costs arising out of exchange rate variations and rupee component.
6. NRIs, and overseas corporate bodies (OCBs) predominantly owned by them, have been allowed

to invest up to 100 per cent equity in high-priority industries. These investments through the automatic approval route of RBI have full benefits of capital repatriation. NRI investments up to 100 per cent of equity is also allowed in export houses, trading houses, star trading houses, hospitals, EOUs, sick industries, hotels etc. Foreign citizens of Indian origin are now permitted to acquire house property without the permission of the Reserve Bank of India.

7. Disinvestment of equity by foreign investors no longer needs to be at prices determined by the Reserve Bank. It has been allowed at market rates on stock exchanges from September 15, 1992 with permission to repatriate the proceeds of such disinvestment.
8. Foreign companies have been allowed to use their trademarks on domestic sales from May 14, 1992.
9. Portfolio investment in any of the listed companies of Indian stock exchanges/Over-the-counter exchange has been allowed by foreign institutional investors as well as NRI/OCBs, without any lock-in period for the remitting of the funds, subject to the condition that the aggregate holding of shares/debentures does not exceed 30 per cent of the voting equity capital of the company. In a bid to provide greater access to Indian companies to foreign portfolio investment, the Union Budget 2000-01 raised this limit to 40 per cent.
10. Foreign investors can invest in Indian companies through the Global Depository Receipts (GDR) route without any lock-in period. These Receipts can be listed on any of the overseas stock exchanges and denominated in any convertible foreign currency.
11. The following are the several measures to boost foreign investment announced in 1998-99:

- whereas previously NRIs were allowed to purchase shares in Indian companies in the secondary market subject to a limit of 1 per cent of the company's total equity with a 5 per cent limit for aggregate NRI/OCB investments in the company, these limits were raised to 5 per cent and 10 per cent respectively;
- The State Bank of India launched a Resurgent India Bond (RIB) scheme denominated in foreign currencies and was open to both NRIs/OCBs and the banks acting in fiduciary capacity on behalf of them. The scheme opened on August 5, 1998 and closed on August 25, 1998. Mobilization under the scheme amounted to $ 4.2 billion;
- Projects for electricity generation, transmission and distribution as also roads and highways, ports and harbors, and vehicular tunnels were permitted foreign equity participation up to 100 per cent under the automatic route, provided foreign equity does not exceed Rs. 1,500 crore;
- Regarding equity participation in private sector banks, multilateral financial institutions were allowed to contribute equity to the extent of the shortfall in the NRI holdings within the overall permissible limit of 40 per cent;
- The government decided to permit foreign direct investment up to 49 per cent of the total equity, subject to license, in companies providing Global Mobile Personal Communication by Satellite (GMPCS) services;
- NRIs/PIOs (Persons of Indian Origin) OCBs were allowed to invest in unlisted companies under certain conditions;

- Foreign institutional investors were allowed to purchase and sell Government Securities and Treasury Bills within overall approved debt ceilings;
- 100 per cent foreign institutional investors' debt funds have been permitted to invest in unlisted debt securities of Indian companies.

12. In March 1999, the Reserve Bank issued a notification granting general permission to Mutual Funds for issuing units to NRIs/PIOs/OCBs subject to certain specified norms, thereby dispensing with the existing procedure of obtaining prior permission. In addition, approval procedures were simplified by the Reserve Bank in respect of NRIs/PIOs/OCBs by granting them general permission in lieu of a case by case approval procedure in a large number of areas. This includes acceptance of deposits by Indian companies, investment in Air Taxi operations, sale of shares in stock exchanges, transfer of shares/bonds/debentures and immovable property to charitable trusts/organizations in India as gift, raising of loans by resident individuals/proprietorship concerns on non-repatriable basis, issue of Commercial Papers by Indian companies to NRI etc.

13. Foreign owned Indian holding companies were hitherto required to obtain prior approval of the FIPB (Foreign Investment Promotion Board) for downstream investment. They have now been permitted to make such investments within permissible equity limits through the automatic route provided such holding companies bring in the requisite funds from abroad. Also, the need to obtain prior approval of the FIPB for increasing foreign equity within already approved

limits has been dispensed with in all cases where the original project cost was up to Rs. 600 crore.

14. With a view to expand the FIIs (Foreign Institutional Investors) category, the government has permitted foreign corporates and high net-worth individuals to invest through SEBI registered FIIs. The government has also permitted SEBI registered domestic fund managers to manage foreign funds for investment in the Indian capital market through the portfolio investment route provided the funds are channeled through internationally recognized financial institutions and subject tot the reporting requirements as applicable to FIIs.
15. In August 1999, a Foreign Investment Implementation Authority (FIIA) was established within the Ministry of Industry in order to ensure that approvals for foreign investments (including NRI investments) are quickly translated into actual investment inflows and that proposals fructify into projects. In particular, in cases where FIPB clearance is needed, approval time has been reduced to 30 days.
16. In December 1999, a notification was issued by the Ministry of Finance, permitting Indian software companies which are listed in foreign exchanges and have already floated ADR/GDR (American Depository Receipts/Global Depository Receipts) issues, to acquire foreign software companies and issue ADRs/GDRs without reference to the Government of India or the Reserve Bank of India up to the value limit of $ 100 million. For acquisitions beyond $ 100 million, proposals would require examination by a Special Composite Committee in the Reserve Bank of India.
17. With a view to further liberalize the operational

guidelines for ADR/GDR issues, it has been decided to dispense with the track record scrutiny process for ADR/GDR issues and the two-stage approval by the Ministry of Finance. Indian companies would henceforth be free to access the ADR/GDR markets through an automatic route without the prior approval of the Ministry of Finance subject to the specified norms and post-issue reporting requirement. Since ADR/GDR are reckoned as part of FDI, such issues would need to conform to the existing FDI policy and permissible only in areas where FDI is permissible.

18. An Insurance Regulatory and Development Act (IRDA) was passed by Parliament in December1999. The Act, which seeks to promote private sector participation in the insurance sector, permits foreign equity stake in domestic private insurance companies up to a maximum of 26 per cent of the total paid-up capital.

19. On January 6, 2000, the Cabinet Committee on Economic Affairs approved the proposal to raise FDI through automatic route up to 74 per cent in bulk drugs, intermediaries and formulations. Hitherto, up to 51 per cent FDI was allowed.

20. On February 1, 2000, the Union Cabinet decided to all9ow automatic FDI in all except a limited number of industries, those relating to acquisition of shares in Indian Companies and those which fall outside notified sectoral policy under sectors in which FDI is currently not permitted.

21. In February 2000, the government took a major decision to place all items under the automatic route for FDI/NRI/OCB investment except a small negative list. To give effect to this decision, the Reserve Bank of India issued a notification on April 5, 2000, which says that all items excluding specific sectors will be eligible for

foreign investment under the automatic route up to even 100 per cent.

22. The government also permitted 100 per cent foreign investment in Film Industry subject to certain criteria. In the Advertising sector, the upper limit has been fixed at 74 per cent. However, it was decided not to allow any FDI in the print and broadcast media sectors.

23. In May 2000, the Union Government allowed 100 per cent FDI in all minerals except diamonds and precious stones. In case of diamonds and precious stones, foreign equity up to 74 per cent will be allowed on an automatic route.

24. On 12th June 2000, the Union Cabinet approved 100 per cent FDI in Petroleum refining and e-commerce sectors.

25. The important decisions taken to further liberalize the FDI policy during 2000-01[16] were as follows:

    - The existing upper limit of Rs. 1,500 crore for FDI in projects involving electricity generation, transmission and distribution (other than atomic reactor plants) has been dispensed with;
    - For facilitating greater inflow of foreign funds in the oil-refining sector, the ceiling for FDI under the automatic route in oil refining has been increased to 100 per cent from the existing 49 per cent;
    - FDI under the automatic route has been permitted up to 100 per cent for all manufacturing activities in Special Economic Zones (SEZs), except for the following activities:

      (i) arms and ammunition, explosives and allied items of defence equipment, defence aircraft and warships;

(ii) narcotics, hazardous, chemicals, etc.;

(iii) distillation and brewing of alcoholic drinks; and

(iv) Cigarettes/cigars and manufactured tobacco substitutes.

- FDI up to 100 per cent allowed with some conditions for the following activities in the telecom sector:

  (i) Internet Service Providers (ISP) not providing gateways;

  (ii) Infrastructure providers providing dark-fiber;

  (iii) Electronic mail; and

  (iv) Voice mail.

- Automatic route is available to proposals in the information technology sector, even when the applicant company has a previous joint venture or technology transfer agreement in the same field; and
- Offshore Venture Capital Funds/Companies allowed investing in domestic venture capital undertakings as well as other companies through the automatic route subject only to SEBI regulations and sector specific caps on FDI.

26. In a notification issued on 21st May, 2001 Government of India has further liberalized the FDI regime. Some of the important changes in the FDI policy are:

- FDI up to 100 percent is permitted on the automatic route for manufacture of drugs and pharmaceutical provided the activity does not attract compulsory licensing.
- FDI up to 100 per cent is permitted in airports,

with FDI above 74 per cent requiring prior approval of the Government.

- The defence industry sector is opened up to 100 per cent for Indian private sector participation with FDI permissible up to 26 per cent, both subject to licensing.
- FDI up to 100 per cent permitted with prior approval of the Government for development of integrated townships, including housing, commercial premises, hotels, resorts, and regional level urban infrastructure facilities such as roads and bridges, mass rapid transit system; and manufacture of building materials.[17]
- FDI up to 100 per cent is permitted on the automatic route in hotel and tourism sector and for Mass Rapid Transport Systems in all metropolitan cities, including associated commercial development of real estate.
- FDI up to 74 per cent is permitted for the following telecom services subject to licensing and security requirements:

  (i) Internet service providers with gateways;

  (ii) Radio paging; and

  (iii) End-to-end bandwidth.

- FDI up to 49 per cent from all sources is permitted in the Banking Sector on the automatic route subject to conformity with guidelines issued by RBI from time to time. Further, the same is raised to 74 per cent during 2002-03.
- Foreign Institutional Investors can invest in a company under the Portfolio Investment route

beyond 24 per cent of the paid up capital of the company with the approval of the general body of the shareholders by a special resolution. In the Union Budget for 2002-03, the Finance Minister announced that FII portfolio investments would not be subject to the sectoral limits for foreign direct investment except in specified sectors.

- In pursuance of government's commitment to further facilitate Indian industry to engage unhindered in various activities, government has permitted, except for a small negative list, access to the domestic route for FDI, whereby foreign investors only need to inform the RBI within 30 days of bringing in their investment, and again within 30 days of issuing any shares.
- Non-Banking Financial Companies (NBFCs) may hold foreign equity up to 100 per cent if there are holding companies.
- Foreign investors can set up 100 per cent operating subsidiaries (without any restriction on number of subsidiaries) without the condition to disinvest a maximum of 25 per cent of their equity to Indian entities, subject to bringing in US $ 50 million.
- Foreign firms have been allowed to pay royalty on brand name/trade mark as a percentage of net sales in case of technology transfers.
- FDI up to 26 per cent is eligible under the automatic route in the Insurance Sector, as permitted in the Insurance Act, 1999, subject to their obtaining license from Insurance Regulatory and Development Authority (IRDA).
- FDI up to 100 per cent is permitted with prior

approval of the Government in Courier Services subject to existing laws and exclusion of activities relating to distribution of letters.

- FDI up to 100 per cent is permitted with prior approval of the government for development of integrated townships and regional urban infrastructure, tea sector (including tea plantation), advertising and films.
- The defence industry sector has been opened up to 100 per cent for Indian Private Sector participation with FDI permitted up to 26 per cent, both subject to licensing.
- FDI in Print Media Sector as allowed up to 26 per cent of paid-up equity capital of Indian entities publishing periodicals and newspapers dealing with news and current affairs.

27. Union Budget 2004-05 has increased the sectoral caps for Foreign Direct Investment (FDI) in Telecommunications from 49 percent to 74 percent; in Civil Aviation from 40 percent to 49 percent; and in Insurance from 26 percent to 49 percent.

1.9.3 An Evaluation of the New Policy

Although the liberalization has increased the inflow of foreign capital to India, it has been much lower than several other developing countries in the Asia. After reaching a highest amount of $3.57 billion in 1997, FDI inflow to India dropped to $2.16 billion in 1997 and marginally increased to $2.63 billion in 2000. India's share of global FDI flows declined from 0.75 in 1997 to 0.24 in 2000. The FDI inflow is nowhere near the annual target of $10 billion set by the Government many years ago. This is because the infrastructural facilities are poor, several factors are costly and the policy and procedural environment in India in several respects is far from encouraging. Not only the foreign capital is shying away from India but also it is feared that there are signs of capital flight from India.

There are many ardent critics of foreign investment and technology, and its related problems. However, the opening up of the economies of a number of nations for foreign companies and the several measures they have taken to woo foreign companies are clear indicators of the positive contribution foreign capital and technology can make.

Government of India had been considering only equity investments and had been excluding factors like reinvested capital in the computation of FDI. However, in 2003 Government aligned the methodology with the internationally accepted practice. As per the revised data,[1818] Since 2000-01, FDI definition has been revised by including reinvested earnings (including earnings of FDI companies) and other direct capital (inter-corporate debt transactions between related entities).

FDI inflow in 2000-01 is reckoned at $4.03 billion against $2.34 billion earlier, while it would be $6.13 billion in 2001-02, $4.67 billion in 2002-03, and $4.68 billion in 2003-04.

The new policy of Government of India is, of course, much better than the old policy. However, in comparison with the business environment in many other countries, India still is not very attractive in the eyes of foreign companies, despite the large and growing Indian market. Now that many countries are competing to lure the foreign capital and technology, the choice is indeed very wide for the foreign firms. Further, many multinationals are keen to establish a foothold in the former 'communist' and 'socialist' countries, which have now widely opened their doors for the foreign capital and technology, besides their interest in several other countries.

One important criticism of the liberalization of foreign investment has been that foreign investment would take place mostly in non-priority sectors. However, about 80 per cent of the foreign investment in India since the liberalization have gone to priority sectors. Now several of the priority industries, including the infrastructural sector, which were earlier exclusively reserved for the public sector, are opened for foreign investment. Foreign investment needs to be directed to priority sectors.

1.10. Organizational Setup for FDI

1.10.1 Foreign Investment Promotion Board (FIPB)

FIPB is a high-powered board operating under the Ministry of Industry, which is specially empowered to engage in purposive negotiation and also consider approvals in totality free from predetermined parameters on procedures.

The reconstituted FIPB comprises of:

(i) Secretary, Department of Economic Affairs – Chairman

(ii) Secretary, Department of Industrial Policy & Promotion –Member

(iii) Secretary, Department of Commerce – Member

(iv) Secretary (Economic Relations), Ministry of External Affairs – Member

The Board would be able to co-opt Secretaries and other top officials of financial institutions, banks and professional experts of industry and commerce, as and when necessary.

The consideration that are normally taken into account by FIPB while granting approvals are:

- The extent of capital needed for the project.
- The nature and quality of technology.

- The requirements of marketing and management skills, and
- The commitment for exports.

As per the guidelines recently announced by the Government, FIPB may consider proposals for 100 per cent foreign equity based on the following criteria:

- Where only holding operations are involved and all subsequent downstream investments to be carried out would require prior approval from the government,
- Where proprietary technology is sought to be protected or sophisticated technology is proposed to be brought in,
- Where at least 50 per cent of the production is exported,
- Proposals for consultancy,
- Where the foreign investor is unable to find a joint venture partner, 100 per cent may be granted on a temporary basis provided the foreign investor divests at least 26 per cent equity stake to Indian parties within a period of 3 to 5 years,
- Where in the case of an existing joint venture, the Indian partner is unable to raise resources for expansion/technological up gradation of the existing industrial activity,
- Proposals for power, roads, ports and industrial parks or estates.

In particular, where FIPB clearance is needed, approval time has been confined to 30 days.

Foreign owned Indian holding companies were hitherto required to obtain prior approval of the FIPB for downstream investment. They have now been permitted to make such investments within permissible equity limits through the automatic route provided such holding companies bring in the requisite funds from abroad. Also, the need to obtain prior approval of the FIPB for increasing foreign equity within already approved limits has been dispensed with in all cases where the original project cost was up to Rs. 600 crore.

The approach of FIPB is liberal for all sectors and all types of proposals. The totality of package proposed is examined and approved on merits within a period of thirty days. RBI has granted general permission under Foreign Exchange Regulation Act (FERA) in respect of proposals approved by the Government. Indian companies getting foreign investment approval through FIPB route do not require any further clearance from RBI for the purpose of receiving inward remittance and issue of shares to the foreign investors. Such companies are, however, required to notify the Regional Office concerned of the RBI of receipt of inward remittances within 30 days of such receipt and to file the required document with the concerned Regional Offices of the RBI within 30 days after issue of shares to the foreign investors.

1.10.2 Foreign Investment Implementation Authority (FIIA)

The Union Budget, 1999-2000 announced the establishment of a Foreign Investment Implementation Authority within the Ministry of Industry, and it was established on August 9, 1999 to facilitate quick implementation of FDI approvals and assist foreign investors in getting necessary approvals. Its major functions are to rationalise and simplify approval and implementation procedures of foreign investment proposals. It also ensures the approvals for foreign investments (including NRI investments) are quickly translated into actual investment inflows and those proposals fructify into projects.

Fast Track Committees have been set up in 30 Ministries/

Departments for regular review of FDI mega projects (with proposed investment of Rs. 1 billion and above), and resolution of any difficulties in consultation with the concerned Ministries/ State Governments. Unresolved issues are brought before FIIA. Details of the Fast Track Committees set up in various Ministries/Departments are available at the website http:// dipp.nic.in.

1.10.3 Foreign Investment Promotional Council

The Government has constituted a Foreign Investment Promotion Council (FIPC) in the Ministry of Industry. It has been set up to have more target oriented approach towards foreign direct investment promotion. Its functions are to identify the sector/project within the country requiring foreign direct investment and target specific regions/countries of the world from where FDI will be brought through.

1.10.4 Insurance Regulatory and Development Act (IRDA)

An Insurance Regulatory and Development Act (IRDA) was passed by the Parliament in December 1999. The Act seeks to promote private sector participation in the Insurance Sector and permits foreign equity stake in domestic private insurance companies up to a maximum of 26 percent of the total paid-up capital.

In February 2000, Government took a major decision to place all items under the automatic route for FDI/NRI/OCB investment except for a small negative list, which includes the following:

(i) items requiring an industrial license under the Industries (Development and Regulation) Act, 1951;

(ii) foreign investment being more than 24 per cent in the equity capital of units manufacturing items reserved for small scale industries;

(iii) all items requiring industrial license in terms of the locational policy notified under the New Industrial Policy of 1991;

(iv) proposals having previous venture/tie-up in India with foreign collaborator;

(v) proposals relating to acquisition of shares in existing Indian company by foreign/NRI/OCB investor;

(vi) Proposals falling outside notified sectoral policy/caps or under sectors in which FDI is not permitted and applications chosen to be submitted through FIPB rather than automatic route by the investors.

This is an important step to dispense with case-by-case approval procedure and to impart greater transparency in the process of foreign investment.

1.10.5 Department of Industrial Policy and Promotion–Committee Report

In an attempt to bring the reporting system of FDI in India into alignment with international best practices, the Department of Industrial Policy and Promotion (DIPP), Ministry of Commerce and Industry, Government of India (GoI), in consultation with RBI, constituted a Committee in May 2002. The committee comprises of Officials from RBI and DIPP to study the issue.

The Committee studied the relevant conceptual and methodological issues and identified the data gaps involved in order to make necessary recommendations for strengthening the collection, compilation and reporting of FDI data and submitted its report in October 2002 and recommended that-

- the FDI statistics should include, besides equity capital, 'reinvested earnings' (retained earnings of FDI companies) and 'other direct capital' (inter-corporate debt transactions between related entities) in accordance with the international best practices; and

- The steps are taken jointly by RBI and DIPP to expand the coverage of FDI statistics in India.

As a follow-up action to the submission of FDI Compilation Report, a Technical Monitoring Group (TMG) with representatives from RBI, DIPP, Department of Economic Affairs (DEA), Department of Company Affairs (DCA), and National Informatics Centre (NIC) was constituted by DIPP in November 2002. The main objective of TMG is to speedy implementation of the recommendations made by the above committee.

The main focus of the TMG was to identify various components of FDI, which are operationally feasible and capture these components in a specified institutional framework and within a specified time period. TMG submitted its first Action Taken Report on June 27, 2003.

TABLE-1.1

Component-wise Revised FDI

($US Million)

S.No	*Item/year*	*2000-01*	*2001-02*	*2002-03*
1.	Revised FDI to India (a+b+c)	4,029	6,131	4,660
	(a) Equity	2,400	4,095	2,700
	(b Reinvested Earnings	1,350	1,646	1,498
	(c) 'Other Capital'	279	390	462
2.	FDI data currently published	2,342	3,905	2,574
3.	Additional Amount on Account of Revision	1,687	2,226	2,086

Source: Economic Developments in India – Volume 68.

RBI and DIPP jointly decided to expand the coverage of data on FDI, both inflow and outflow for 2000-01 and 2001-02. The revised data on FDI include all items indicated under equity capital (except non-cash acquisitions); all items under the reinvested earnings have been included except reinvested earnings indirectly held direct investment enterprises; and data under 'other capital' relate short-term and long-term borrowing trade credit (more than 180 days), suppliers' credit (more than 180 days) and financial leasing.

The revised data for 2000-01 to 2002-03 are shown in the above tables:

TABLE-1.2

Foreign Direct Investment Outflows

(US $ million)

S.No	*Item*	*2000-01*	*2001-02*	*2002-03*
1.	Revised FDI Abroad(a+b+c)	757	1,390	1,049
	(a) Equity	344	570	424
	(b) Reinvested Earnings	339	699	519
	(c) 'Other Capital'	74	121	106
2.	FDI Abroad data currently	514	639	590
3.	Published Additional Amount on Account of Revision	243	751	459

Source: Economic Developments in India – Volume 68

1.10.6 Investment Comission

The Cabinet Committee on Economic Affairs (CCEA) approved the proposal for the creation of an Investment Commission on 27th October 2004. The Prime Minister, Dr. Man Mohan Singh decided that it would be located in the Finance Ministry and would enjoy operational autonomy and Government support. As originally proposed in the Union Budget by the Finance Minister P. Chidambaram, the Commission will comprise one Chairperson, two members and three professional groups and will initially have a three-year term.

While suggesting the creation of the Commission, the Finance Minister stated that it would solicit both foreign and domestic investments and act as a facilitation group between the potential investor and the official machinery. Specific problems faced by the investors would be brought to the notice of the Government for speedy resolution so that investments in India rise significantly.

The Commission will also make recommendations to the Government on policy and procedures to facilitate greater foreign direct investment (FDI) flows into India and all policy recommendations emerging from its recommendations will be brought before the CCEA for approval.

1.11 Review of Literature

In the recent past, there have been discussions and research in various parts regarding the coverage of foreign direct investment (FDI) studies in India.

Prof. Gangadhar & Yadagiri[19] have made study on "Trends of Foreign Direct Investment in India". The objectives of the study are to analyse the approval of Foreign Direct Investment according to investing country-wise, state-wise, sector-wise with a view to highlight their pattern and diversities; and also examining actual inflows of Foreign Direct Investment vis-à-vis approvals to identify variations between them and discuss the reasons for such variations.

The study revealed, USA was the biggest investment country followed by U.K., Oman, Switzerland, U.A.E., Thailand, Netherlands, Japan, Mexico and Germany. A close examination of the data pertaining to approval of Foreign Direct Investments reveals that more than half of the total approved investments was concentrated in five states, namely Maharastra, West Bengal, Delhi, Tamil Nadu and Gujarat. It has been found service sector has registered a significant increases from Rs. 5.81 crores in 1991 of approvals to Rs.283.57 crores and Rs. 874.72 crores in 1992 and 1993 respectively, since this sector has attracted several approvals. The total actual inflow of

Foreign Direct Investment in 1991 was Rs. 351.43 crores out of the total approvals of Rs. 534.11 crores. The inflows increased to Rs. 675.22 crores and Rs. 1,388.90 crores out of Rs. 3,887.54 crores in 1992 and Rs.7, 990.62 crores up to November 1994 respectively of total approvals.

• Studies by Reserve Bank of India (1998) on *Finances of FDI Companies* have released disturbing trends. The export intensity of sales (export to sales ratio) of such companies has been steadily falling and the import intensity of exports (imports to exports ratio) has been steadily rising during the period 1993-94 to 1996-97. The import intensity of exports has not only been increasing but it is also higher than 100 per cent.[20] These companies have also faced a decline in growth in their exports. Traditional sectors like textiles and tea have fared much better than the modern sectors like engineering and chemicals. Export intensity of sales and import intensity of exports differs not only across the sector but also across the source countries.

If this trend of high import intensity of exports of FDI companies persists for a long period than the very purpose of attracting FDI will be defeated. Rather than solving the problem of foreign exchange, the FDI inflows may accentuate the problem of rising current account deficits.

Behaviour of FDI Companies

Year	*Rate of growth of exports (%)*	*Exports intensity of Sales (%)*	*Import intensity of Exports (%)*
1993-94	29.4	10.4	80.6
1994-95	10.7	9.9	107.5
1995-96	14.6	9.2	139.1
1996-97	12.1	9.2	177.0

Source: Compiled from RBI Bulletin (various issues), Finances of FDI Companies.

• A press release(2000) issued by the Commerce Ministry claimed that the first two months of the year 2000 have seen FDI inflows amounting to $600 million, of which about $481 million have come in February alone. This is against the average inflow of $230 million a month in the past.[21]

• According to Nagesh Kumar[22] (2000), the expansion in the magnitude of FDI inflows during 1990s is not due to reform alone. It reflects, in part, the dramatic expansion in the global FDI flows to developing countries from about $35 billion per year on average during 1987-92 to $166 billion in 1998.

Majority foreign ownership, which was restricted to certain exceptional cases during the 1970s and 1980s because of regulations, is becoming more popular again. As noted by Nagesh Kumar, majority of approvals in the 1990s have been in the range of 50-100 per cent foreign ownership range with a third accounted for by wholly foreign owned subsidiaries. A number of multinational corporations (MNCs) have taken advantage of the new rules to increase their stake in the existing affiliates in the country. The importance of joint venture mode of operations has declined with liberalization. Moreover, many MNCs are opting the route of acquisition of existing enterprises to enter India.

• In a study on FDI, Confederation of Indian Industry (2001) has estimated the FDI approvals over the seven-year period 1991-98 at $55.1 billion while actual inflows have been estimated at $11.9 billion. This implies that only 21.7 per cent of the FDI cleared during the period 1991-98 have actually been brought into the country. Thus, almost 80 per cent of the FDI approved between 1991 and 1998 did not fructify and remained only on paper.[23]

• According to John Degnbol-Mortinussen[24] (2001), seen in the broader context of India's macro-economic policies,

FDI and other external resources have been used as a soft option in lieu of mobilising domestic resources through taxation. FDI has further been used as a soft option in lieu of a pro-active R&D policy. The authorities have seen FDI as the main career of technology transfer neglecting the indigenous R&D.

• He also argues that the entire approach of the Government of India towards FDI may imply serious problems for industrial development. According to him, the policy framework in practice encourages portfolio investment over FDI, and the industrial constraints that affect implementation of new projects encourage investment in existing assets, meaning that a significant part of the capital actually flowing into India is used to take over or buying shares in existing undertakings rather than to promote industrial expansion and competition. The focus on attracting rentiers – NRIs especially – to hold portfolio investments in India has not contributed much to real capital formation, merely implied that ownership of existing income-bearing paper assets have changed hands.

• C.P.Chandrasekhar and Jayati Ghosh[25] (2002) pointed out that an important objective of promoting FDI has been to promote efficiency in production and increase exports. However, any increase in the equity stake of the foreign investors in existing joint ventures or purchase of a share of equity by them in domestic firms would not automatically change the orientation of the firm. That is, "the aim of such FDI investors would be to benefit from the profit earned in the Indian Market." As a result, in such cases FDI inflows need not be accompanied by any substantial increase in exports, whether such investment leads to the modernisation of domestic capacity or not.

• Dr. C.L.Chandan & Dinesh Sharma of Institute of

Management Studies, H.P.University, Shimla (2002)[26] studied *the need for New Policy initiatives of FDI in India*. While analyzing the FDI scenario in India, they have noticed that there is a huge gap between approvals and actual inflows of FDI. There is delay for the inflow of approved FDI into India. The total FDI approval in India during the period 1991 to 2000 (Jan-Apr) was Rs. 2,16,171 crore, whereas the actual inflow was Rs. 75,852 crore only. The percentage of FDI inflow over approval is35.09 per cent only over the entire period under consideration. However, the improvement in the inflow rate has been encouraging since 1998.

It has also been stated that, in order to get maximum benefit from FDI; the host country must implement policies to maximize the linkage effects created by foreign firms. This is to ensure full integration of local firms into the foreign investment sector so as to prevent the formation of a foreign enclave leading to an increasing degree of foreign dependency. Foreign Direct Investment (FDI) flow has set a new record in 1999 when global inflows touched $865 billion. FDI flows to developing countries reached a level $208 billion. There was an increase of 16 per cent over 1998. The World Development Report 2000 indicate that over the period 1991-99, 94 per cent of the 1035 changes world-wide in the laws governing FDI created a more favourable framework for FDI.

Keeping in view the crucial importance of FDI in the economic development in the present globalised economy, the Government of India needs to provide a new orientation to the FDI policy. Certain new policy initiatives and commitment is urgently needed in this regard. The policy should be further liberalized and procedures should be enormously simplified. The low approval/inflow rate is a serious cause of concern. The delay in getting post-FIPB clearances is the main hurdle. The government should set up a Foreign Investment Implementation Authority that will look into delays at the State Government-level.[27] The success story of China and other East Asian countries should be an eye opener for the policy makers. The high growth rates attained by the Asian Tigers have been on the back of strong foreign direct investment in these countries. In China and Singapore, FDI accounts for 25 per cent of the total fixed capital formation as compared to India's 3.6 per cent. A small country like Singapore attracts four times the FDI India is able to attract. It is the case with China, which attracts 20 times the FDI India is able to attract. India should follow the Chinese model earnestly if it wants to be benefited by FDI.

- Rajat Acharyya[28] (2002), made a review of the Report and observes, both the quantity and distribution of foreign direct investment (FDI) flows in the developing countries are not very encouraging. China, Indonesia, Thailand, Malaysia, Brazil and Mexico attract almost 80 per cent of such FDI flows. Moreover, the quantity of FDI flow, which seems to matter more than the quantity of it, is poor. The typical example is the FDI flow in Mexico. Though the trade data shows that exports, particularly the high-technology exports, as a percent of GDP has risen to over 30 percent by the end of the 1990s, the FDI flows that caused such surplus in exports had almost no feed back effect on the rest of the economy either in terms of dissemination of new technology or in terms of the positive impact on the level of skill. This is because such FDI flows, drawn there primarily due to cheap unskilled labour, have been concentrated mainly in assembling of automobiles and in electronics and computer industries, with negligible linkages between exporters and local producers. Moreover, Mexico's export success has been dependent only on the US market.

In other developing countries also, the FDI flows into the Export Processing or Special Economic Zones, attracted primarily by cheap labour and tax holidays, has mostly been concentrated in low-quality category of the manufacturing activities. They have no impact on the technological capacity of the rest of the economy.

• Mousumi Duttaray, Amitava Krishna Dutt, and Kajal Mukhopadhyay[29] of USA (2003) have studied the relation between FDI and growth. The study examined the causality between FDI and growth for ten developing countries viz., Argentina, Brazil and Mexico from Latin America, South Korea, Indonesia, India, Malaysia, Philippines and Thailand from Asia, and Kenya from Africa. The study revealed that FDI affects growth in several ways: by augmenting saving and investment; by affecting the balance of payments directly and by promoting exports; through technology transfers which improve productivity; and changing industrial structure, income distribution, and broader political economy factors. Of these, exports and productivity are the obvious variables to include in their analysis. Since the importance of FDI in capital accumulation is quantitatively negligible for most Less-Developed Countries (LDCs), and the effects of FDI on growth through changes in industrial structure, income distribution and political economy factors are too complex to be clear.

Although FDI can cause growth, causation can also run the other way. Higher growth in a country may include higher FDI by expanding markets, by signaling to transnational corporations that the country is following policies favorable towards them and by making possible improvements in education and infrastructure, which increases the profitability of FDI. Moreover, FDI can be expected to increase after investors know that the country has export capability and technological base, which warrants advantageous product relation, so that exports and productivity increase, can also cause FDI.

• Nadeem M. Firoz Farahmand Rezvani (Montclair State University), Taghi Ramin (William Patterson University) and

Wagdy Abdallah (Seton Hall University)[30] (2003) have made a study in China, which uses different kinds of Zones to attract Foreign Investment. China is using the Foreign Trade Zone (FTZ) concept exceptionally to their advantage. This country is a centrally planned economy and uses protectionism to control its imports and foster its exports.[31] China restricts foreign investment outside the designated zones. Today one can invest in the zones but not freely outside the zones.

Foreign Trade Zones are sometimes called Free Trade Zones because they are considered foreign territory for the purpose of customs entry procedures.[32] Tariffs and other taxes or duties are not collected when goods and materials enter the zone from outside the country; they enter 'free'. That is, they enter the zones free of customs duties as long as they stay there. Duties are levied when goods leave the FTZ to enter the domestic country, such as from China's FTZ to China's territory.

They have observed that in developing countries, there have been many free zone-sites established in recent years (NAFTZ, March 22, 2000). Most of them offer customs-related privilege resulting in customs-cost saving. They tend to exist as part of capital investment programmes created to boost exports and to promote exports and export-related activities within their boundaries.

- Nadeem M. Firoz and H. Amy Murray[33] (Montclair State University) (2003) have made research in China, which tries to bring about economic development through Economic Development Zones (EDZs). Economic Development Zones in China viz., Special Economic Zones (SEZs), Foreign Trade zone (FTZ), Economic Trading Development Zones (ETDZs) and Coastal Open Cities (COCs) have been interchangeably for all economic zones.

The percapita income of China's neighbours Hongkong and Taiwan ranges between $ 10,000 and $ 20,000, while People's Republic of China (PRC) income is $ 350. In Purchasing Power Parity (PPP) terms[34], the PRC income is about $ 2,000. According to experts, the PRC per capital income will increase drastically in the near future, due to economic development. PRC is developing much faster than many other developed nations. In the USA the GNP will grow @ 157 per cent by the year 2020, while in the UK it will grow @ 160 per cent and in china growth is predicted to be 567 per cent. To bring about economic development PRC has been designed to increase their exports to finance these projects. In 1995 china's exports were about $ 155 billion, and imports were about $ 140 billion. This means that in 1995, China had a positive balance of trade of $ 15 billion. Imports are controlled with tight measures that create unjustified trade barriers. Therefore investor cannot export goods to China freely. The only option that remains open for investors is to develop Joint Ventures in SEZ, COC, EDTZ, or FTZ, and take advantage of low tax rates and tax holidays. Joint Ventures can provide a way for investors to export and re export goods back to their home countries, and around the world. This policy of tight control on imports in China is meant to increase investment in the private sector, to provide many incentives and encourage foreign investment for major projects in China. These projects will help PRC to become an industrialized nation. Investors can also take advantage of China's resources, which are cheap labour, a large market of 1.3 billion consumers, and an abundance of raw materials. In view of this the countries from all parts of the world are rushing to invest in China.

The authors have concluded that Free Trade Zones offer many advantages both for the home and the host country. For many, the FTZ might be a new word in their international vocabulary, but its origin is eight centuries old; although in

China the term has only been used a decade ago. Economic Development can be recognized by an increased standard of living, opportunity for a good life, industrialization, and increase in employment, increase in per capita income, increase in gross national products, technological progress and increase in the literacy level. The Free Trade Zones (FTZs) assist in enhancing all of these indicators in any country.

• Sadhana Srivastava[35] (2003) emphasized on the true level of FDI flows to India as compared to that of China. It is often noted that India is widely regarded as an 'underperformer'. When it comes to attracting foreign direct investment (FDI), particularly in comparison with China and the rest of East Asia.[36]

The analysis suggests that the failure of India to adopt international guidelines on measuring FDI statistics implies that aggregate FDI data for India are not directly comparable to those of most of the other countries. More specifically, the fact that FDI inflows in India are entirely evaluated on equity investments while ignoring other components implies that FDI inflows into India have been systematically undervalued by quite a significant proportion of the total volume of inward FDI. For instance, in China reinvested earnings and intra-company loans together accounted for about 30 per cent of total FDI inflows during 1997 and about 51 per cent of total FDI inflows during 1998.[37] Accounting for these components in FDI statistics would bring India's FDI figures much closer to those of China. While Hong Kong has been a major direct investor part of the investments may be due to 'round-tripping' from the mainland as domestic (Chinese) investors try to take advantage of tax and tariff benefits extended to foreign investors.[38]

• According to the IFC's World Business Environment Survey, 2002 (WBES), the FDI gap between India and China is not nearly as huge as may be suggested by official figures. According to the Report, if FDI figures are adjusted for both round-tripping in case of China and underestimation of FDI inflows in case of India, the difference in terms of ratio of adjusted FDI to GDP is quite closer, only about 15 per cent during 2000. This adjustment takes account of nearly 50 per cent of total FDI flows round-tripped to China during 1999-2000; which reduces FDI net inflows from $40 billion to $20 billion,[39] and also takes into account India's adoption of a standard computation of FDI, which raises the latter's net FDI inflows from $2-3 billion a year to about $8 billion. In cumulative terms, China's FDI levels obviously remain for higher than India's by virtue of the fact that the former liberalized its trade and investment regime a decade before India did.

• The Steering Committee on FDI set up by the Planning Commission, which presented its report in August 2002, addressed its concern regarding improvement in data coverage on FDI. The National Statistical Commission has recommended conducting periodical surveys on dividends and profits arising out of foreign direct investment and portfolio investment separately. In pursuance of the recommendation, a survey is being launched by the Reserve Bank of India to collect detailed information on FDI that will include reinvested earnings. It is expected that this survey will improve the international compatibility of FDI data in India while providing much more detailed information on FDI flows than currently exists.

• Dr. Neetu Prakash[40] (2004), whose study aims at analyzing the role and performance of FDI in India, stressed on analyzing the different routes through which FDI comes in India; dimensions and trends of FDI vis-à-vis actual inflows in India; and evaluating the reasons for low FDI in India vis-à-vis some selected Asian Countries.

The study suggested that in response to the policy on liberalization, the FDI has now been allowed in all sectors (except a small negative list), such as power, oil, refinery, electronics and electrical equipment, chemicals, hotels, food processing industries, telecommunications, infrastructure, industrial machinery, etc., resulting inflows of FDI increased from US $129 million in 1991-92 to US $3,904 million in 2001-02. But the performance regarding inflows as a percentage of total approvals as well as inflows as compared to other South East Asian Countries especially China is not satisfactory. Further, in this context, the study also made some of the following suggestions to encourage FDI in India:

(a) To expedite the process of disinvestment and privatization;

(b) To reduce the fiscal deficit by cutting down unproductive expenditures of Government Departments;

(c) To use Information Technology (IT) and modern marketing techniques to attract FDI;

(d) To remove evils of corruption, redtapism and bureaucratic system from the Government Departments;

(e) To build a strong financial structure;

(f) To increase the efficiency of labour by providing proper work conditions and training, etc.;

(g) To accept the recommendations of Steering Committee (set up by the Planning Commission in August 2001). Few of them are as follows:

- To enact Foreign Investment Promotion Law (FIPL) to incorporate and integrate relevant aspects for promoting FDI;
- To empower Foreign Investment Promotion Board

(FIPB) for granting initial central level registrations and approvals wherever possible for speeding up the implementation process;

- To enact a special investment law relating to infrastructure in States in order to increase investment in infrastructure as well as remove hurdles in process of promoting infrastructure;
- To empower Foreign Investment Implementation Authority (FIIA) for expediting administrative and policy approvals; and
- To develop Special Economic Zones (SEZs) as internationally competitive destinations for export-oriented FDI.

If these suggestions are implemented, FDI is expected to play a more important role in near future.

1.12 Host Country Determinants of Foreign Direct Investment

It is widely agreed that foreign direct investment (FDI) takes place when three sets of determining factors exist simultaneously: the presence of ownership-specific competitive advantages in a transnational corporation (TNC); the presence of locational advantages in a host country; and the presence of superior commercial benefits in an intra-firm as against an arm's-length relationship between investor and recipient.

- The ownership-specific advantages (e.g. proprietary technology) of a firm – if exploited optimally – can compensate for the additional costs of establishing production facilities in a foreign environment and can overcome the firm's disadvantages vis-a-vis local firms.
- The ownership-specific advantages of the firm should be combined with the locational advantages of host

countries (e.g. large markets or lower costs of resources or superior infrastructure).

- Finally, the firm finds greater benefits in exploiting both ownership-specific and locational advantages by internalization, i.e. through FDI rather than arm's-length transactions. This may be case for several reasons. For one, markets for assets or production inputs (technology, knowledge or management) may be imperfect, if they exist at all, and may involve significant transaction costs or time lags. For another, it may be in a firm's interest to retain exclusive rights to assets (e.g. knowledge) which confer upon it a significant competitive advantage (e.g. monopoly rents).

While the first and third conditions are firm-specific determinants of FDI, the second is location-specific and has a crucial influence on a host country" inflows of FDI. If only the first condition is met, firms will rely on exports, licensing or the sale of patents to service a foreign market. If the third condition is added to the first, FDI becomes the preferred mode of servicing foreign markets, but only in the presence of location-specific advantages. Within the trinity of conditions for FDI to occur, locational determinants are the only ones that host governments can influence directly.

To explain differences in FDI inflows among countries and to formulate policies to capture inbound investment, it is necessary to understand how TNCs choose investment locations. This need has become all the more topical as discussions and negotiations on international investment framework – whether at the bilateral, regional or multilateral levels – have gathered momentum and the possibility of a multilateral framework on investment has raised questions as to whether, why and how international investment agreements matter for the location of FDI and the activities of TNCs. In particular, a key question (one similar to that faced by the creators of the Post-Second World War multilateral trading system) is what effect, if any, a multilateral framework on investment might have for the growth and pattern of FDI.

The objective of this study is therefore to review the location-specific (host-country) determinants of FDI inflows and stocks and to analyze how these have changed in a liberalizing and globalizing world economy. The impact of international investment frameworks on FDI is examined separately, since that is a matter of special interest to countries in the light of recent international discussions.

On the basis of Dunning (1998), the host country determinants can be classified into three categories, viz. Policy Framework of Foreign Direct Investment; Economic Determinants; and the Facilitation Factors. This view of host-country determinants begins with the role of national policies and especially the liberalization of policies (a key factor in globalization) as FDI determinants. Then follows a review of business facilitation measures: as the world economy becomes more open to international business transactions, countries compete increasingly for FDI not only by improving their policy and economic determinants, but also by implementing pro-active facilitation measures that go beyond policy liberalization. While not as important as the other two sets of determinants, these measures are receiving increased attention. Economic determinants and, in particular, their changing significance in the context of liberalization and globalization are reviewed next, and also reviewed the issues related to the impact of international investment frameworks.

Several caveats are required before reviewing the FDI determinants, analyzed below:

- Direct investment abroad is a complex venture. As

distinct from trade, licensing or portfolio investment, FDI involves a long-term commitment to a business endeavour in a foreign country. It often involves the engagement of considerable assets and resources that need to be coordinated and managed across countries and to satisfy the principal requirements of successful investment, such as sustainable profitability and acceptable risk/profitability ratios. Typically, there are many host country factors involved in deciding where an FDI project should be located and it is often difficult to pinpoint the most decisive factor. Although the analysis that follows treats each of the three sets of determinants separately, the interrelationships among them must be borne in mind.

- The relative importance of different location-specific determinants depends on at least four aspects of investment: *the motive for investment* (e.g. resource-seeking or market-seeking FDI); *the type of investment* (e.g. New or sequential FDI); *the sector of investment* (e.g. services or manufacturing) and *the size of investors* (small and medium-sized TNCs or large TNCs). The relative importance of different determinants also changes as the economic environment evolves over time. It is therefore entirely possible that a set of host country determinants that explains FDI in a particular country at a given time changes as the structures of its domestic economy and of the international economy evolve. At the same time, there are also location-specific determinants that remain constant.
- As a general principle, host countries that offer what TNCs are seeking, and host countries whose policies are most conducive to TNC activities stand a good chance of attracting FDI. But, firms also see locational determinants in their interaction with ownership-

specific and internalization advantages in the broader context of their corporate strategies. These strategies aim, at spreading or reducing risk, pursuing oligopolistic competition, and matching competitors' actions or looking for distinct sources of competitive advantage. In the context of different strategies, the same motive and the corresponding host country determinants can acquire different meanings.

1.12.1 The National FDI Policy Framework

Core FDI policies consist of rules and regulations governing the entry and operations of foreign investors, the standards of treatment accorded to them, and the functioning of the markets within which they operate. These policies can range from outright prohibition of FDI entry to non-discrimination in the treatment of foreign and domestic firms – and even preferential treatment of foreign firms. They typically satisfy various objectives – reducing or increasing FDI, influencing its sectoral composition or geographical origin, encouraging specific contributions to the economy and affecting ways in which these contributions are made. To achieve these objectives, FDI policies are usually accompanied by other policies that also influence investors' decisions.

Among these supplementary policies used to influence locational decisions, trade policy plays the most prominent role. The study revealed that, to attract FDI and to maximize its contributions to their import-substituting development strategies, countries in Latin America used a mix of protectionist trade policies combined with policies allowing FDI in manufacturing. Asian countries, in contrast, used both FDI and trade policies to encourage TNCs to contribute to their export-oriented economic strategies. Hong Kong, China pursued laissez-faire trade and FDI policies. On the other hand, the FDI policies of such economics as the Republic of Korea, Taiwan Province of China and Japan were embedded in a broader set of industrial policies guiding and selectively inducing TNCs to link up with local firms to help increase local innovative and export capacities.

Other related policies may include privatization policies and policies determined by the international agreements a country has signed:

- Privatization is a special case of acquisition, as it involves purchases of firms from the state. It has two dimensions: an FDI-policy dimension and a competition-policy dimension. If privatization welcomes foreign investors, it broadens the scope of FDI. The competition-policy dimension becomes relevant if, in industries characterized as natural or near-natural monopolies, the sale of a privatized company to a domestic or foreign investor only means the transfer of a monopoly from the state to a private agent.
- International investment agreements provide an international dimension to national FDI policies. Some of them focus on insurance and protection, while others deal with broader issues.

(a) The Impact of Globalization

The relationship between FDI policies and globalization runs both ways: each affects the other. Indeed, it was the liberalization of national policy frameworks that helped unleash one of the key driving forces of globalization, as we know it today: increasing international production by TNCs. At the same time, progress in the liberalization of trade, as well as technological progress in telecommunications and transportation, permitted TNCs to pursue increasingly regional and global strategies, and to integrate their production structures on a regional or global basis, which in turn creates incentives to liberalize FDI policies. This mutually reinforcing process has in fact shaped international production in recent years and led to its integration at a deeper level than the shallow integration based on arm's-length trade and flows of financial capital.

The accelerating process of FDI liberalization led countries to extend more open policies into industries, long considered sensitive and to permit forms of FDI entry previously considered less desirable, such as the establishment of fully owned subsidiaries, Mergers and Acquisitions and participation in privatization programmes. This has, in turn, provided TNCs with an ever-increasing choice of locations and they have become more selective and demanding as regards other host country determinants.

The liberalization of FDI frameworks has contributed to an acceleration of FDI flows by creating more "space" for them, a process of diminishing returns has set in and liberal FDI policy is increasingly losing its effectiveness as a locational determinant of FDI. Competing intensely with one another for FDI and finding that liberal policies are no longer enough, host countries have increasingly come to realize the importance of adopting proactive measures to facilitate business transactions by foreign investors and of improving the economic determinants of FDI.

The speeding up of liberalization and the simultaneous weakening of its effectiveness as a determinant of FDI has extended the scope of FDI policy frameworks. In particular, it has drawn attention to other policies that may affect FDI but that have not been specifically considered in this context in the past. These could be seen as constituting the "outer ring" of policies in the FDI context, as distinct from the core policies directly used to influence FDI. The outer-ring policies can be divided into macro-economic and macro-organizational policies:

Macro-economic policies: These are mainly monetary and fiscal policies, including those affecting taxes and exchange rates:

- Monetary and fiscal policies, which determine the parameters of economic stability such as the rate of inflation and the state of external and budgetary balances, influence all types of investment. Since they determine interest rates and thus the cost of capital in a host country, they directly affect one of the determinants of the investment decision, although the effects of; interest rates on FDI are smaller than on domestic investment because TNCs normally have a greater choice of sources of financing.
- Fiscal policies also determine general tax levels, including corporate and personal tax rates and thereby influence inward FDI. Other things being equal, a country with lower corporate tax rates should stand a greater chance of attracting FDI projects than a country with higher rates. Personal tax rates may affect managers' choices as regards the location of regional headquarters and may affect the hiring of foreign personnel.
- Exchange-rate policy is related to stability and may influence FDI decisions by affecting the prices of host country assets, the value of transferred profits, and the competitiveness of foreign affiliate exports.

Macro-organizational policies: These affect patterns of resource allocation as well as the structure and organization of economic activities and include the following:

- First, there are structural policies influencing the industry composition of manufacturing, the spatial composition of economic activities, the functional composition of activities, and the composition of activities by type of ownership and intensity of competition. Some of these policies have been used in the FDI context for some time, although with different degrees of intensity.

- There are also policies determining the functioning of factor markets, such as labour-market policies that may have either a discouraging or an encouraging impact on inward FDI.
- Finally, there are policies that affect the supply and quality of productive resources in a host country. Such policies can affect not only the quantity of FDI a country receives but also its quality. Thus, educational and health policies that raise the supply and quality of human capital in a country or policies that promote infrastructure development can improve a country's locational advantages substantially and give it an edge over others.

To sum up, one of the consequences of the worldwide trend towards the liberalization of FDI policies has been the realization by countries that, as their FDI policies proper become similar, the value of these policies as tools to influence locational decisions becomes less pronounced. Host countries are instead increasingly evaluated by potential foreign investors on the basis of a broader set of policies within which FDI policies are embedded.

1.12.2. Economic Determinants of FDI

The economic determinants of inward FDI can be grouped for analytical convenience into three clusters, each of them reflecting the principal motivations of TNCs for investing in foreign countries: *resource-seeking, market-seeking* and *efficiency-seeking*. As with the evolution of FDI regulations, these determinants have changed in response to the forces of liberalization and globalization. This section reviews the economic determinants of inward FDI, focusing on the principal ones, and analyses how they have changed over time.

(a) Natural Resources

Historically, the most important motivation of FDI has been the exploitation of natural resources. The FDI inflow is nowhere near the annual target of $10 billion set by the Government many years ago. This is because the infrastructural facilities are poor, several factors are costly and the policy and procedural environment in India in several respects is far from encouraging. Not only the foreign capital is shying away from India but also it is feared that there are signs of capital flight from India. Besides the decline in the importance of the primary sector in world output, this decline was caused by factors such the development of the indigenous enterprises in this sector. In a number of developing countries the public sector came to play an important role in the resources based industries. Public sector efforts also included equity or technical collaborations with MNCs.

Although, the share of the primary sector in FDI has declined, there has been a substantial increase of the FDI in this sector in absolute terms. The FDI stock in the primary sector of developed countries increased more than five-fold during 1975-1990, while in the developing countries it increased more than six-fold. Though declining in importance, the availability of natural resources is still a determinant of FDI and continues to offer important possibilities for inward investment in resource-rich countries. Natural resources still explain much of the inward FDI in a number of countries, developing (countries in sub-Sahara, Africa), developed (Australia) and countries in transition (Azerbaijan, Kazakhstan and Russian Federation).

(b) National Markets

Another important traditional determinant of FDI has

been market seeking. Markets protected from international competition by high tariffs or quotas triggered *tariff jumping* FDI. The market access became the predetermining motive for investing in the manufacturing sector of developed countries between the two world wars and of developing countries in the 1960s and 1970s, during the heyday of import substitution industrialization. This motive was paramount in the wave of United States investments in Europe, especially in the United Kingdom, during the early post war period and in Japanese investments in the United States after the mid 1980s, following voluntary export restrictions and the possibility of further protectionist measures in the automobile industry.

It is very relevant to note here that the largest market in the world, the U.S., is the largest recipient of FDI, followed by China, a huge market by the size of the economy, population and very high economic growth rate. It is being pointed out that some of the largest national markets remain unmatched in size by the largest regional markets or even by entire continents.

The lion's share of FDI flow to the developing countries goes to the larger markets with comparatively good infrastructure and political stability in general.

The growing importance of the service sector has also been resulting in increasing FDI because of the fact that most services are not tradable and, therefore, the only way to deliver them to foreign markets is through establishment abroad. However, the highly regulated nature of the services sector has been a deterrent to the FDI flow in its full potential.

(c) Efficiency Seeking

Another important motivation of FDI is efficiency seeking. Low cost of production, deriving mostly from cheap labour, is the driving force of many FDIs in developing countries. Export processing zones have been developed by developing countries mostly to take advantage of the efficiency seeking FDI flows.

It may be noted that the presence of any of the three determinants mentioned above alone need not attract FDI. Even if a country has natural resources or abundance of cheap labour, FDI would not take place in the absence of required infrastructural facilities to develop the industry or trade. Besides, several other factors like the political environment; government policies, bureaucratic culture, social climate etc. are also important determinants of FDI.

1.12.3. The Impact of International Policy Frameworks

In the efforts to attract FDI and to influence its quality, countries increasingly conclude international agreements dealing with an expanding set of issues. A number of these instruments may influence some of the FDI determinants and thus exert an impact on FDI flows. This section discusses the extent to which the most important of the existing or potential agreements – bilateral, regional, plurilateral and multilateral – do indeed affect FDI determinants and, if so, whether they can also influence FDI flows, either alone or together with other determinants.

(a) Bilateral Investment Treaties

Bilateral Investment Treaties (BITs) were originally concluded between developed and developing countries, with a view to promoting investment between the treaty partners. Increasingly, BITs are also concluded between developed and developing countries on the one side and economies in transition on the other; they are also being concluded between developing countries. The number of these treaties increased significantly in the 1990s: about three-quarters of the over 1,500 treaties in existence at the end of 1997 date from the 1990s.

BITs exert some influence on the policy framework for

FDI, by contributing to the improvement of an investment climate. They do so, in particular, by strengthening the bilateral standards of protection and treatment of foreign investors and establishing mechanisms for dispute settlement. In this manner, they help to reduce the risk of investing in countries' party to these treaties. BITs do not alter the economic determinants of FDI, and they seldom provide for proactive promotion measures by governments.

Since FDI flows are determined by a variety of factors, it would be unreasonable to expect that any improvements in the investment climate brought about by BITs, which relate only to parts of the FDI policy framework, could exert a significant impact on FDI flows. Even such important economic determinants as large and growing markets or an abundant labour force do not work alone as FDI determinants, but only in tandem with other factors. And, just as there are cases of countries receiving substantial FDI flows without putting business facilitation measures into place, so there are examples of countries with large FDI flows and few, if any, BITs. Conversely, there are also examples of countries that have concluded many BITs but have attracted only modest amounts of FDI.

A comprehensive recent statistical analysis confirmed the relative insignificance of BITs in determining FDI. Both an analysis of time-series data on bilateral FDI flows in relation to 200 BITs; and a cross-sectional analysis of 133 countries investigating the relationship between total FDI flows and stocks; the number of BITs; and other independent economic variables, showed that variables such as market size and growth, exchange rates and country risk are more important than BITs as FDI determinants. At best, BITs play a minor and secondary role in influencing FDI flows and explaining differences in their size among countries. Moreover, with the rapid proliferation of BITs in the 1990s, the distinctive influence of BITs as a signal to attract additional investment may have been eroded, as compared to a period when such treaties were still comparatively rare. Indeed, foreign investors increasingly regard BITs, as a standard feature of the institutional structure introduced in the past decade.

None of this means that BITs do not support the existing level of investment or prevent it from declining; the analysis mentioned above focused on the impact on FDI growth. There is some evidence that foreign investors encourage governments of home countries to conclude BITs with host countries in which they already have FDI. Furthermore, BITs may matter as a protective device for small projects, undertaken by small and medium-sized enterprises, even if the amounts involved are too small to affect the total or even bilateral flows of the host countries investigated in these analysis. Finally, while it may be quite reasonable to expect the impact of a BIT on FDI flows to occur soon after its conclusion, it cannot be ruled out that an impact may only occur many years later. This may well happen if important locational determinants of FDI are not yet in place in a host or home country. This is in line with earlier conclusions concerning policy determinants, namely, that they are enabling in character: by themselves, they have little or no effect, because they have to be complemented by economic determinants and, in specific circumstances, can be helped by investment facilitation measures.

(b) Regional Integration Frameworks

The impact of Regional Integration Frameworks (RIFs) – which range from free-trade areas to complete economic integration – on FDI determinants depends on a variety of factors. The first and foremost is the scope and depth of the integration envisaged by a RIF, which determines the extent of policy harmonization and varies by type of RIF. At the one extreme, a shallow RIF that entails no more than tariff reductions among members and external tariffs on non-members can have an impact on FDI determinants through trade or strategic responses to competitors (static effects) and growth (dynamic effects). A deeper RIF that also allows for the movement of capital (including FDI) would be expected to have effects on the investment determinants of TNCs beyond those induced by trade liberalization or growth alone. In general, as a region becomes more integrated as the result of a RIF, the influence of the RIF on FDI determinants can work through more channels. In addition, as regulatory FDI frameworks become more harmonized within a region, more importance is attached by TNCs to economic determinants in deciding their precise location. To a lesser extent, the importance of business facilitation also rises.

The credibility of RIFs, manifested in the extent to which RIF's provisions are actually implemented, is another factor determining the impact of RIFs on FDI determinants. Failure to implement RIFs fully means that their impact on FDI determinants cannot be pronounced, as illustrated by the failure of numerous RIFs in the 1960s and 1970s to exert any discernible influence on TNCs. More recent RIFs, such as NAFTA, MERCOSUR and earlier the European Union, have exerted greater influence on FDI determinants, especially those related to policy and economic conditions, precisely because they have been implemented more strictly than their predecessors. If member countries choose to be exempted from RIF's provisions and continue to restrict access to certain industries, retain high tariffs for certain products or keep low environmental standards, such exemptions can also influence FDI determinants, even if they are temporary. They also place in doubt the member countries' commitment to adhere to a given RIF. Similarly, the speed with which a member country implements RIF provisions – for instance, abolishing tariffs – also influences the country-specific impact of the RIF on FDI determinants.

A third factor is the prior interdependence of member countries and the established linkages among them, as indicated by the levels of trade and FDI barriers. For countries that have already established significant links, the principal influence of a RIF on FDI determinants would depend on how they address divergences in domestic policy. The Free Trade Agreement between the United States and Canada (1989), had very little impact on FDI flows to Canada, partly because bilateral trade between the two countries had already been considerably liberalized prior to the Agreement, either through multilateral rounds of tariff reduction or through sectoral agreements like the Canada-United States Auto Pact. The Free Trade Agreement meant that cross-penetration of markets through FDI was not especially required and this was evident in a decline in Canadian outward FDI to the United States.

A distinction needs to be drawn here between RIFs confined to developed countries and those involving developing countries. For most recent RIFs among developed countries (e.g. the case of the enlargement of the European Union), the pre-existing, largely open, FDI framework remains in effect after the implementation of the RIF. Not addressing the movement of capital explicitly in the RIF does not therefore necessarily detract from its impact on economic and business facilitation determinants. For most RIFs that involve developing countries, the pre-existing FDI framework is typically not open to the same degree for all members, with the restrictions often reflecting the level of development and structural characteristics of their economies. Therefore, in the case of NAFTA, MERCOSUR and the revised Andean Pact, FDI provisions are included explicitly on both the inward and the outward side, even if no provisions on the movement of other factors of production are included. In these cases, RIFs can have a direct impact on the host countries' policy frameworks for FDI, in addition to their impacts on other categories of FDI determinants.

Even if RIFs have a positive impact on FDI determinants for the region as a whole, not all member countries necessarily benefit to the same extent. For some countries, membership in RIFs will enhance their location-specific advantages. For small countries, the size of their domestic market will no longer deter market-seeking foreign investors in tradable since they will now have access to the region's market, and no just the host country market. For the same reason, the size of the domestic market of large countries will no longer be as attractive and, therefore, will become less of a bargaining asset for host county governments. Economic determinants specific to individual member countries or business facilitation at the local level can thus become important.

The analysis that follows looks at the ways in which RIFs influence each of the three categories of FDI determinants, namely, the policy framework for FDI, the set of economic determinants, and the factors pertaining to the facilitation of business.

The Impact of Regional Integration Frameworks on FDI Determinants

(i) The policy Framework

As analyzed earlier, the majority of RIFs do not explicitly address FDI policy, although there is an increasing tendency for free a trade agreement to include investment. Even RIFs postulating a high degree of integration among members, including provisions regarding the movement of capital may not necessarily contain explicit FDI policy provisions. The overall impact of RIFs on the policy framework for FDI therefore, depends on whether a RIF contains provisions liberalizing the movement of capital (including FDI capital); on how restrictive the capital movement and investment regimes of the member countries had been prior to the implementation of the RIF; and on other policy-liberalization provisions contained in the RIFs, notably trade policy. Of these conditions, whether or not a RIF contains explicit FDI provisions may be the least important for developed countries and most developing countries as far as inward FDI is concerned, because inward investment regimes are typically open even prior to the implementation of RIFs. The OECD member countries adopted the Code of Liberalization of Capital Movements in 1961, though capital-movement liberalization did not accelerate until after the mid-1970s. Even in many developing countries, at least partially open FDI policies have typically been in place prior to the implementation of a RIF, as the example of Mexico prior to joining NAFTA illustrates. So, the direct impact of explicit FDI provisions contained in RIFs on FDI policy determinants is likely to be small in many instances, unless they result in a considerable liberalization of investment regimes.

Other policy provisions contained in RIFs, especially those relevant to trade liberalization, are likely to be more important in determining FDI. In the overwhelming majority of RIFs, the central elements and the most important factors influencing market-seeking FDI are the liberalization of trade barriers and the granting of preferential market access to members. Trade liberalization and trade policy condition among RIF's members contribute to a policy framework conducive to FDI because they create favourable conditions for foreign affiliates within the region to access regional markets for final and intermediate products. They also allow TNCs to establish regionally integrated production networks to enhance their efficiency. In the case of customs unions and free-trade areas, trade discrimination against non-members in the form of tariff barriers makes the size of a regional market more appealing and encourages market-seeking FDI by TNCs not present in the region. The removal of non-tariff barriers, or their harmonization, also exerts a positive influence on market-seeking FDI.

Finally, RIFs may also influence the speed of FDI (and trade) policy liberalization. The prospective NAFTA Agreement promoted Mexico to liberalize its FDI framework even before the Agreement was signed, even though the liberalization of services and parts of the primary sector accelerated only after Mexico became a signatory. In some cases, however, member countries that are ready to deregulate a particular industry (e.g. financial services in the case of the European Union) may be obliged to wait until the other members of the RIF have reached a similar point. In the European Union, not all countries were ready to deregulate their financial services at the same time, and a tier system was introduced to resolve that. But, the reverse may also take place: countries that are lagging behind in terms of deregulation of industries and liberalization of policies may be pressured to move faster by other RIF members. Even if pressures to liberalize do not apply to FDI policies per se, they can affect the overall policy framework of a member country in a manner that encourages FDI.

More generally, RIFs can reaffirm their members' commitments to adhere to liberal policies and bring about a momentum to continue the liberalization process in both FDI and trade. To put it differently: unless RIFs substantially alter national FDI policy frameworks, they will not have a major impact on FDI policy determinants from the point of view of individual countries. Their contribution to FDI policy determinants lies in ensuring member countries' commitment to adhere to a liberal existing policy framework, or to liberalize it if is restrictive, to harmonize policies, to lock in liberalizing changes, to increase momentum to liberalize further, to strengthen standards of treatment and protection, and to encourage policies that ensure the proper functioning of markets.

(ii) Economic Determinants

Market size and growth are the FDI economic determinants that are most affected by the implementation of a RIF. Dynamic effects of RIFs in encouraging higher rates of economic growth can help boost inward FDI. Most importantly, the size of the market is redefined under a RIF as the size of the region's market. The possibility of accessing a market wider than that of a single country for tradable goods and services becomes an inducement to invest in the region. The United States FDI in the European Union exemplifies this. A part of United States affiliate sales in the European Union are geared to the regional market: their sales in the European Union in countries other than the host countries other than the host country itself accounted for 31 percent of their total sales in 1995. All this is made possible by the removal of intra-regional trade barriers within the region, which carries the implication that a single host country's market size is no longer as significant a determinant of market-seeking FDI as it used to be before the implementation of the RIF. With the implementation of a RIF, the accessibility of a region's market from a given location becomes an important FDI locational determinant. In addition to abolishing customs-clearance procedures that help speed up border crossings, good physical infrastructure, especially in transport and communications, facilitates access to regional markets. The importance of infrastructure as an FDI determinant is therefore enhanced considerably when a RIF comes into effect, for both market-seeking and efficiency-seeking TNCs.

As the importance of market size- as an FDI determinant becomes more uniform for all countries that are members of a RIF and as the removal of cross-border barriers within the region increases competitive pressures, determinants related to enhancing efficiency come to play a bigger role for all types of FDI. Increased market-size – from national to regional or global – is in itself an efficiency-inducing determinant because it provides the demand dimension that gives rise to the possibility of exploiting economies of scale and scope in production and distribution. Indeed, one of the primary advantages of enlarged markets under RIFs is that they create the demand conditions that allow TNCs to reap economies of scale and scope in all parts of the value chain. On the production side, cost considerations are especially important for efficiency-seeking TNCs. RIFs allow such TNCs to locate each value-added activity of the production process in the most cost-efficient location within the region in order to rationalize operations regionally by taking advantage of productivity-adjusted cost differences in labour, technology, and other resources. In sum, RIFs help to create both the demand conditions and the production conditions needed to improve efficiency in production.

Furthermore, RIFs give foreign investors the opportunity to be close to clusters of companies producing similar products or having similar R&D facilities and thus to exploit regional as well as sub-national agglomeration economies and obtain access to created assets. Proximity to a cluster of companies producing similar products or having similar R&D facilities, need not necessarily require that a TNC invests in the same country where these companies or facilities are physically located. It may very well invest in a bordering country in close physical proximity to the cluster of companies or R&D facilities. Thus, within regions, a greater concentration of FDI in a few supranational clusters may develop that allows FDI to be more dispersed in terms of country distribution, but more concentrated in terms of geographical space.

Finally, RIFs promote greater competition to capture expanded markets or increase market shares within the region.

Firms may respond to the increased competition for markets by establishing a physical presence, especially if arm's-length competition through trade is hindered by a common external tariff. Increases in intra-regional and extra-regional cross-border acquisitions designed to access resources or defend competitive positions often accompany RIFs. About one-quarter of Japanese manufacturing affiliates in Western Europe established during the mid-1990s were established through acquisitions, compared to 10 per cent of those established in 1990.

(iii) Business Facilitation

The primary effect of RIFs on business facilitation is to reduce intra-regional business transaction costs. Such costs arise directly from inadequacies of information, asymmetries in doing business in different countries, the heterogeneity of administrative procedures, and differences in business support measures. Recognizing the importance of business facilitation obstacles, some RIFs seek to harmonize efforts to remove them or replace them with comprehensive region-wide programmes for FDI facilitation. In the case of the European Union, the removal of internal tariff barriers was not sufficient for creating a unified regional market because of other obstacles to intra-regional transactions, especially in services. The European Economic Community identified 280 barriers to cross-border transactions in 1985, and removed about 90 per cent of them in 1993 as part of the single market programme.

Since RIFs allow a region's market or many of its resources to be more easily accessible by TNCs from any location within the regional bloc, and policy coordination and harmonization gives rise to a more level playing field, business facilitation factors become increasingly important, as they concern matters which individual members countries – and, increasingly, sub-national authorities – can address to distinguish themselves from one another when competing for FDI. Even if some business facilitation measures are harmonized across members, there still remain important differences among members that allow them to compete for FDI. Measures aimed at targeting specific investors, providing social amenities and marketing a country as an investment location usually fall outside the scope of RIFs, and can therefore be used by each RIF member to enhance location-specific advantages. One result is precisely a proliferation of incentives used to attract FDI.

1.13. Objectives of the Study

The present study is aimed at examining the following:

- Firstly, to study the global FDI flows vis-a-vis the FDI flows in India in order to identify the position of India in the overall global FDI flows along with presenting the bottlenecks if any for low rate of FDI flows.
- Secondly, to analyse and present FDI flows at aggregate level, in the context of pre and post liberalization periods with a view to bring out the diversities if any as well as to identify the measures of the Government for such position.
- Thirdly, to examine sectoral differences if any in the FDI flows and to bring out the important sectors which have attracted major FDI flows.
- Fourthly, to discuss the state-wise FDI flows to highlight the dominant state which has attracted major share of FDI flows as well as to analyse the factors for such position.
- Fifthly, to study the pattern and elements of FDI flows, in order to bring out the relative differences in the flows of component-wise FDI and their pattern.
- Sixthly, to discuss the role of mergers and acquisitions and foreign equity participation in India with reference to FDI flows.

- Seventhly, to study the impact of FDI flows in Indian economy in general and Indian Industry in particular in order to highlight the growth and performance.
- Eighthly, to present the impact of FDI flows on the industrial development in India.
- Finally, to present summary of the finding along with identifying various issues raised in the study and to suggest suitable suggestions for such issues.

1.14. Hypotheses of the Study

An industrializing economy like India can greatly benefit in different ways by welcoming foreign capital into the country. The following are the main hypotheses:

(a) India can have better technology to exploit the unutilized national resources;

(b) Foreign Investment will enable technology up gradation and modernisation of Industry to improve quality and productivity;

(c) Foreign Investment will supplement domestic savings and capital formation towards accelerating the rate of investment for economic development;

(d) Foreign Investment will help to build up the much-needed infrastructure for the development of agriculture and industry;

(e) Foreign Investment will bring marketing expertise which would enable Indian goods to penetrate the international market on a larger scale; and

(f) Foreign Investment will promote employment generation by absorbing the relatively economical, particularly skilled labour force.

1.15. Significance of the Study

India's foreign investment policy has come long way

since independence. Through Foreign Investment was welcomed initially, the subsequent strain on the foreign exchange reserves due to dividend repatriation, royalty payments, etc. and complaints of repetitive import of same technology prompted the Government to go for a selective and restricted approach. But the failure of the Indian industry to develop technology as its own and the consequent decline of competitiveness, made the Government to liberalize the Foreign Investment Policy. But these policy changes during 1948-90 did not make any major and significant dents on the trend of foreign investment. FERA continued to be a major deterrent for foreign investment.

It is in the 1990s' that the Government has gone for an overhaul of Foreign Investment Policy. FERA-1973 has been diluted largely and foreign investment is welcomed in a wide range of sectors. Foreign investors have responded positively to India's policy changes.

There has been a gradual and steady measure in foreign investment approvals as well as actual inflows. Since the post-liberalization, the Government of India has opened the doors for the foreign investment into various sectors in the country.

1.16. Scope of the Study

This study covers the following:

(a) The analysis of FDI inflows and outflows;
(b) Sector/Industry/Region-wise analysis of FDI;
(c) FDI as global prospective;
(d) The measures and machinery of the Government to attract FDI;
(e) The role of mergers and acquisitions for FDI flows;
(f) A comparative analysis of global FDI flows vis-à-vis FDI flows in India;

(g) The analysis of Foreign Aid and Foreign Collaboration in India; and

(h) The impact of FDI flows on Industrial Development in India.

1.17. Methodology

In order to conduct the research study on the Impact of Foreign Direct Investment flows in India, the following methodology is adopted:

A. Sources of Data

The study will be based on both primary and secondary sources of data.

Primary Data: The primary source of data is being collected by administering well designed questionnaires to various people involved in policy making, industry and other agencies.

Secondary Data: The secondary source of data relevant to the study was being collected from various libraries, FDI Board, Ministry of Finance, Government of India. In this context, I have made use of reports of CMIE, RBI Reports, Economic Survey, World Investment Report, India Development Report, Asia Development Report, and other journals.

B. Research Techniques

In order to analyse and present the data collected both from primary and secondary sources, the research analysis techniques such as Ratio Analysis, Percentages, Trend Analysis, Averages, Techniques of Regression, Correlation, Multiple Regressions, Chi-square test, Student's T-test and Scaling techniques, etc. have been used.

1.18. Organization of the Study

The study of "THE IMPACT OF FOREIGN DIRECT

INVESTMENT ON INDUSTRIAL DEVELOPMENT IN INDIA" has been divided into the following chapters:

Chapter – I is an introductory in nature and deals with the Overview of Foreign Direct Investment, review of literature, objective, scope, methodology, hypothesis and limitations of the study.

Chapter – II discusses the Foreign Collaborations in India, and its impact on the Indian Economy.

Chapter – III is concerned with Foreign Direct Investment – Global perspective. This also covers flows of FDI at the region-wise i.e., Developed, Developing, and Central and Eastern Europe Countries.

Chapter – IV analyses the Aggregate flows of FDI in India as to review the country-wise inflows of FDI.

Chapter – V deals with State and Industry–wise Analysis of FDI as to point out the sector, which attracts majority of FDI flows.

Chapter – VI highlights the Prospects and Opportunities of FDI with a view to present the Policy of the Government by sector.

Chapter – VII presents the Impact of FDI on various facets of Industrial Development, viz., Exports, Foreign Exchange Reserves, Balance of Payments, Employment, etc.

Chapter – VIII presents a summary of findings of the earlier chapters in the form of conclusions and offers suggestions for improvement of FDI flows to India.

REFERENCES

1. Sanjaya Lal, "Less-Developed Countries and Private Foreign Investment", *Economic and Political Weekly,* August 3, 1974.

2. International Monetary Fund, *Balance of Payments Manual*, Washington, DC, 1977, p. 408
3. This general definition of FDI is based on Organisation for Economic Co-operation and Development (OECD) detailed benchmark definition of Foreign Direct Investment, Second Edition (Paris, OECD,1992) and International Monetary Fund, Balance of Payments Manual, Fifth Edition (Washington, D.C., IMF, 1993).
4. United Nations Conference on Trade and Development (UNCTAD), World Investment Report 2003.
5. Direct Investment comprises not only the initial transaction establishing the relationship between the investor and the enterprise but also all subsequent transactions between them and among affiliated enterprises, both incorporated and unincorporated (IMF, Balance of Payments Manual, Fifth Edition, 1993, p. 86).
6. FDI can take the form of green-field investment in a new establishment or Merger & Acquisition (M&A) of existing local enterprises.
7. Modechai E. Kreinin, *International Economics* (New York: Harcourt Brace Jovanovich Inc., 1971, p. 332.
8. Quoted from various sources by United Nations, World Investment Report, 1998, p.106.
9. Quoted from different sources by WTO, *Annual Report*, 1998, p. 33.
10. World Bank, *World Development Report 1992*, p. 96.
11. Press Release on Revised Data on Foreign Direct Investment, Ministry of Commerce & Industry, Govt. of India, August 2004.
12. Charles Kindleberger, American Business Abroad (New Haven Yale University Press, 1969).
13. Modechai E. Kreinin, *International Economics* (New York: Harcourt Brace Jovanovich Inc., 1971), p. 332.
14. The two gap means the gap between savings and investments and gap between foreign exchange availability and import needs.
15. Total Foreign Exchange Reserves accounted for US $ 119.5 billion as on 25th June, 2004 – *RBI Bulletin* July 2004; and reached $129.55 billion as on 31st December 2004 – *Times of India,* January 31, 2005.
16. From the speech of Shri Yashwant Sinha, Finance Minister of

India, presenting Central Government Budget 2001-02 in the Parliament on 28th February 2001.

17. Wide guidelines issued on 4th January 2002, Press Note No. 3 (2002 Series).
19. Prof. V. Gangadhar & Yadagiri; "Trends of Foreign Direct Investment in India", the *Chartered Accountant*, December 1995.
20. *Alternative Economic Survey 1998-2000*, p. 73
21. *Ibid.*, p. 72
22. Nagesh Kumar, "Economic Reforms and their Macro-Economic Impact", *Economic and Political Weekly*, March 4, 2000, p. 807.
23. *Business Standard*, January 5, 2001, p. 1.
24. John Degnbol-Martinussen, *Policies, Institutions and Industrial Development* (Delhi, 2001), p. 194.
25. C.P. Chandrasekhar and Jayati Ghosh, *The Market that Failed: A Decade of Neoliberal Economic Reforms in India* (Delhi, 2002), p. 133.
26. *Shimla Management Journal*, Volume 2, No. 2. May 2002.
27. Rukmini Parthasarathy, "FIPB No Red tape...", *Business Today*, February 22-March 6, 2000, pp. 24.
28. Rajat Acharyya, "Globalization, Rigged Rules and Double Standards – A review of Oxfam International 2002, Rigged Rules and Double Standards: Trade, Globalization and the Fight against Poverty", Washington Oxfam International Advocacy Office, *Decision*, Indian Institute of Management, Kolkata, Volume 29, July-December 2002.
29. "The Relation between Foreign Direct Investment and Growth: Causality and Mechanisms", *Indian Journal of Economics*, Volume LXXXII, No. 330, January 2003.
30. "Investing in China's Economic Development Zones: A Managerial Guide", *International Journal of Management*, Volume 2Q, No. 2, June 2003.
31. Ball, Don and McCulloch, Wendell, *International Business*, Irwin Mc GrawHill. (2001).
32. Onkvisit Sak and John J. Shaw, *International Marketing*, Prentice Hall, NJ. 2000, p. 358.
33. Foreign Investment Opportunities and Customs Laws in China's Special Economic Zones, *International Journal of Management*, Volume 20, No.1 – March 2003.
34. Bellur, V. Venkatakrishna & Meidu – "Privatization and free

market in the PRC: Implication to Multinational" *Business Research Year Book*, Global Business Perspectives, Publication of International Academy of Business Disciplines, 1997, Volume IV.

35. Sadhana Srivastava, "What is the True level of FDI flows to India", *Economic and Political Weekly*, Volume XXXVIII, No. 7 February 15, 2003, p. 608.

36. FDI inflows in China accounted for US $ 44,846 million whereas US $ 3,403 million in India during the year 2001. The share of India in Developing Countries stood at 5.2 percent, whereas that of China is 72.1 percent. *Economic Survey 2002-03*, Government of India.

37. *World Investment Directory, 2000*, p. 113.

38. E.M. Graham and E. Wada, "Foreign Direct Investment in China: Effects on Growth and Economic Performance" in P. Drysdale (ed), *Achieving High Growth: Experience of Transitional Economies in East Asia*, Oxford University Press.

39. World Bank, *Global Development Finance 2002: Financing the Poorest Countries*, Washington DC.

40. Dr. Neetu Prakash, "Foreign Direct Investment in India", *The Management Accountant*, Volume 39, No. 4. April 2004.

2

Foreign Colloborations in India

2.1 Introduction

India is on the threshold of a business revolution favored by political, economic, social and demographic factors. In the light of the recent economic liberalization the Indian economy has been integrated with the world economic system. In the Indian context, this implies opening up the economy to foreign direct investment by providing facilities to foreign companies to invest in different fields of economic activity in India; removing constraints and obstacles to the entry of Multinational Corporations (MNCs) in India (through dilutions and ultimate scrapping of restrictive laws like FERA); allowing Indian companies to enter into foreign collaborations in India and also encouraging them to set up joint ventures abroad; carrying out massive import liberalization programmes by switching over from quantitative restrictions to tariffs in the first place, and then bringing down the level of import duties considerably; and instead of a plethora of export incentives (like duty drawbacks, cash compensatory support, replenishment licenses and other fiscal incentives, etc.) opting for exchange rate adjustments for promoting exports.

A common form of MNC's participation in Indian industry is through entering into collaboration with Indian industrialists.

Foreign collaboration is one of the forms of foreign private investment in India. In recent years, as a result of New Economic Policy 1991 of the Government of India, this form of foreign private investment is becoming more popular as compared to direct foreign investment. Under this form, there is joint participation of foreign and domestic (Indian) capital. Foreign collaborations may be in the form of:

(i) Joint participation between foreign Governments and Indian Government;

(ii) Participation between foreign private firms and Indian Government; and

(iii) Participation between foreign private firms and Indian private firms.

2.2. Foreign Collaborations in the Post-Independence Period

Before independence, the attitude towards foreign private capital (FDI and Foreign Collaborations), was one of fear and suspicion. It was, of course, natural being on account of the previous exploitative role played by foreign investors in 'draining away' resources from India. Though this fear and suspicion to some extent reflected in our first Industrial Policy Resolution of 1948, yet the role of foreign private investment was equally recognized and it, thus, made clear that: i) There will be no discrimination between foreign and Indian capital; ii) The foreign companies will have full opportunities to earn profits without subjecting them to under controls; and iii) In case of compulsory acquisition or nationalization, compensation will be paid on a fair and equitable basis. Although, certain relaxations in the direction of foreign investment were made in the Industrial Policy Resolution of 1956, but in an overall sense, our policy towards foreign investment remained quite restrictive and selective.

During the early phase of the planning era, the national policy towards foreign capital did recognize the need for foreign capital, but decided not to permit it a dominant position. Consequently, foreign collaborations had to keep their equity within the ceiling of 49 per cent and allow the Indian counterpart a majority stake. Moreover, foreign collaborations were to be permitted in priority areas, more especially those in which we had not developed our capabilities

As a result, during the period 1948-60, only 1080 foreign collaborations were approved whereas during 1961-70 the number of such approvals was 2475. In fact, it was during the eighties and nineties that Indian Government liberally relaxed its policy towards foreign collaboration, specifically in respect of investors from oil exporting countries. In January 1983, under the Technology Policy Statement (TPS), a number of policy measures were announced liberating the licensing and investment provisions. Consequently, the number of collaborations rose to the order of 7436 during 1981-90. As a result of New Economic Policy 1991 of the Government of India, the total number of foreign collaboration approvals raised to 26332 during the period 1991-2004.

It was only during the eighties that Government relaxed its policy towards foreign collaborations. This was done specifically in respect of investors from Oil Exporting Developing countries with a well-defined package of exemptions:

(i) Investment up to 40 per cent in equity of new ventures could be made by investors from Oil Exporting Developing countries in specified segments without being linked to technology transfer.

(ii) Investments by Non-Resident Indians (NRIs) were allowed in Indian Industrial Units under the defined scheme within the framework of the conditions laid down by the Government.

This was followed by Technology Policy Statement (TPS) in January 1983. The objective of the policy was to acquire imported technology and ensure that it was of the latest type appropriate to the requirements and resources of the country. Under this policy, a number of policy measures were announced liberalizing the licensing provisions:

(a) All but 26 industries were exempted from licensing in case of non-MRTP and non-FERA companies;

(b) Private sector was allowed to participate in the manufacture of telecommunications equipment;

(c) A number of electronic items were exempted from MRTP Act;

(d) Foreign companies were allowed to manufacture electronic components;

(e) MRTP companies were allowed to set up industries in backward areas;

(f) A number of new items were added to the list of industries allowed to be set up by FERA and MRTP units;

(g) Broad banding of a license for a number of industries was allowed; and

(h) MRTP companies could commercialize the results of their R& D or of those of national laboratories.

As a consequence of the measures taken by the Government, during August 1991 and August 1998, there should be no complacency about the policy of foreign collaborations. Foreign collaborations do have a positive role in certain fields like power generation, steel, aluminum, petroleum, cement etc., but they should not be allowed to proliferate in consumer goods, needed by the upper strata of Indian society. Besides this, the activities of multinationals, which increase our dependence on foreigners and drain away our resources, should be restricted. But a much bolder and persistent policy has to be followed to get rid of them. The stakes are high because multinationals are even known for toppling governments wherever they feel that the regime has become an obstacle to the achievement of their aspirations. The idea of the economic power of the multinationals can be had from the fact that "today, with the solitary exception of India whose national income is only twice the annual income of General Motors, economic resources of all other underdeveloped countries are much less than those of multinational corporation."

The liberalization of policy towards foreign technology and collaborations is enabling Indian companies to upgrade their production facilities or to establish new facilities, which help them to enter/expand the foreign market. A number of companies have thus increased their foreign business. A number of Indian companies are also setting up units abroad, either alone or in collaboration with foreign firms. Indian companies have also been acquiring firms in foreign countries. More and more Indian firms have been taking advantage of the international souring by becoming suppliers of parts and components to companies abroad. Technological and marketing tie-ups with foreign firms will play a major role in internationalization of the Indian business.

2.3. Foreign Collaborations (Financial and Technical) in India

It is proposed to analyse the pattern of approvals of Foreign Collaborations in post-liberalization of Indian Economy. Foreign collaborations are of two types — *Financial Collaborations* and *Technical Collaborations*. In *Financial Collaborations*, the foreign partner participates in equity capital and eligible for profits. More often, the foreign partner enjoys a greater degree of influence than his represented shareholding. In most cases, shares shall be given to the foreign partner against the supply of machinery, raw-materials, patents, technical know-how and technical assistance. In *Technical Collaboration*, the foreign partner does not participate in equity capital or sharing profits. He only supplies expertise and technical know-how against the payment of fees, royalty, etc.

The Industry Ministry accords approval up to Rs. 600 crores on the advice of Foreign Investment Promotion Board (FIPB), but larger projects over this limit are approved by Cabinet Committee on Foreign Investment.

The purpose of this analysis is to bring out the pattern of Foreign Collaboration Approvals and year-wise diversities therein. The Government of India in the process of liberalization has implemented various measures such as, increasing equity participation of Foreign Companies to 51 per cent, FII's were allowed to invest in all the securities traded on the primary and secondary markets, change of FERA rules, Tax incentives and permitting Foreign Collaboration mergers and acquisitions, etc. These measures have given rise to boosting effect for Foreign Collaborations in India. Several Multinational Corporations (MNCs) have increased their equity participation to 51 per cent of their Indian counterparts.

The Table 2.1 presents the data pertaining to Approvals of Foreign Collaborations in India from 1991 to 2004.

A close examination of the data of the Table 2.1 reveals that up to August 2004 there were 26,332 Foreign Collaborations with Rs. 2476.9 billions of foreign investment approved.

Trend of liberalization in the 1980s gave a substantial spurt to foreign collaborations. This would be clear from the fact that of the total 12,760 foreign collaboration agreements approved in 40 years between 1948 and 1988, as many as 6,615 (i.e. 48.3 percent) were approved during the eight years between 1981 and 1988. As a result of liberalized foreign

Table 2.1 FOREIGN COLLABORATION APPROVALS IN INDIA DURING 1991-2004

Year	Total number of Forreign collaborations approved			% share of Financial Collaborations	Investment Approved (Rs. billion)
	Technical	Financial	Total		
1981-85	**2740**	**688**	**3428**	**20.1**	**37.5**
1986-90	**2853**	**1154**	**4007**	**28.8**	**89.9**
1991-95	3954	4157	8111	51.3	531.2
1996	744	1545	2289	67.5	308.9
1997	660	1654	2314	71.5	503.9
1998	595	1184	1779	66.6	275.9
1999	498	1720	2218	77.5	251.4
2000	418	1702	2120	80.3	172.4
2001	288	1976	2264	87.3	209.2
2002	307	1963	2270	86.5	110.6
2003	321	1550	1871	82.8	54.2
2004*	86	1010	1096	92.2	59.9
1991-2004	**7871**	**18461**	**26332 (100.0)**	**70.1**	**2476.9**

Source: SIA, News Letter September 2004 ** Figures in brackets indicate percent to total.

* data for 2004 covered till the end of August

investment policy announced in July-August 1991, there has been a further spurt of foreign collaborations. The data in the table shows that over the period August 1991 to August 2004, the government approved 7,871 foreign technology collaborations and 18,461 foreign direct investment proposals. The total amount of foreign investment approved in the process amounted to Rs. 2,476.9 billion.

The data in Table 2.1 also reveals:

(a) Financial Collaborations were just 20.1 per cent during 1981-85, their share improved to 28.8 per cent during 1986-90, but rose sharply to 70 per cent during 1991-2004.

(b) The amount of Approved Investment also increased sharply from Rs. 89.9 bullions during 1986-90 to Rs. 2476.9 billions during 1991-2004.

Obviously, there is a shift from technical approvals to financial approvals during the post-liberalization phase. However, Government has been successful in attracting more foreign investment in the post-liberalization phase as compared to the earlier period.

Thus, it can be concluded that the post reforms period has witnessed much fold increase in Foreign Collaborations both of Financial and Technical from year to year. This shows an enormous encouraging trend for Foreign Direct Investment in India. This is a very welcoming trend for rapid industrialization and economic development of the country.

2.4. Component-wise Analysis of Foreign Collaboration Approvals

In India as per the rules of liberalization the FDI comes through three different routes. The first is with automatic approvals by the Reserve Bank of India provided the investment is in an industry that belongs to one of the 35 "priority" industries earmarked for up to 51 per cent FDI (Annexure III in the July, 1991 Industrial Policy). MNC's or their Indian partners want to invest in an industry outside these 35 sub-sectors or when an FDI holding of more than 51 per cent is sought, permission has to be taken from the Secretariat of Industrial Approvals or the Foreign Investment Promotion Board. This is the second route for FDI. A third route is investment by NRIs.

Now, it is decided to examine the position of number of category-wise Foreign Collaboration Approvals from 1991 to 2004. Table 2.2 presents the data pertaining to number of Foreign Collaboration Approvals.

TABLE 2.2

Component-wise Number of Foreign Collaboration Approvals

(in numbers)

YEAR	SIA	RBI	FIPB	TOTAL
1991	760 (80.0)	188 (19.8)	2 (0.2)	950 (100.0)
1992	585(38.5)	736 (48.4)	199 (13.1)	1520 (100.0)
1993	307 (20.8)	676 (45.8)	493 (33.4)	1476 (100.0)
1994	382 (20.6)	702 (37.9)	770 (41.5)	1854 (100.0)
1995	631 (27.0)	845 (36.2)	861 (36.8)	2337 (100.0)
1996	410 (17.9)	719 (31.4)	1160 (50.7)	2289 (100.0)
1997	167 (7.2)	801 (34.6)	1346 (58.2)	2314 (100.0)
1998	193 (10.8)	432 (24.3)	1154 (64.9)	1779 (10C.0)
1999	221 (10.0)	571 (25.7)	1426 (64.3)	2218 (100.0)
2000	197 (9.3)	551 (26.0)	1372 (64.7)	2120 (100.0)
2001	207 (9.1)	1132 (50.0)	925 (40.9)	2264 (100.0)
2002	420 (18.5)	1010 (44.5)	840 (37.0)	2270 (100.0)
2003	230 (12.3)	898 (48.0)	743 (39.7)	1871 (100.0)
2004	67 (6.1)	536 (48.9)	493 (45.0)	1096 (100.0)
1991-04	4739 (18.0)	9751 (37.0)	11842 (45.0)	26332 (100.0)

Source: SIA, News Letter September 2004.

Figures in brackets indicate percent to total.

It is observed from the data of the Table 2.2 that, out of the 26,332 total number of approvals of Foreign Collaborations during August 1991 to August 2004, the share of RBI (Reserve Bank of India approval) and FIPB (Foreign Investment Promotion Board) jointly put together was at 82 percent and SIA (Secretariat for Industrial Assistance) route has accounted for remaining 18 percent. Contrary to this in 1991, the first year of economic reforms, there was total 950 numbers of Foreign Collaboration Approvals; SIA route has claimed 760 number of approvals accounting for 80 percent of the total approvals, whereas RBI and RIPB accounted for only 20 percent.

The notTe feature of component-wise number of Foreign Collaboration Approvals is that the proportion of SIA in the total approvals has fluctuated from 80 percent in 1991 to 18.5 percent in 2002, after witnessing a further decline at 12.3 percent in 2003 and 6.1 percent in 2004. As against this phenomena, the approvals from RBI automatic route was moved between 20 percent and 50 percent during the period under review showing further fall in latter year's of the study. However, the number of approvals through FIPB has gained momentum and shown significant increase in total number of approvals from 0.2 percent in 1991 to 39.7 percent in 2003 and further 45.0 percent in 2004.

Thus, this analysis highlights that, in early years of economic liberalization, the SIA route was dominating over the others; whereas in latter years of liberalization, RBI and RIPB was dominating; and between these two, FIPB route was more prominent than that of the RBI route of approvals.

2.5. Industry-wise Analysis of Foreign Collaboration Approvals

During the post-liberalization era since 1991 the Government of India has been allowing Foreign Direct Investment and Foreign Technology/Financial Collaborations are most of the sectors of Indian Economy. Now this is turn to analyse the industry-wise foreign collaborations approved during the period August 1991 to August 2004. The data presented in Table 2.3.

TABLE 2.3

Industrywise Distribution of Foreign Collaboration Approval

INDUSTRY	F.C. APPROVALS (in number)	PERCENTAGE SHARE (in percent)
Electrical Equipment	5,904	22.6
Chemicals (other than fertilizers)	1,923	7.4
Transportation	1,777	6.8
Industrial Machinery	1,527	5.8
Service Sector	1,378	5.3
Misc. Mechanical & Engg. Industry	1,079	4.1
Fuels (Power & Oil Refinery)	1,002	3.8
Consultancy Services	950	3.6
Food Processing Industries	943	3.6
Telecommunications	926	3.5
Textiles	813	3.1
Metallurgical Industries	789	3.0
Hotels & Tourism	749	2.9
Others	6,357	24.5
TOTAL	**26,117**	**100.0**

Source: SIA News Letter - September 2004.

An industry-wise analysis of the distribution of foreign collaboration approvals in Table 2.3 depicts that Electricals and Electronics (including Telecommunications 3.5 per cent) accounted for 26.1 percent of the total approvals, indicating highest priority to this sector, followed by Chemicals (other than fertilizers) 7.4 percent. Foreign Collaborations in Transport

Industry were third in importance with 6.8 percent. By and large, it may be stated that the priority sectors like Metallurgical, Power, Oil Refinery, Electrical Equipment, Transportation, Communications, and Chemicals account for about 70 percent of total approvals and the non-priority sectors like Food Processing, Service Sector, Hotels and Tourism, etc. account for about 30 percent of the total approvals. It implies that foreign collaborations approvals were more or less in conformity with the general climate towards foreign capital in the country.

2.6. Foreign Collaborations and MNCs

Multinational Corporations (MNCs) are huge industrial organizations which extend their industrial and marketing operations through a network of their branches or their Majority Owned Foreign Affiliates (MOFAs). MNCs are also known as Transnational Corporations (TNCs). Instead of aiming for maximization of their profits from one or two products, the MNCs operate in a number of fields and from this point of view; their business strategy extends over a number of products and over a number of countries. There are now 40,000 TNCs whose tentacles straddle the international economy through some 2,50,000 overseas affiliates.

As MNCs enter the Indian industry through collaboration with Indian industrialists, Foreign collaboration agreements are made between Indian companies and foreign parties, involving sale of technology, as well as use of foreign brand names for the final products. The enormity of foreign collaborations entered into by the Indian companies would be clear from the fact that in nearly all of the new industries in the large or medium size group, privately or publicly owned, set up after Independence, some collaboration agreement was present.

The policy of the government in the field of foreign collaboration has been criticized on the following counts:

(1) A large number of agreements were concluded for the manufacture of products which are non-essential or which could be produced with the help of local technology. These items included vaccum flasks, lipstick, toothpaste, cosmetics, ice-creams, biscuits, dry batteries, readymade garments etc. Clearly such collaborations were directed to serve the needs of high income groups and to take advantage of a foreign brand name;

(2) The government permitted multiple collaborations, i.e. repetitive import of the same or similar technology. This resulted in repetitive payments without adding to the stock of technical knowledge in the country;

(3) The terms of agreements were mostly weighted in favour of the foreign collaborators and were against Indian interests. This arose on account of the lack of bargaining power in the Indian side and the government's eagerness to acquire foreign participation in the face of foreign exchange shortage;

(4) Since the responsibility of specification and supply of equipment was entrusted to the foreign collaborators, there was close tie-up between the designers and suppliers resulting not only in price markup but also in over-import of equipment. Sometimes equipments were imported even when they were available locally, sometimes they remained idle for want of spares, and often the processes were more highly mechanized and sophisticated than was desirable or necessary. At times, obsolete technology was imported;

(5) The terms of payment were also drawn up so as to squeeze out the maximum payments under one head or other. Generally 5 per cent of the annual turnover for 10 years as royalty plus 5 per cent of the imported

plant cost as technical fees in the case of royalty-cum-technical fees, or 10 per cent of the issued capital as lump sum payment for technical fees alone, was the limits of official policy. However, these tended to become routine;

(6) The most important part related to the presence of various restrictive clauses in the agreements. Some restrictions imposed were:

   (a) The technology cannot be passed on to any one else, in some cases even after the expiry of the agreement;

   (b) Manufacturing is to be carried out according to the specifications laid down by the collaborator and no local adaptations can be made;

   (c) Control over overseas purchase was exercised through the provision that it had to be made directly or indirectly through the collaborator;

   (d) Production was tightly controlled at times through the posting of foreign technicians;

   (e) Controls over the pricing and marketing of the products were exercised by requiring that a part of the production was to be sold to the collaborator's subsidiary in India at a fixed commission or that specified firms were to be made the sole selling agents; and

   (f) Right to export was also restricted by the provision that exports could be done only to specific countries or on certain preconditions; and

(7) Foreign collaborations have helped the growth of monopolies and concentration. They joined hands with the big business houses and the latter were only too eager to enter into understanding with them since

the presence of foreign links often conferred certain strategic advantages (patent, resources, foreign exchange, etc.) enabling the big business houses to diversify and expand.

2.7. Takeovers and Implementation of Foreign Collaborations

Indian entrepreneur seems to have lost his bargaining power and well-known Indian brands have been taken over by TNCs. It needs to be emphasized that takeovers do not add to new production capacities. On the contrary, they are likely to add to higher outflow of foreign exchange.

In foreign collaborations, transfer of superior technology has not been the main consideration.

Some Recent Takeovers:

- ICI (UK) attempted to takeover Asian Paints.
- Hindustan Lever took over TOMCO.
- Premier Automobiles transferred two of its plants to Peugeot.
- Transfer of Lakme's brand to a 50:50 Joint Venture with the Levers.
- TVS-SUZUKI takes up Hero Honda.
- Whirlpool took over TVS Whirlpool.
- Suzuki's attempted to gain majority control in Maruti Udyog.
- Bridgstone increasing its stake from 51 to 74 per cent in Joint Venture with ACC.
- Bausch & Lomb increasing its share in the Indian venture to 69 per cent.
- Henkel increasing its share to 70 per cent.
- Blue Star edged out of Motorola Blue Star and Hewlett Packard India.

- Shriram's share got reduced in Shriram Honda Power.

Once the Indian partners transferred the units, they neither had the money nor the marketing network with them.

2.8. Impact of Foreign Collaborations in India

It would be worthwhile to examine how far foreign collaborations have been beneficial for the growth of our economy. At the time of Independence, most of our industries were concerned with consumer goods. Barring two steel mills, we had hardly any capital goods or intermediate goods industries. Today, the Indian industrial scene presents quite a different picture. Petroleum refining, chemicals and pharmaceuticals, light and heavy engineering, steel, man-made fibre manufacture and several other industries have been established and are working on a profitable basis. These industries would not have come into existence or would have taken many years to expand but for the technical know-how and skills obtained from abroad. The gain is not merely in terms of physical output, but in the training of technicians and developing the skills of modern management.

The important conclusions are:

- An overwhelming number of foreign subsidiaries operating in India originate from U.K. and U.S.A. Out of 171 subsidiaries, 116 had their parent company in the U.K. and 25 in the U.S.A.
- Most of the foreign subsidiaries have raised financial resources from within India and the transfer of capital, by way of contribution to share capital or loans from the parent company, has been marginal.
- Nearly all the branches and subsidiaries of foreign companies have accepted the Indianization scheme and a large number of them have already taken measures to reduce the degree of foreign shareholding.

Many of the foreign subsidiaries in India, which have accepted the policy of equity dilution, have, however, succeeded in obtaining the Government approval to enter into perpetual legal agreements with their parent companies, under which the management control, even when the parent company held only a minority in the total shares, would continue to rest in foreign hands.

- Large foreign companies in India are fast acquiring the character of multi-product and multi-industry enterprises. For instances, Imperial (now Indian) Tobacco Company (ITC) recently diversified its activities to hotel industry and is already having a chain of luxury hotels in India. The Union Carbide of India has entered into agricultural and marine products. To demonstrate its respect for the national priorities, the Imperial Chemical Industries have taken up rural uplift programme in a village of Uttar Pradesh. On the one hand, diversification helps the foreign subsidiaries to expand in new and more profitable areas, but on the other, they escape any likelihood of attracting anti-monopoly legislation and public resentment. There has been an increasing tendency on the part of foreign companies to diversify their activities into areas like hotels, cosmetics and other industrial products, which constitute an important part of the budget of the affluent sections of the society.
- The assumption that the entry of Transnational Corporations (TNCs) would ensure transfer of sophisticated technology to developing countries has not been found valid in practice. In India, there is sufficient evidence to suggest that the transfer of technology is only from one industrial project in a

developed country to another 'project site' but it makes no contribution to the low technology-oriented system of production to the poor country. In such cases, transfer of technology is a myth and TNCs in practice do not permit such transfer but keep process and technologies a well-guarded secret.

3

Foreign Direct Investment: Global Perspective

3.1. Introduction

The past decade has witnessed a remarkable process of liberalization of Foreign Direct Investment (FDI) policies worldwide. This has been part of a broader liberalization of international trade in goods and services and flows of finance, technology and knowledge.

The ultimate objective of FDI liberalization is to enhance economic growth and welfare. Developing countries, in particular, have increasingly turned to FDI as a source of the capital, technology, managerial know-how and market access needed for sustained economic growth and development. The move towards more open FDI regimes has been accompanied by a shift in many countries towards greater deregulation of economic activity and greater reliance on market forces in their domestic economies, as well as on international trade and factor movements. Liberalization has contributed to increased FDI flows to countries with those economic characteristics that TNCs find attractive, and has promoted more complex and integrated patterns of international production by TNCs.

As countries liberalize their foreign-direct-investment (FDI) regimes, and firms increase international investment and production, it is important to consider how the local and marketing strategies of transnational corporations (TNCs) interact with the competitive structure and behaviour of the markets in which they operate.

This chapter has been focused on analysis of FDI flows at global context, the reasons for down-turn of FDI in recent years, i.e. since 2001, and also the trends of FDI flows at regional level, i.e. Developed, Developing and Central and Eastern European (CEE) countries. It examines recent trends in inter-firm agreements/Cross-Border Mergers and Acquisitions as these are assuming increasing importance in certain industries. Subsequently, the host country determinants of Foreign Direct Investment as well as the benefits of FDI to Host Countries have also been discussed.

3.2. Overall Trends – International Production

The size and distribution of international production by TNCs – and their role in the world economy – can be gauged from estimates of the worldwide FDI stock*, assets, sales, gross product and exports of these firms.[1] The role of FDI and TNC activity in the global economy continues to grow, as reflected in the sales, assets, value-added (gross product), employment and exports of foreign affiliates. The degree of transnationalization is increasing for both TNCs and the countries in which they operate. Each of the above variables has resumed an upward trend since 2002. (Table 3.1)

Indeed, all major indicators (Table 3.1) related to FDI and TNC activities showed higher rates of growth till 2000. Then, the GDP and exports, compensating for the decline in growth during 2001, that reflected the recession of the early 2000. More specifically, world FDI stock, which constitutes the capital base for TNC operations, rose by over 11.8 percent in 2003, to reach an estimated $8.2 trillion.[2]

---

* FDI stock refers to 'the total accumulated value of foreign owned assets at a given time.

TABLE 3.1

Selected Indicators of FDI and International Production, 1982-2003

(Billions of dollars and per cent)

Item	Value at current prices ($ billion)			Annual growth rate (Percent)						
	1982	1990	2003	1986-1990	1991-1995	1996-2000	2000	2001	2002	2003
FDI inflows	59	209	560	22.9	21.5	39.7	27.7	-41.1	-17.0	-17.6
FDI outflows	28	242	612	25.6	16.6	35.1	8.7	-39.2	-17.3	2.6
FDI inward stock	796	1 950	8 245	14.7	9.3	16.9	19.1	7.4	12.7	11.8
FDI outward stock	590	1 758	8 197	18.1	10.7	17.1	18.5	5.9	13.8	13.7
Cross-border M&As [a]	..	151	297	25.9[b]	24.0	51.5	49.3	-48.1	-37.7	-19.7
Sales of foreign affiliates	2 717	5 660	17 580[c]	16.0	10.2	9.7	16.7	-3.8	23.7[c]	10.7[c]
Gross product of foreign affiliates	636	1 454	3 706[d]	17.4	6.8	8.2	15.1	-4.7	25.8[d]	10.1[d]
Total assets of foreign affiliates	2 076	5 883	30 362[e]	18.2	13.9	20.0	28.4	-5.4	19.6[e]	12.5[e]
Exports of foreign affiliates	717	1 194	3 077[f]	13.5	7.6	9.9	11.4	-3.3	4.7[f]	16.6[f]
Employment of foreign affiliates (thousands)	19 232	24 197	54 170[g]	5.6	3.9	10.8	13.3	-3.2	12.3[g]	8.3[g]
GDP (in current prices) [h]	11 737	22 588	36 163	10.1	5.1	1.3	2.7	-0.9	3.7	12.1
Gross fixed capital formation	2 285	4 815	7 294	13.4	4.2	2.4	3.8	-3.6	-0.6	9.9
Royalties and licence fee receipts	9	30	77[i]	21.3	14.3	7.7	9.5	-2.5	6.7	..
Exports of goods and non-factor services [h]	2 246	4 260	9 228	12.7	8.7	3.6	11.4	-3.3	4.7	16.6

Source: UNCTAD, based on its FDI/TNC database (www.unctad.org/fdistatistics) and UNCTAD estimates.

a Data are available only from 1987 onward.

b 1987-1990 only.

c Based on the following regression result of sales against FDI inward stock (in $ million) for the period 1980-2001: Sales = 1 542.5036+1.945042*FDI inward stock.

d Based on the following regression result of gross product against FDI inward stock (in $ million) for the period 1982-2001: Gross product = 493.8792+0.389537*FDI inward stock.

e Based on the following regression result of assets against FDI inward stock (in $ million) for the period 1980-2001: Assets = -1 389.4785+3.850915*FDI inward stock.

f For 1995-1998, based on the regression result of exports of foreign affiliates against FDI inward stock (in $ million) for the period 1982-1994: Exports = 288.4750+0.454011*FDI inward stock. For 1999-2003, the share of exports of foreign affiliates in world exports in 1998 (33.3 per cent) was applied to obtain the values.

g Based on the following regression result of employment (in thousands) against FDI inward stock (in $ million) for the period 1980-2001: Employment = 1,5162.6220+4.731003*FDI inward stock.

h Based on data from the International Monetary Fund, *World Economic Outlook*, April 2004.

i 2002.

3.3. Global Foreign Direct Investment Flows

The past 20 years have seen a marked increase in both the *flow* and *stock* of FDI in the world economy. The average yearly inflow of FDI increased from about $254 billion in 1991-96 to a record $1.39, trillion in 2000, which is at a growth rate of 29.1 percent over the last year (Table 3.2). The flow of FDI not only accelerated over the last quarter century, but it also accelerated faster than the growth in world trade. For instance, between 1990 and 2000, the total flow of FDI from all countries increased about fivefold, i.e., by 57.3 percent, while world trade grew by some 82 per cent and world output by 23 per cent. As a result of the strong FDI flow, by 2000 the global stock of FDI exceeded $5.7 trillion.

FDI is growing more rapidly than world trade and world output for several reasons. Much of the recent increase in FDI is being driven by the dramatic political and economic changes that have been occurring in many of the world's developing nations. The general shift toward democratic political institutions and free market economies has encouraged FDI. Across much of Asia, Eastern Europe, and Latin America, economic growth, economic deregulation, privatization programs that are open to foreign investors and the removal of many restrictions on FDI have all made these countries more attractive to foreign investors. The globalization of the world economy, a phenomenon is also having a positive impact on the volume of FDI.

3.3.1. Analysis of FDI Inflows

The data in Table 3.2 shows that there was a steady rise in the global FDI flows in the Nineties. This rise was more marked during the period 1998, which was $691 billion, rose to $1087 billion in 1999 with a growth rate of 57.3 percent. However, this growth rate has been declined to 27.7 percent during 2000, inspite of the global FDI inflows increased from $1087 billion in 1999 to $1388 billion in the year 2000.

TABLE 3.2

GLOBAL INFLOWS OF FDI BY HOST REGION, 1991-2003

Host Region	Value at current prices (Billions of dollars)									Percentage distribution								
	1991-96 (Avg)	1992-97 (Avg)	1998	1999	2000	2001	2002	2003	1998-03 (Avg)	1991-96 (Avg)	1992-97 (Avg)	1998	1999	2000	2001	2002	2003	1998-03 (Avg)
World Total	254.3	310.9	691.0	1086.8 (57.3)	1388.0 (27.7)	817.6 (-41.4)	678.8 (-17.0)	559.6 (-17.6)	870.3	100.0	100.0	100.0	100.0	100.0	100.0	100.0	100.0	100.0
Developed Economies	154.6	180.8	472.5	828.4 (75.3)	1108.0 (33.8)	571.5 (-48.4)	490.0 (-14.3)	366.6 (-25.2)	639.5	60.8	58.1	68.4	76.2	79.8	69.9	72.2	65.5	73.5
Developing Economies	91.5	118.6	194.1	231.9 (19.5)	252.5 (8.87)	219.7 (-13.0)	157.6 (-28.3)	172.0 (9.2)	204.6	36.0	38.2	28.1	21.3	18.2	26.9	23.2	30.7	23.5
Central & Eastern Europe	8.2	11.5	24.3	26.5 (9.1)	27.5 (3.7)	26.4 (-4.1)	31.2 (18.4)	21.0 (-32.9)	26.2	3.2	3.7	3.5	2.4	2.0	3.2	4.6	3.8	3.0

Source: UNCTAD, World Investment Report 2004

Note: Figures in brackets indicate annual growth rate over the previous year.

Global inflows of foreign direct investment (FDI) declined in 2003 for the third year in a row, by 18% to $560 billion (Table 3.2). This follows a massive fall of 41% in 2001 (from $1.4 trillion in 2000 to $818 billion) and another 17% in 2002 (to $679 billion). This was prompted again by a fall in FDI flows to developed countries at $367 billion; they were 25 per cent lower than in 2002. Worldwide, 111 countries saw a rise in flows, and 82 countries observed a decline. It was only developing countries as a group that experienced a recovery, with FDI inflows rising by 9 percent, to $172 billion overall. But in this group, the picture was mixed: Africa and Asia and the Pacific saw an increase, while Latin America and the Caribbean experienced a continuing decline. The group of 50 Least Developed Countries (LDCs) continued to receive little FDI ($7 billion). FDI flows to Central and Eastern Europe (CEE) also slumped, from $31 billion to $21 billion for the period of study.

As for as percentage distribution of Global FDI inflows is concerned, the developed countries attracted 74 percent on an average during 1998-2003 as compared to 61 percent during 1991-96. The share of developing countries being declined to 24 percent during the period of study (1998-2003) as it was 36 percent in 1991-96; and the CEE attracted just 3 percent of the total global inflows.

It has been observed from the Table 3.2 that the FDI inflows into Developed Countries, Developing Countries and CEE countries rushed towards high growth till 1999 and declined shortly during the year 2000. Further, FDI inflows into these countries found tremendous fall in 2001 and 2002. Driving the most significant downturn of the past three decades were weak economic growth, tumbling stock markets and institutional factors such as the winding down of privatization in several countries. The drop in FDI inflows was confined to the developed countries and Central and Eastern Europe

(CEE). However, inflows to developing countries rose by 9%. Among the global countries, Luxembourg, China was the world's largest host country in 2003, followed by France, United States, whereas Canada stood at 20th place (figure 3.1). Among the top 20 recipients of FDI inflows, China, Belgium, Ireland, Italy, Hong Kong, Switzerland, Singapore, Bermuda, and Australia have found hike of flows in 2003 as compared in 2002, and the rest of the countries observed decline.

The decline in FDI flows in 2001 followed rapid increases during the late 1990s. There was similar pattern during the late 1980s and early 1990s, and in 1982-1983. Thus, this is the third downward cycle in FDI, each punctuating a long upward trend in FDI every ten years. These swings reflect changes in several factors. The main ones are business cycles, stock market sentiment and M & As. These short-term factors (including factors such as the terrorist attack of September 11, 2001) work in tandem with longer-term factors, sometimes offsetting and at other times reinforcing them. There is, on the other hand, a stable and positive relationship between global FDI flows and the level and growth of world GDP. Technological change, shrinking economic distance and new management methods favour international production. Their impact is, however, countered by cyclical fluctuations in income and growth. The decline in FDI in 2001 reflected a slow down in the world economy. More than a dozen countries – including the world's three largest economies fell into recession. On the supply side, FDI is affected by the availability of investible funds from corporate profits or loans, which is in turn affected by domestic economic conditions. On the demand side, growing overseas markets lead TNCs to invest, while depressed markets inhibit them. The more interdependent host and home economies become, and the more widely a recession or upswing spreads, the greater are the corresponding movements in global FDI.

Figure 3.1: The Top 20 Recipients of FDI Inflows, 2002 and 2003

(Billions of dollars)

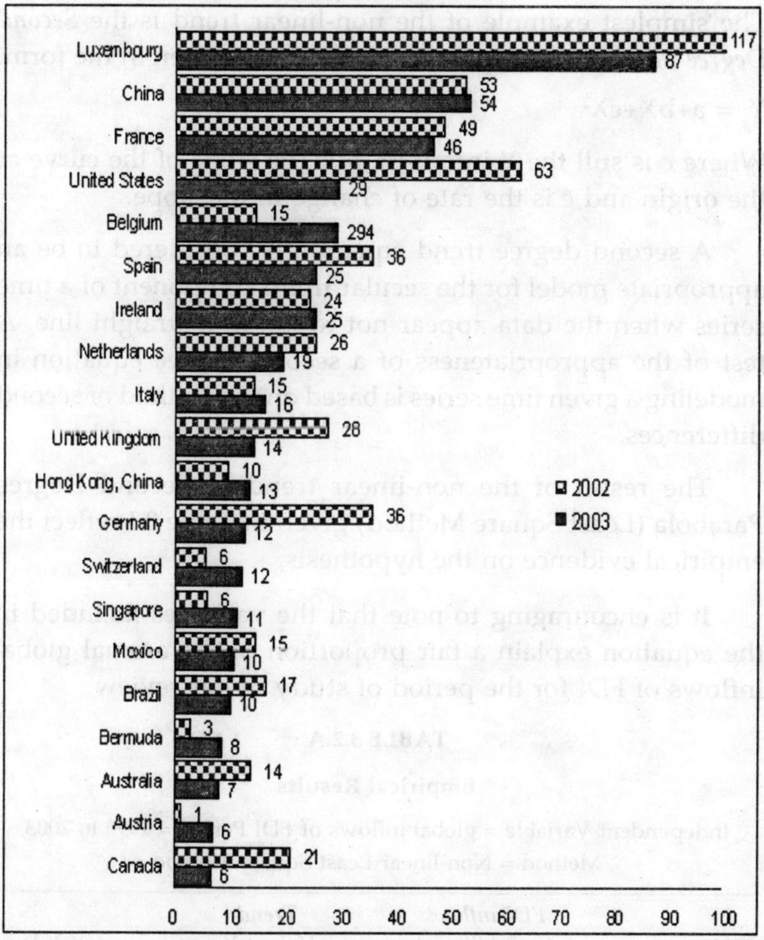

Empirical Analysis

The global inflows of Foreign Direct Investment are being tested through the Method of Least Squares. It is a mathematical method and with its help a trend line is fitted to the data in such a manner that the following two conditions are satisfied:

$E(Y-Y_c)=0.$

i.e. the sum of deviations of the actual values of Y and the computed values of Y is zero.

The simplest example of the non-linear trend is the *Second Degree Parabola,* the equation of which is written in the form:

$Y_c = a+bX+cX^2$

Where c is still the Y intercept, b is the slope of the curve at the origin and c is the rate of change in the slope.

A second degree trend equation is considered to be an appropriate model for the secular trend component of a time series when the data appear not to fall in a straight line. A test of the appropriateness of a second degree equation in modeling a given time series is based on the method of second differences.

The result of the non-linear trend of Second Degree Parabola (Least Square Method) given in Table 3.I reflect the empirical evidence on the hypothesis.

It is encouraging to note that the variables included in the equation explain a fair proportion of the annual global inflows of FDI for the period of study under review.

TABLE 3.2.A

Empirical Results

Independent Variable = global inflows of FDI Period = 1996 to 2003
Method = Non-linear Least Square Method

Year	*FDI inflows (in $ billions)*	*Trend Values* Y_c	$(Y-Y_c)$
1998	691	787.09	-96.09
1999	1087	1026.76	59.24
2000	1388	1111.65	276.35
2001	818	1041.76	-228.76
2002	679	817.09	-138.09
2003	560	437.64	122.36
N=6	ΣY=5222		

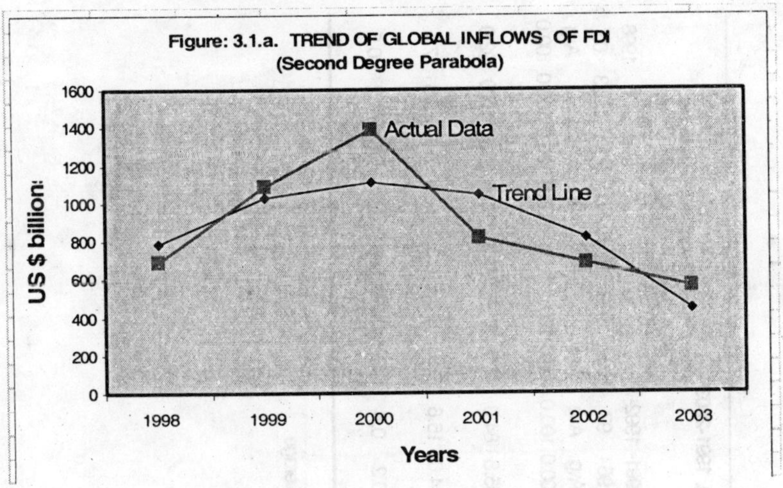

Therefore, the non-linear equation is:

$$Y_c = 1111.65+7.5X-77.39X^2$$

Hence, it can be inferred that the trend of global inflows of FDI had been recovering since 2000 and decreasing since 2001. The variation in Actual data and the trend values ($Y - Y_c$) shows negative in 2001 and 2002. However, the same is found positive during 2003.

To conclude, it can be suggested that world wide FDI policy regime should be further liberalized as to attract high degree of flows to cater to the needs of industrial development at the global context.

3.3.2. Analysis of FDI Outflows

Analysis of the data of Table 3.3 shows that the world wide FDI outflows have been increased from $597 billions in 2002 to $612 billions in 2003 with an annual growth rate of 2.6 percent. The average global outflows of FDI during 1998-2003 found at $816 billion, out of which, Developed countries dominated with outflow of $751 billion (i.e. 92 percent of total world FDI outflows). Developing countries shared $61

TABLE 3.3

GLOBAL OUTFLOWS OF FDI BY HOST REGION, 1991-2003

Host Region	Value at current prices (Billions of dollars)									Percentage distribution								
	1991-96 Avg	1992-97 Avg	1998	1999	2000	2001	2002	2003	1998-03 Avg	1991-96 Avg	1992-97 Avg	1998	1999	2000	2001	2002	2003	1998-03 Avg
World Total	280.6	328.2	687.2	1092.3	1186.8	721.5	596.5	612.2	816.1	100.0	100.0	100.0	100.0	100.0	100.0	100.0	100.0	100.0
				(58.9)	(8.7)	(-39.2)	(-17.3)	(2.6)										
Developed Economies	240.7	275.7	631.5	1014.3	1083.9	658.1	547.6	569.6	750.8	85.8	84.0	91.9	92.9	91.3	91.2	91.8	93.0	92.0
				(60.6)	(6.9)	(-39.3)	(-16.8)	(4.0)										
Developing Economies	39.4	51.3	53.4	75.5	98.9	59.9	44.0	35.6	61.2	14.0	15.6	7.8	6.9	8.3	8.3	7.4	5.8	7.5
				(41.3)	(31.3)	(-39.5)	(-26.5)	(-19.1)										
Central & Eastern Europe	0.5	1.2	2.3	2.5	4.0	3.5	4.9	7.0	4.1	0.2	0.4	0.3	0.2	0.4	0.5	0.8	1.2	0.5
				(5.9)	(63.6)	(-11.9)	(37.5)	(44.3)										

Source: UNCTAD, World Investment Report 2004

Note: Figures in brackets indicate annual growth rate over the previous year. Avg=Annual Average

billion and the CEE $7 billion, which could be just 7.5 percent and 0.5 percent respectively of the total world FDI outflows.

Unlike inflows, FDI outflows from developed countries rise in 2003, albeit marginally by 4 percent to $570 billion over the previous year, which was $548 billion. Firms from developing countries, too, are increasingly becoming outward investor till the year 2002, and gradually declined during 2001-2003. However, the outflows from CEE found increase by 44 percent to $7 billion in 2003 over the previous year of the study.

Figure 3.2: The Top 20 Economies for Outflows of FDI 2002 and 2003 (Billions of dollars)

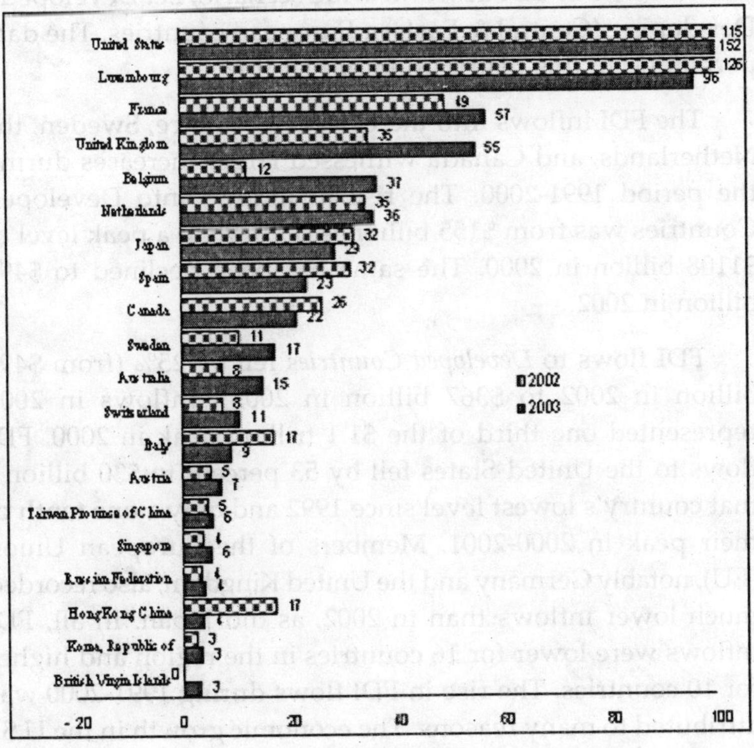

Source: UNCTAD, World Investment Report 2004.

While uneven performance characterized outward FDI by developed countries, the world's 100 largest TNCs showed signs of resumed growth in terms of sales and employment in 2002, the latest year for which complete data on the companies are available. Nine of the top 10 among the 100 largest TNCs in the world ranked by foreign assets are based in three countries (France, U.K and US).

Of the total world FDI outflows, the U.S. stood at top one investor country (with a 32 per cent increase in 2003), followed by Luxembourg, France, U.K. (Figure 3.2).

3. Regional Distribution of FDI Inflows and Outflows

Now, it is proposed to analyse the performance of inflows and outflows of FDI at world wide scenario, i.e. Developed/ Developing/Central & Eastern European countries. The data pertaining to this distribution of FDI flows.

The FDI inflows into the U.S., U.K., France, Sweden, the Netherlands, and Canada witnessed larger increases during the period 1991-2000. The rise in inflows into Developed Countries was from $155 billion in 1991-96 to a peak level of $1108 billion in 2000. The same has been declined to $490 billion in 2002.

FDI flows to *Developed Countries* fell by 25% (from $490 billion in 2002 to $367 billion in 2003). Inflows in 2003 represented one third of the $1.1 trillion peak in 2000. FDI flows to the United States fell by 53 percent to $30 billion - that country's lowest level since 1992 and only a one tenth of their peak in 2000-2001. Members of the European Union (EU), notably Germany and the United Kingdom, also recorded much lower inflows than in 2002, as did Japan. In all, FDI inflows were lower for 16 countries in the region and higher for 10 countries. The rise in FDI flows during 1991-2000 was attributed to many reasons. The economic growth in the U.S., and Europe was robust and investment opportunities were attractive, Transnational Corporations have adopted a spate of mergers, take-overs and acquisitions in the world over as a route to financial strengthening and for expansion and growth. The financial and economic crisis in some developing countries has forced the MNCs to invest more in developed countries in the last few years (1997-2000).

Flows to Developing Countries as a group rose by 9% (from $158 billion in 2002 to $172 billion in 2003), but they varied by region. Africa recorded 28 percent increased inflows in 2003 ($15 billion, up from $12 billion in 2002), driven mainly by natural-resource projects. There was an increase in flows to 36 countries and a decline to 17. FDI flows to the Asia-Pacific region reached $107 billion, up from $95 billion in 2002, with 36 countries receiving higher flows than in 2002 and 21, lower inflows. Latin America and the Caribbean, however, experienced a fourth consecutive year of decline. But the decline was marginal - from $51 billion in 2002 to $50 billion. Of 40 countries in the region, 19 received lower inflows. The share of developing countries in global FDI inflows rose by 8 percentage points, to 31% in 2003.

The lowest inflows of FDI funds took place in the case of emerging *Central and Eastern European* Countries of Czech Republic, Poland, Slovakia and Russia. Central and Eastern Europe (CEE) resisted the global decline, with its FDI inflows rising by 15 percent, although flows to 10 countries in the region fell during 2002. After a record year in 2002, when inflows reached $31 billion, FDI flows to CEE fell sharply in 2003, to $21 billion. FDI inflows were higher for 10 countries in the region and lower for 9. Inflows into the "accession-eight" — the Czech Republic, Estonia, Hungary, Latvia, Lithuania, Poland, Slovenia and Slovakia — declined from $23 billion to $11 billion. FDI inflows to the Russian Federation also plunged, from $3.5 billion in 2002 to $1.1 billion in 2003.

The US was again the main investor country (having lost this position to Luxembourg in 2002), with a 32% increase in outflows in 2003 (figure 3.2). Outflows from the EU were down by 4%, even though outflows from France and the UK rose by 16% and 57%, respectively. Outflows from Germany declined by 70%, as parent company loans to their foreign affiliates fell. Japan's outflows continued to fall (-11%), mainly in the services sector, having also declined in 2002.

In 2002:

- Inflows in the developed world declined by 22 percent, with nine countries experiencing increases and 16 countries decreases. The U.S., and U.K. alone accounted for more than 50 percent of the fall in the countries with reduced inflows;
- The decline in the developing world (23 per cent) which faced even sharper declines in other private external capital flows, was steepest in Africa (41 percent), followed by Latin America and the Caribbean (33 percent). Flows to the world's most populous region, Asia and the Pacific, fell only a little, thanks to higher flows to China;
- Central and Eastern Europe (CEE) resisted the global decline, with its FDI inflows rising by 15 percent, although flows to 10 countries in the region fell; and
- Both manufacturing and services were hit hard, while FDI flows to the primary sector rose.

In 2003:

- FDI flows to developed countries fell by 25 per cent from $490 billion in 2002 to $367 billion in 2003. This latter figure represents only two-thirds of the peak of $1.1 trillion reached in 2000. Flows to the United States declined (from $159.5 billion in 2001 to $29.8

billion in 2003) to the lowest level since 1992, only one-tenth of their peak in 2000-2001.

- Flows to developing countries, on the other hand, rose by 9 percent from $158 billion in 2002 to $172 billion in 2003, but they varied by region. Africa recorded 28 percent higher inflows in 2003 ($15 billion, up from $12 billion in 2002); Asia-Pacific region reached $107 billion, up from $95 billion (hiked by 14 percent). Latin America and the Caribbean, however, experienced a fourth consecutive year of decline, although it was marginal, from $51 billion in 2002 to $50 billion.
- The share of developing countries in global FDI inflows rose by 8 percentage points, to 31 percent in 2003 (from 23 percent in 2002). The top ten recipients accounted for almost three-fourths of total flows to developing countries – 11 percentage points less than in 2000 when concentration was the highest.
- FDI flows to Central and Eastern Europe (CEE) fell sharply in 2003, to $21 billion (which was $31 billion in 2002).

3.5. Dispersion of Foreign Direct Investment

The percentage distribution of global inflows of FDI in Table 3.2 & Figure 3.3 shows that the major amount of the FDI flows received among the developed countries. For nearly three decades till the early 1990s, about three-quarters of the FDI flows have gone to the developed countries. These countries attracted FDI inflows of 65.51 percent out of the world total flows in 2003, whereas, the developing countries attracted 30.74 percent and the Central & Eastern European Countries at 3.75 percent of the world total flows. The average FDI flows during 1998-2003 showed that, of the global FDI inflows, Developed countries dominated by attracting 73.5 percent; Developing countries 23.5 percent; and the CEE 3 percent.

Nearly two-thirds of the flows take place between the countries of the *Triad* – the U.S., the European Community and Japan. In 1999, the United States and the United Kingdom were the leaders as investors and recipients. With $199 billion, the UK became the largest outward investor in 1999, forging ahead of the U.S.

FDI is concentrated in a handful of countries – ten countries received 74 per cent of global FDI flows in 1999. Just ten developing countries received 80 per cent of total FDI flows to the developing world. More importantly, there are no signs that the concentration of international production across countries has been declining over time. Developed countries have attracted 58.14 percent of world inflows in 1992-97, tremendously increased its share to 79.83 percent in 2000. However, this share has been declined to 72.18 percent and 65.51 percent during 2002 and 2003 respectively. However, in many least developed countries that have received only small amounts of FDI, such investment is important vis-a-vis the size of domestic investment. What remains a challenge for these countries is the ability to attract not only more, but also higher quality FDI – broadly defined as investment with strong links to the domestic economy, export orientation, advanced technology and skill or spillover effects.

The share of the FDI going to the developing countries was at 38 percent during 1992-97, has been gradually declined to 19 percent in 2000. However, there was an increase with a share of 23.22 percent in the absolute amount of FDI flows to the developing countries in 2002. The economic liberalization in the developing countries has helped for increased share of the FDI. Further, the year 2003 marked with global FDI inflows share at 30.74 percent.

FDI in developing countries has been larger than official inflows for every year since 1993. It was 10 times larger than

Figure 3.3 PERCENTAGE DISTRIBUTION OF WORLD FDI INFLOWS 1992-2003

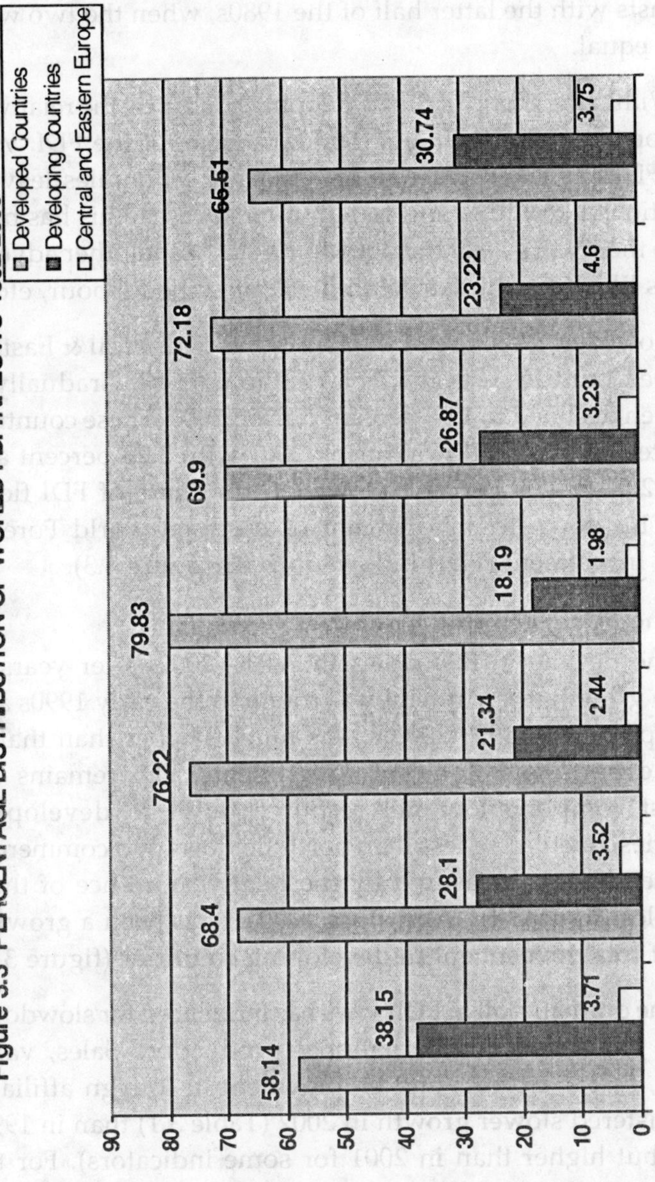

Source: UNCTAD, World Investment Report 2004 and previous issues

bilateral Official Development Assistance (ODA) in 2000; this contrasts with the latter half of the 1980s, when the two were about equal.

Within the group of the developing countries, the relatively developed among them get the lion's share of the FDI. Very little FDI has taken place in low-income economies leaving exceptions like China and India. In most cases, this has been due to the small size of the domestic market and other adverse factors like poor infrastructure, lack of skilled labour, etc.

However, the share of world inflows of Central & Eastern Europe Countries was at 3.7 percent in 1992-97. Gradually, it has been declined to 1.98 percent during 2000. These countries attracted more FDI flows during 2001 with 3.23 percent and in 2002 with 4.60 percent. However, the share of FDI flows into CEE down to 3.75 percent of the total world Foreign Direct Investment (FDI) inflows in 2003 (figure 3.3).

3.6. The FDI Declining Countries

The decline in FDI flows in 2001—2002, after years of steady growth interrupted by a trough in the early 1990s and a sharp spurt in 1999-2000 – was much steeper than that in GDP, exports and domestic investments. FDI remains the biggest component of net resource flows to developing countries, fluctuating less than portfolio flows and commercial bank lending as measured by the relative variance of these variables (figure3.4)[3]. And since 1990, it has been a growing part of total investment in developing countries (figure 3.5).

The dramatic fall in FDI flows has influenced for slowdown in the expansion of international production. Sales, value added, assets, exports and employment of foreign affiliates all registered slower growth in 2002 (Table 3.1) than in 1996-2000 (but higher than in 2001 for some indicators). For the largest transnational corporations (TNCs) most indicators of the size of foreign operations declined slightly in 2001, the beginning of the FDI downturn period.

Figure 3.4: Total Resource Flows[a] to Developing Countries[b], by type of flow, 1990-2002 (*Billions of dollars*)

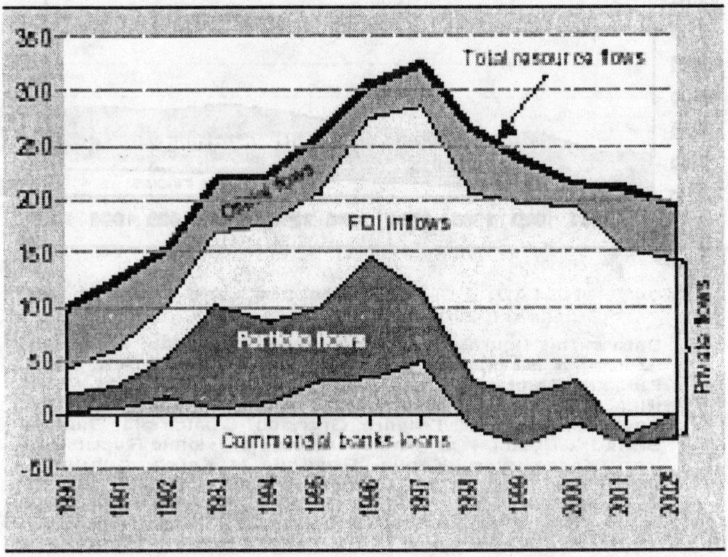

Source: UNCTAD, based on World Bank, 2003.

a Defined as net liability transactions or original maturity of greater than one year.

b The World Bank's classification of developing countries is different from that of UNCTAD. Central and Eastern Europe is included in the former classification.

c Preliminary.

Figure 3.5: FDI Inflows, Private Domestic Investment and Public Investment in Developing Countries and Central and Eastern Europe[a], 1990-2000

(*Billions of dollars*)

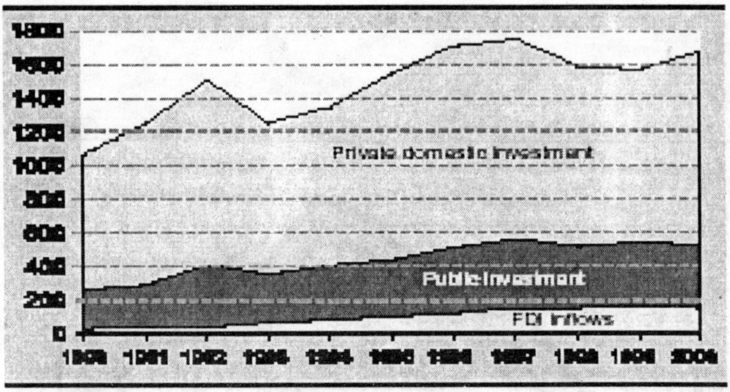

Source: UNCTAD, FDI/TNC database; and Everhart and Sumlinski, 2001.

[a] Data in this figure cover the following countries: Argentina, Azerbaijan, Bangladesh, Barbados, Belize, Benin, Bolivia, Brazil, Bulgaria, Cambodia, Chile, China, Colombia, Comoros, Costa Rica, Côte d'Ivoire, Dominica, Dominican Republic, Ecuador, Egypt, El Salvador, Estonia, Grenada, Guatemala, Guinea-Bissau, Guyana, Haiti, India, Indonesia, Islamic Republic of Iran, Kazakhstan, Kenya, Republic of Korea, Lithuania, Madagascar, Malawi, Malaysia, Mauritania, Mauritius, Mexico, Morocco, Namibia, Nicaragua, Pakistan, Panama, Papua New Guinea, Paraguay, Peru, Philippines, Poland, Romania, Seychelles, South Africa, Saint Lucia, Saint Vincent and the Grenadines, Serbia and Montenegro, Thailand, Trinidad and Tobago, Tunisia, Turkey, Uruguay, Uzbekistan and Venezuela.

The slower growth of the foreign activities of TNCs in 2001-2002 could translate into lower ratios of the transnationalisation of economic activities for host countries. In 2000, reflecting the FDI boom, the transnationality index continued to rise, with a noticeable increase over the previous year.[4] The decline was broad-based: 108 out of 195 economies saw lower inflows in 2002 than in 2001 (Table 3.4).

TABLE 3.4

Number of Countries with Declines in FDI Inflows, 2002

Region	Number of countries with declines	Total number of countries
World	108	195
Developed countries	16	26
Developing countries	82	150
Africa	23	53
Latin America and the Caribbean	28	40
Asia and the Pacific	31	57
Central and Eastern Europe	10	19
Memorandum: Least developed countries	25	49

Source: World Investment Report 2003

3.6.1 The Causes for the Decline

The decline in FDI inflows in 2001 and 2002 was uneven in four ways:

- *Geographically:* Regions fared differently, and a handful of countries accounted for the bulk of the decline worldwide.
- *Sectorally:* Flows to both manufacturing and services fell, but not those to the primary sector. Finance, transport, storage and communications were severely affected, while FDI in other industries remained virtually unchanged (health and social services) or even rose (mining, quarrying and petroleum).
- *Financially:* The decline in intra-company loans

exceeded that in equity flows (in 2001 all the financial components of FDI declined about half).

- *Mode of entry:* Cross-border Mergers and Acquisitions (M&As) fell more than Greenfield Investment.*

The decline in *Outflows* was also uneven.

3.6.2. Geographical Variations in Declining FDI

Different regions fared differently, and a handful of countries accounted for the bulk of the decline worldwide. The slump in the developed world (22%) was concentrated in the US and the UK (figure 3.6), which together accounted for 54% of the fall in the 108 countries with reduced inflows. The decline in the developing world (23%), which faced even sharper cuts in other private external capital flows, was steepest in Africa (41%) and in Latin America and the Caribbean (33%). In the latter region, 2002 was the third consecutive year of declining inflows. Flows to the world's most populous region, Asia and the Pacific, fell minimally, thanks to record high flows to China, the largest FDI recipient globally (figure 3.7).

The United States alone accounted for nearly 90 percent of the decline in inflows to developed countries in 2002 (as it did in 2001) (Table 3.4a). Among developing regions the fall was steepest in Africa (41 percent), a return to normalcy after the exceptionally large inflows registered by two countries in 2001. Flows to Latin America and the Caribbean dropped for the third year in a row, this time by a third. The decline in flows to the Asia-Pacific region (which includes West Asia) was quite small (11 percent). And flows to CEE rose by 15 percent.

Despite the high concentration, the decline was widespread, with 108 of the total of 195 host economies receiving less in 2002 than in 2001. With FDI inflows of $53

* Green-field Investment refers to the establishment of a wholly new operation in a foreign country.

Figure 3.6

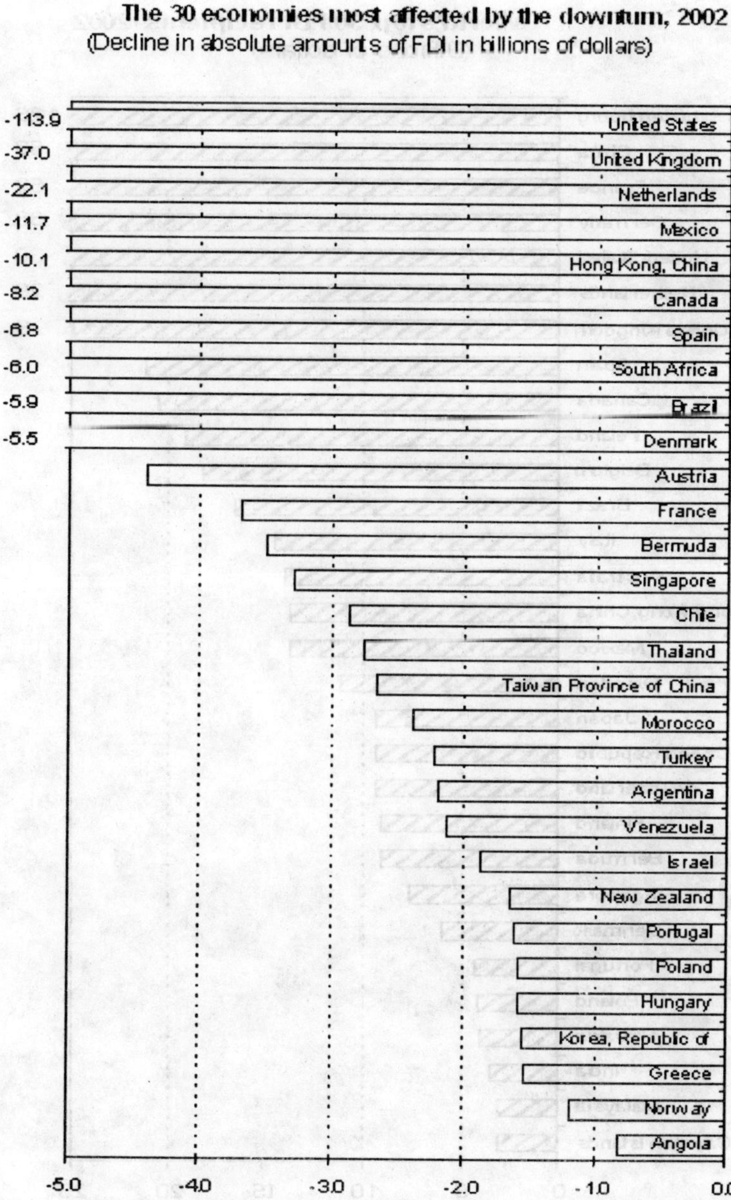
The 30 economies most affected by the downturn, 2002
(Decline in absolute amounts of FDI in billions of dollars)
-113.9
-37.0
-22.1
-11.7
-10.1
-8.2
-6.8
-6.0
-5.9
-5.5
United States
United Kingdom
Netherlands
Mexico
Hong Kong, China
Canada
Spain
South Africa
Brazil
Denmark
Austria
France
Bermuda
Singapore
Chile
Thailand
Taiwan Province of China
Morocco
Turkey
Argentina
Venezuela
Israel
New Zealand
Portugal
Poland
Hungary
Korea, Republic of
Greece
Norway
Angola
-5.0
-4.0
-3.0
-2.0
-1.0
0.0

Figure 3.7

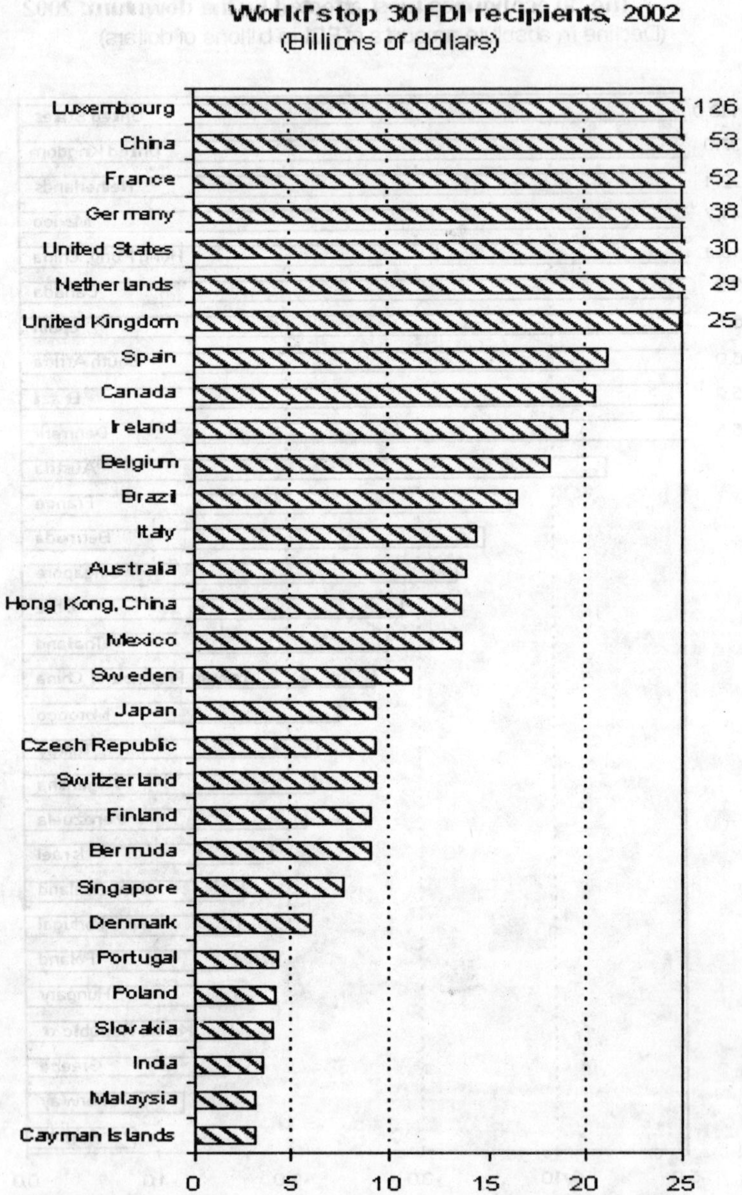
World's top 30 FDI recipients, 2002
(Billions of dollars)
Luxembourg
China
France
Germany
United States
Netherlands
United Kingdom
Spain
Canada
Ireland
Belgium
Brazil
Italy
Australia
Hong Kong, China
Mexico
Sweden
Japan
Czech Republic
Switzerland
Finland
Bermuda
Singapore
Denmark
Portugal
Poland
Slovakia
India
Malaysia
Cayman Islands
126
53
52
38
30
29
25
0
5
10
15
20
25

billion, an average of $144 million a day, China overtook the United States ($30 billion) to become the world's second largest recipient (after Luxembourg), (Table 3.4b) strengthening its position in world manufacturing exports. India and Malaysia also attracted larger FDI flows (which was $3.4 and $0.6 billion in 2001, increased to $3.45 and $3.2 billion respectively in 2002), while flows to the major host countries declined in Latin America (Argentina, Brazil, Chile, Mexico, Venezuela). In Africa, flows to Morocco and South Africa, the two largest recipients in 2001, fell considerably. In the CEE, the Czech Republic boosted its inflows to more than $9 billion (Table 3.4a).

TABLE 3.4A

FDI Inflows to Major Economies, 2001 and 2002

(Billions of Dollars)

	Host region/economy	*2001*	*2002*
World		**823.8**	**651.2**
Developed countries		**589.4**	**160.3**
European Union		**389.4**	**374.4**
	France	55.2	51.5
	Germany	33.9	38.0
	Luxembourg	—	125.6
	United Kingdom	62.0	24.9
	United States	144.0	30.0
Developing Countries		**209.4**	**162.1**
Africa	**18.8**	**11.0**	
	Algeria	1.2	1.1
	Angola	2.1	1.3
	Nigeria	1.1	1.3
	South Africa	6.8	.08
Latin America and the Caribbean		**83.7**	**56.0**
	Argentina	3.2	1.0

Brazil	22.5	16.6
Mexico	25.3	13.6
Asia and the Pacific	**106.9**	**95.1**
China	46.8	52.7
Hong Kong, China	23.8	13.7
India	3.4	3.45
Korea, Republic of	3.5	2.0
Malaysia	.06	3.2
Philippines	1.0	1.1
Singapore	10.9	7.7
Taiwan Province of China	4.1	1.4
Central and Eastern Europe	**25.0**	**28.7**
Czech Republic	5.6	9.3
Poland	5.7	4.1
Russian Federation	2.5	2.4

Source: UNCTAD, World Investment Report 2003- FDI database.

TABLE 3.4B

World FDI Inflows: Top 5 Countries

(Millions of Dollars)

Country	*2000*	*2001*	*2002*
Luxembourg	—	—	1,25,660
China	40,772	46,846	52,700
France	43,250	55,190	51,505
Germany	2,03,080	33,918	38,033
United States	3,14,007	1,43,978	30,030

Source: UNCTAD, World Investment Report 2003

3.6.2.1. Sector

FDI inflows in 50 countries, which together accounted for roughly 90 percent of the total, declined by more than 45 percent in both manufacturing and service sectors in 2001, compared to 1999-2000. But, FDI in the primary sector rose by 70 percent, down in developing countries but up significantly in the developed countries (figure 3.8). Services are the single largest sector for FDI inflows. In the peak years 1999-2000, most large cross-border M & As were in services (particularly telecommunications), a pattern sustained in 2001-2002, through at a much lower level.

The slow recovery from the global economic slump hit both manufacturing and services hard, while FDI in the primary sector rose. Finance, transport, storage and communications were severely affected; FDI in other industries remained virtually unchanged (health and social services), or even rose (mining, quarrying and petroleum).

Figure 3.8: Inward FDI Flows by Sector, 1999-2000 and 2001 (Per cent)

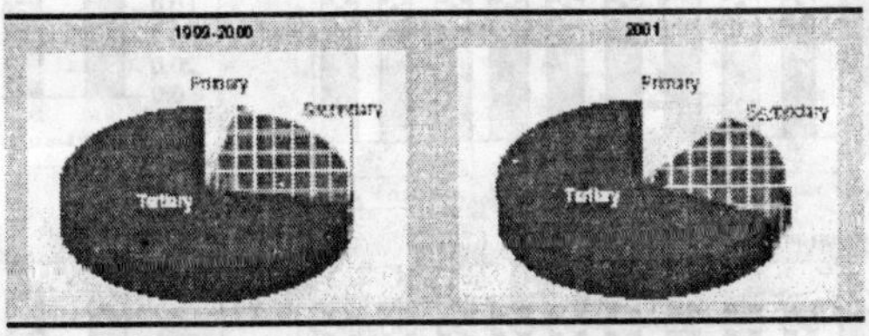

Source: UNCTAD, FDI database and annex table A.I.4.

Notes: Data cover 50 countries for which data are available for 1999, 2000 and 2001. They account for 94 % and 89 % of world inward flows in 1999-2000 and 2001, respectively. In the absence of actual data, approval data were used in some countries.

3.6.2.2. *Financing*

The role played by the three modes of FDI *financing* (equity investment, intra-company loans and reinvested earnings) has shown a decline in 2002 (as well as in the preceding year) and was also uneven. The 2002 decline in intra-company loans (by 77 percent) was much larger than that in equity investments (by 12 percent) for the 30 countries (accounting for two thirds of total FDI flows), (figure 3.9). Intra-company loans by parent firms to their foreign affiliates have fallen since 2001 and were negative in 2003. They were negative for United States, FDI inflows in both 2002 and 2003 (-$21 billion and -$34 billion, respectively) and fell in 2003 in countries as diverse as Argentina, Indonesia, Sweden and Switzerland. The 21 percent fall in FDI flows to the United States in 2002 involved declines of $50 billion in new equity investment and $80 billion in intra-company loans – and a rise of $30 billion in reinvested earnings. The fall in intra-company loans was due to large repayments of loans by foreign affiliates in the United States to their parent companies. Interest rates in the United States were lower than in other areas, especially the EU.[5] And parent firms reduced loans to

Figure 3.9: FDI Inflows, by Type of Financing, 1990-2002 (*Per Cent*)

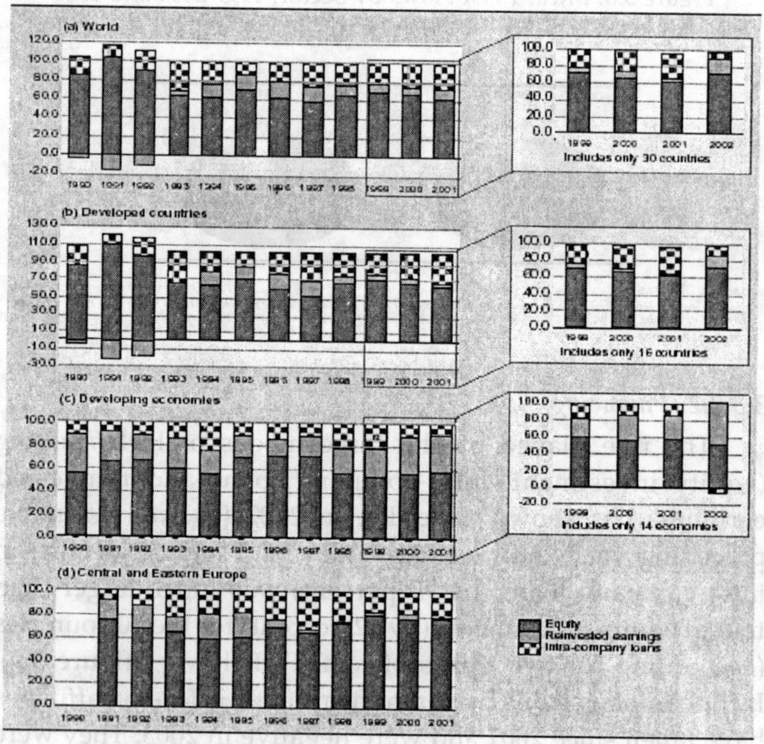

Source: UNCTAD, based on IMF, *Balance of Payments Statistics*, April 2003 CD-ROM and UNCTAD FDI/TNC database.

their foreign affiliates, particularly to EU affiliates in the United States, because of the reduced need to finance M & As in the United States.[6]

Equity investment remained volatile. Reinvested earnings were the single largest component of FDI in developing countries, accounting for about 40 percent (compared to 17 percent in developed countries) of total FDI inflows to that part of the world. This underlines the importance of policies aimed at retaining established foreign affiliates through appropriate aftercare services.

3.6.2.3. Mode of Entry

Cross-border M&As fell more than Greenfield FDI. In fact, most of the decline in FDI came from a dramatic drop in cross-border M&As - from $1.1 trillion in 2000 to $594 billion in 2001 and $370 billion in 2002. The average value per transaction was also declined - from $145 million in 2000 to $98 million in 2001 and $82 million in 2002 - as the number of mega deals (worth over $1 billion) fell from 175 in 2000 to 113 in 2001 and only 81 in 2002, the lowest since 1998. A slowdown in corporate restructuring reinforced the impact on M&As. Further aggravating the decline in M&As was a pause in privatization.

The continued decline in inward FDI flows in 2003 reflected the impact of a combination of macro, micro and institutional factors.

At the macroeconomic level, growth prospects for many countries remained uncertain. In spite of some recovery in the second half of the year, major stock markets remained well below their historical peak of early 2000.[7] At the microeconomic level, increased profitability starting from the latter half of 2003 helped, but did not move FDI inflows upwards.[8] High debt-equity ratios[9] continued to force large companies to downsize their operations. At the institutional level, several new accounting scandals in 2003 may have deterred investors. Reflecting the interaction of these factors, the value of M&As fell from $370 billion in 2002 to $297 billion in 2003 (Table 3.1) – a decline of 20 percent.

An important factor in the decline of FDI, and particularly of Mergers and Acquisitions (M&As), has been a slowdown or end in privatization. The total sale of State-owned assets fell from about $50 billion in 2000 to less than $20 billion in 2003 (World Bank 2004). Privatization-related FDI in developing countries fell to one-tenth of the level of 1998, from a record $33 billion that year to $3.5 billion in 2003[10]. Liquidity and other problems at home lowered TNCs' interests in privatization. At the same time, some developing countries, particularly in Latin America, became more skeptical of its benefits. Privatization-related FDI in CEE declined as well.

3.7. Indices of Inward FDI Performance

Inward FDI Performance Index is a measure of the extent to which host countries receive inward FDI. The Index ranks countries by the amount of FDI they receive relative to their economic size, calculated as the ratio of a country's share in global FDI inflows to its share in global GDP. A value greater than one indicates that the country attracts more FDI in proportion to its economic size, a value below one shows that it receives less (a negative value indicates that foreign investors disinvested in that period). Thus, a higher index implies success in the competition, explicit or implicit, to attract FDI.[11]

3.7.1. Region-wise Analysis

The group of developed countries suffered a slight decline in its relative position, reflecting the large drop in FDI (on account of the slowdown in M&As) in these countries. Within the group, the largest declines were in the EU and North America. "Other developed countries" – mainly Japan, Australia – improved (Table 3.5).

All of the developing regions improved their performance index rank in 2001-2003, but remained below the peak reached in 1993-1995 (except Latin America). This is in contrast to the relative stagnation of the developed regions. However, large regional variations exist.

The best performer in the Index was Central Asia, both in the index score and its rise over the previous period; the sharp rise in its index reflects lumpy resource-based (oil and gas) foreign investments in a few countries. The second best performer in index value was East and South-East Asia and, in terms of improvement over the previous period, "other

Table 3.5

Inward FDI Performance Index, by region, 1988-2003

Region	1988-1990	1993-1995	2000-2002	2001-2003
World	1	1	1	1
Developed regions	1.03	0.76	0.99	0.92
Western Europe	1.33	1.11	1.87	1.84
European Union	1.33	1.12	1.91	1.88
Other Western Europe	1.31	0.95	1.1	1.12
North America	1.13	0.76	0.67	0.45
Other developed countries	0.29	0.21	0.16	0.21
Developing regions	0.99	1.99	1	1.25
Africa	0.7	1.09	0.73	1.16
North Africa	0.85	1.05	0.55	1
Other Africa	0.59	1.12	0.89	1.28
Latin America and the Caribbean	0.9	1.6	1.18	1.42
South America	0.74	1.23	1.24	1.42
Other Latin America and the Caribbean	1.3	2.52	1.08	1.43
Asia	1.09	2.34	0.96	1.19
West Asia	0.3	0.36	0.18	0.31
Central Asia	...	3.11	2.26	4.49
South, East and South-East Asia	1.31	2.74	1.11	1.33
East and South-East Asia	1.73	3.25	1.3	1.54
South Asia	0.11	0.43	0.21	0.37
The Pacific	7.35	6.12	0.65	1.01
Central and Eastern Europe	1.04[b]	1.36	1.17	1.35

Source: UNCTAD, World Investment Report 2004.

(a) Three-year averages.

(b) 1992-1994. As most of the countries in this region did not exist in their present form before 1992, the period for the index is adjusted.

Africa" (i.e. sub-Saharan Africa). Over the period as a whole, however, South America showed the largest improvement in the index.

Two regions had indices below unity in the last period: West Asia and South Asia. Since the former region saw high political instability, its low ranking may not be surprising. South Asia underperformed for other reasons, mainly a historic legacy of inward-looking industrialization, poor infrastructure and (in some countries) political uncertainties.

3.7.2. *Country-wise Analysis*

The analysis of country-wise inward FDI performance Index (Table 3.6) shows Belgium/ Luxembourg continued to lead the performance index, having been the leader since 1998-2000. In part, this reflects Luxembourg's regime that favours financial FDI and involves transshipped FDI. Azerbaijan came third (having risen from 35th place in 1999-2001 and 13th in 2000-2002) as a result of large investments in its oil and gas industry. In fourth place was Ireland, which had held the same rank in 1998-2000 and third place in the previous period; Ireland is a success story, with a history of steadily improving its locational advantages and competitiveness over time (it held 50th place in the mid-1990s). The bottom place continued to be held by Suriname, with Indonesia just ahead.

Of the top 20 performers, 3 were developed countries, 2 mature East Asian newly industrializing economies, 5 transition economies and 10 other developing countries. The spread of countries over the Index reflects a mixture of economic, political and policy-induced factors; the ranks do not appear to reflect any consistent correlation with levels of development. Of the highly developed countries, Japan continued to come last, at 132nd place, a continuing legacy of its small FDI receipts, despite recent proactive FDI policies. The United States also ranked relatively low (112th place), a sharp deterioration over the previous period when it came 92nd (and from even earlier when it was 77th). The decline reflects a sharp drop in inward M&As, with GDP remaining relatively steady.

Over the long term, despite being the largest recipient of FDI, the United States has always ranked comparatively low relative to its GDP. Other developed countries performed better, with Sweden at 42nd place, France 50th, the United Kingdom 83rd, Italy 98th and Germany 102nd.

Among the major developing economies, China ranked 37th, an improvement over its previous rank of 50th. Rather like the United States, China is a small recipient of FDI relative

TABLE 3.6

Ranking by Inward FDI Performance Index, 2001-2003

1	Belgium and Luxembourg	36	Spain	71	Portugal	106	Paraguay
2	Brunei Darussalam	37	China	72	Venezuela	107	Niger
3	Azerbaijan	38	Dominican Republic	73	Ukraine	108	Norway
4	Ireland	39	Viet Nam	74	Congo, Democratic Republic of	109	Malawi
5	Angola	40	Denmark	75	Malaysia	110	Turkey
6	Singapore	41	Latvia	76	Zambia	111	Ethiopia
7	Gambia	42	Sweden	77	South Africa	112	United States
8	Kazakhstan	43	Finland	78	Austria	113	Uzbekistan
9	Hong Kong, China	44	Albania	79	Australia	114	India
10	Estonia	45	Panama	80	Papua New Guinea	115	Kyrgyzstan
11	Bolivia	46	Brazil	81	Malta	116	Libyan Arab Jamahiriya
12	Slovakia	47	United Republic of Tanzania	82	Tajikistan	117	Taiwan Province of China
13	Czech Republic	48	Costa Rica	83	United Kingdom	118	Argentina
14	Trinidad and Tobago	49	Switzerland	84	Jordan	119	Russian Federation
15	Mongolia	50	France	85	Myanmar	120	Korea, Republic of
16	Netherlands	51	Bahrain	86	Uruguay	121	Syrian Arab Republic
17	Nicaragua	52	Mali	87	Thailand	122	Sierra Leone
18	Namibia	53	Slovenia	88	El Salvador	123	Egypt
19	Croatia	54	Togo	89	Iceland	124	Yemen
20	Jamaica	55	Lithuania	90	Lebanon	125	Guinea
21	Bulgaria	56	Bahamas	91	Algeria	126	Oman
22	Congo	57	Botswana	92	Benin	127	Greece
23	Mozambique	58	Tunisia	93	Cameroon	128	Rwanda
24	Cyprus	59	Honduras	94	Ghana	129	Kenya
25	Moldova, Republic of	60	Israel	95	Gabon	130	Nepal
26	Guyana	61	Mexico	96	Philippines	131	Burkina Faso
27	Georgia	62	Romania	97	Pakistan	132	Japan
28	Ecuador	63	Peru	98	Italy	133	Bangladesh
29	Sudan	64	Colombia	99	Belarus	134	Haiti
30	Armenia	65	New Zealand	100	Guatemala	135	Zimbabwe
31	TFYR Macedonia	66	Côte d'Ivoire	101	United Arab Emirates	136	Iran, Islamic Republic of
32	Morocco	67	Qatar	102	Germany	137	Kuwait
33	Hungary	68	Poland	103	Senegal	138	Saudi Arabia
34	Chile	69	Nigeria	104	Sri Lanka	139	Indonesia
35	Uganda	70	Canada	105	Madagascar	140	Suriname

Source: UNCTAD calculations.

to its GDP, even though it dominates the developing world as an FDI host. Brazil ranked 46th, a worsening over 37th the two previous years. India ranked 114th, a gradual improvement over 121st in the previous year (and roughly the same as the previous few years). Mexico gained its ranking steadily from 73rd in the four earlier periods to 61st in the most recent period. One striking feature of the Index calculation is the sharp deterioration in Malaysia's FDI performance. From ranking among the top 10 till the mid-1990s, Malaysia fell in ranking every year in the latter part of the decade, reaching 75th place in 2001-2003. For an economy that depends heavily on FDI to drive its exports, this may be cause for concern, especially since the reasons are not clear.

In the South-East Asian region, Indonesia continued to perform poorly, coming 139th in the last two periods; however, the reason here is clearer – the persistence of political and financial uncertainty following the Asian financial crisis. The two mature Asian Tigers that have, like Japan, been fairly restrictive towards FDI, are the Republic of Korea and Taiwan Province of China; they continued to rank low on the Index, at positions 120 and 117 respectively.

3.8. Inward FDI Potential Index, consisting mainly of structural variables, is far more stable than the Performance Index. Of the 12 variables comprising the Potential Index, only country risk and, to a lesser extent, trade-related measures, tend to vary sharply from one period to the next. Thus, the correlation coefficient between the Potential Index values for the sample countries over previous years is high and rises steadily over time. This testifies to the structural nature of the measure. Inward FDI Potential Indices averaged across different groups of countries: the world as whole, developed countries, developing economies and Central and Eastern Europe (as shown in Table 3.7).

Table 3.7

Inward FDI Potential Index, by group of economies, average scores, 1988-2002a

Period	World	Developed Countries	Developing Countries	Central and Eastern Europe
1988-1990	0.187	0.374	0.138	...
1989-1991	0.186	0.373	0.137	...
1990-1992	0.208	0.371	0.169	...
1991-1993	0.208	0.372	0.172	...
1992-1994	0.209	0.373	0.173	0.184
1993-1995	0.225	0.407	0.185	0.201
1994-1996	0.221	0.395	0.184	0.187
1995-1997	0.217	0.393	0.18	0.18
1996-1998	0.224	0.398	0.186	0.203
1997-1999	0.224	0.402	0.184	0.204
1998-2000	0.221	0.403	0.179	0.204
1999-2001	0.22	0.4	0.178	0.211
2000-2002	0.22	0.396	0.177	0.221

source: UNCTAD, World Investment Report 2004

(a) Three-year moving averages.

Note: Data for the world and the major country groups shown above are averages of the scores for 140 economies as follows: 24 Developed countries; 99 Developing countries; and 17 Central and Eastern Europe economies. They are based on 12 economic and policy variables.

For the world as a whole, the average potential for attracting FDI has remained fairly stable. At the country level, the United States remained in first place throught the period 1988-2002 (according to Table 3.8). Among the 25 leading economies, the countries showing biggest improvements in rank were Ireland and Qatar. The leading economies in the Potential Index were, as before, developed countries, the four Asian Tigers and, in the period 2000-2002, two oil-rich economies from West Asia. China, the largest recipient of FDI in the developing world, was 39th by FDI potential ranking.

Table 3.8

Top 25 Rankings by the Inward FDI Potential Index, 1988-2002

Economy	1988-1990	1996-1998	2000-2002
United States	1	1	1
Norway	4	3	2
United Kingdom	3	5	3
Singapore	12	2	4
Canada	2	4	5
Belgium and Luxembourg	10	8	6
Ireland	24	18	7
Qatar	22	20	8
Germany	7	6	9
Sweden	5	7	10
Netherlands	9	9	11
Hong Kong, China	17	14	12
Finland	8	13	13
France	6	10	14
Iceland	15	19	15
Japan	13	12	16
United Arab Emirates	29	11	17
Korea, Republic of	20	21	18
Denmark	16	16	19
Switzerland	11	17	20
Taiwan Province of China	21	24	21
Australia	14	15	22
Israel	27	25	23
Austria	19	22	24
Spain	25	26	25

source: UNCTAD, World Investment Report 2004

3.9. Indices of Outward FDI Performance

The Index of Outward FDI Performance calculated in the same way as the Inward FDI Performance Index: the world share of a country's outward FDI as a ratio of its share in world GDP. The Outward FDI Index captures two aspects of performance:

- A high index value indicates that a country's firms have strong "ownership advantages" that they are exploiting abroad, or wish to augment through foreign expansion. Ownership advantages are firm-specific competitive strengths of TNCs (or potential TNCs) arising from e.g. innovation, brand names, managerial and organizational skills, privileged access to information, financial or natural resources, historical or cultural links and size and network advantages.
- A high index value may also indicate that a home country may be less desirable as a place to undertake (specific) productive activities relative to foreign locations; hence firms choose to deploy ownership advantages elsewhere. These "location factors" may reflect purely economic factors in home and host economics (e.g. relative market size, production or transport costs, skills, supply chains, infrastructure, technology support), but they can also reflect policy and institutional differences (such as protection, taxes or labour regulations and FDI-related policies).

The Outward FDI Performance Index for flows for 2000-2002 is considered in Table 3.9, taking top 20 performers. As expected, the list of leaders contains several tax havens and offshore financial centres, the outward FDI of which originates elsewhere. Apart from these, most of the leaders are high-income economies. Of 11 economies with ratios above two, six are European; the remaining five are developing economies, including Hong Kong (China) and Singapore, both of which are rich and also act as conduits for investment from elsewhere. The larger developed economies – Germany, the United States, and Japan – have low values, suggesting that even these major outward investors have some way to go before they reach the levels of outward FDI that would be expected of them.

Table 3.9

Outward FDI Performance Index for the 20 Leading Investor Economies, 1988-2003[a]

Rank	Economy	1988-1990	1993-1995	1999-2001	2000-2001	2001-2003
1	Belgium and Luxembourg	2.676	2.087	12.62	16.16	22.741
2	Panama	7.243	2.671	1.254	3.049	6.548
3	Singapore	2.892	4.783	3.579	3.695	5.104
4	Netherlands	3.872	3.964	4.904	5.09	4.643
5	Azerbaijan	...	...	0.993	1.057	3.764
6	Hong Kong, China	3.37	14.911	5.76	6.813	3.477
7	Sweden	4.54	2.688	3.035	3.12	2.329
8	Bahrain	0.559	1.203	0.54	0.647	2.309
9	Switzerland	3.442	3.562	4.04	3.541	2.303
10	France	1.844	1.292	2.996	2.914	2.209
11	Spain	0.429	0.636	2.317	2.5	2.178
12	Denmark	1.107	1.65	3.624	3.524	1.921
13	Canada	0.905	1.402	1.459	1.865	1.869
14	United Kingdom	2.963	2.927	3.559	2.791	1.603
15	Portugal	0.161	0.357	1.718	2.052	1.487
16	Australia	0.947	0.722	0.343	0.687	1.421
17	Iceland	0.059	0.277	1.091	1.462	1.407
18	Cyprus	0.036	0.181	0.649	0.966	1.382
19	Botswana	0.076	0.405	0.776	1.022	1.334
20	Ireland	1.895	0.778	1.579	1.397	1.251

source: UNCTAD, World Investment Report 2004

(a) Three-year moving averages.

Note: Economies are ranked in descending order of their performance index in 2001-2003. Figures were calculated based on outward flows.

Most developed countries have seen an increase in their outward FDI indices over time. The faster rise in FDI than their share of global GDP indicates that their enterprises are building ownership advantages more rapidly and/or are choosing to exploit their advantages in foreign locations. Some, such as Finland, are going overseas at a particularly fast pace, driven in this case by Nokia, a firm in an industry that is highly dynamic and transnationalized. The index for

Hong Kong (China) has risen at an exceptionally fast pace, but this reflects in part its peculiar situation as a staging post for FDI into China and as a recipient of round tripping by Chinese enterprises.

The Index based on outward FDI stock shows similar patterns: there are nine economies with performance ratios above two, of which six are European; and the other three are Hong Kong (China), Panama and Singapore. Belgium-Luxembourg and Hong Kong (China) are again out performers. Germany is not below average by this measure, but the United States and Japan are under-performers. Among developing economies other than the three mentioned above, the highest performance ratios are seen for Malaysia, Bahrain and Bahamas, followed by Taiwan Province of China, Botswana and South Africa.

3.10. Regional Trends in Foreign Direct Investment

This section analyses recent trends of foreign direct investment (FDI) and developments in the various regions of Developed, Developing and Central & Eastern Europe Countries.

3.10.A. Developed Countries

Inflows of Foreign Direct Investment (FDI) to developed countries fell by 25%, from $490 billion in 2002 to $367 billion in 2003 (Table 3.2).

Inflows in 2003 represented one third of the $1.1 trillion peak in 2000. FDI inflows were higher for 10 countries in the region and lower for 16. As a result of transshipped FDI, Luxembourg[12] was once again the largest FDI recipient worldwide, followed by China, France and the United States(figure 3.8). FDI inflows into the United States declined by 53 percent for the third year in a row, to a low of $30 billion – its lowest value since 1992. There were large repayments of intra-company debt ($34 billion), as foreign affiliates in the United States reduced the debt they had accumulated with their parent firms abroad during the M&A boom of 1998-2001. Equity flows also declined (to $62 billion). Reinvested earnings rose because of improved profitability, but their level was low ($2 billion). FDI flows into the EU and Japan have been declined by 21 percent and 32 percent respectively (Table 3.5). In 2003, only two developed countries were ranked in the top ten in Inward FDI Performance Index: Belgium-Luxembourg and Ireland, ranked first and fourth respectively (Table 3.7). Belgium's FDI inflows doubled in 2003, with equity capital being the main source. FDI flows to Italy rose by 13 percent as a result of an increase in M & A activity, while in Ireland, they grew by 4 percent due to high equity inflows and reinvested earnings. However, in the case of both Italy and Ireland, these increases were more than offset by the depreciation of the dollar vis-à-vis the euro. FDI flows to the United Kingdom were down by nearly half, mainly as a result of the continued downturn in cross-border M&As and a net repayment of loans to foreign parent companies. As a result, since 2000, FDI inflows to the United Kingdom have plunged by $104 billion.

Unlike inflows, FDI outflows from developed countries rose in 2003, by 4 percent, to $570 billion. Overall. Outflows from 10 of 25 developed countries increased. The United States regained its position as the main investor country (having lost this position to Luxembourg in 2002), with a 32% increase in outflows in 2003 (figure 3.9), followed by Luxembourg, France and the United Kingdom. Outflows from the EU were down by 4%, even though outflows from France and the UK rose by 16% and 57%, respectively. In these countries, this was largely due to increases in intra-company loans. Outflows from Germany slumped by 70%, due to reduced parent company loans as well as the weak performance of German enterprises to their foreign affiliates fell. Japan's outflows

Table 3.10

DEVELOPED COUNTRIES: FDI INFLOWS, TOP 10		
country	2002	2003
Luxembourg	117	88
France	49	47
United States	63	30
Belgium	15	29
Spain	36	26
Ireland	24	25
Netherlands	26	20
Italy	15	16
United Kingdom	28	15
Germany	36	13
European Union	374	295

Figure 3.10: DEVELOPED COUNTRIES: FDI INFLOWS, TOP 10 COUNTRIES,2002, 2003 (Billions of dollars)

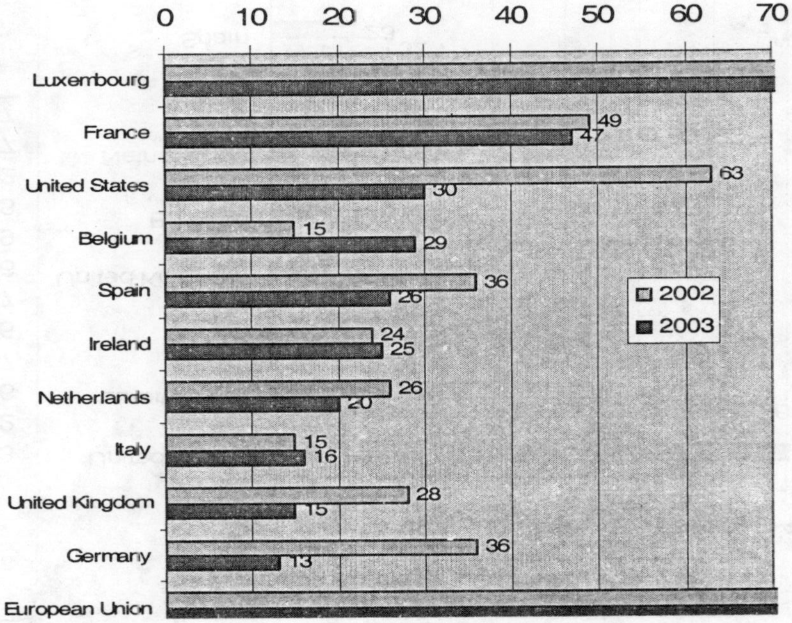

Table 3.11 DEVELOPED COUNTRIES : FDI OUTFLOWS - TOP TEN, 2002 & 2003

(Billions of dollars)

country	2002	2003
United States	115	152
Luxembourg	126	96
France	49	67
United Kingdom	35	55
Beldium	12	37
Netherlands	35	36
Japan	32	29
Spain	32	23
Canada	26	22
Sweden	11	17
European Union	351	337

source: World Investment Report 2004

Figure 3.11: DEVELOPED COUNTRIES : FDI OUTFLOWS : TOP TEN, 2002 & 2003

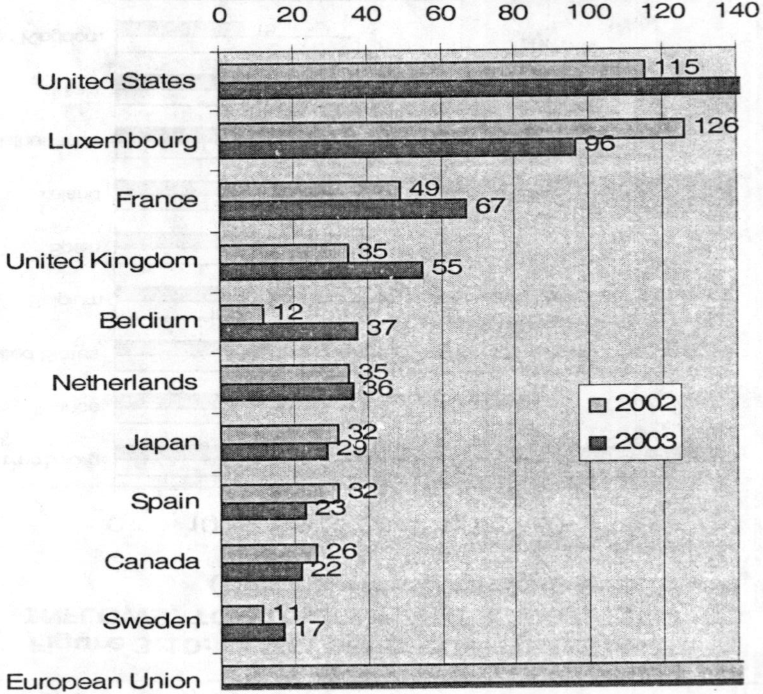

continued to fall (-11%), having also declined in 2002. They were mainly in the tertiary sector, with Europe being the main destination. However, the trend is towards increased investment in manufacturing in Asia and the United States.

Developed Countries: Sectoral distribution of FDI flows

Services dominated the changing pattern of FDI in developed countries as a group, accounting for more than two-thirds of both inflows and outflows in the 2000-2002 periods. FDI in the primary sector was still of importance (albeit declining) in countries such as Australia (18 percent in 2001), the Netherlands (19 percent in 2001) and Norway (28 percent in 2001). Manufacturing sector still accounted for a large share of total FDI stock in some countries, notably Canada (52 percent in 2002), Iceland (54 percent in 2002), Italy (40 percent in 2001) and Sweden (68 percent in 2001), with chemicals, automobiles and machinery being the largest industries.

Developing countries are the prime source as well as destination of FDI in services. Between 1996 and 2002, inward and outward stocks in services rose in 10 and 13 developed countries, respectively.[13]

In absolute and relative terms, the United States accounted for the highest outward and inward FDI stocks in services (amounting to $1,050 billion and $826 billion, respectively, at the end of 2002, or 69 percent and 61 percent of the totals, respectively, led by finance, trade, business activities and transportation, storage and telecoms.

Other countries with a large share of services in their inward stock are Denmark, Switzerland, Luxembourg and France (above 80 percent); countries with the largest outward share in services are Denmark, France, Austria and the United States (ranging from 69 percent to 78 percent).

3.10.B. Developing Countries

• ***Inward Foreign Direct Investment***

In 2003, FDI flows to the developing countries as a group that experienced a recovery, rising by 9 percent to $172 billion overall, following two years of decline. But in this group, the picture was mixed: Africa and Asia and the Pacific saw an increase, while Latin America and the Caribbean experienced a continuing decline.

1. Africa: A Turnaround

FDI inflows to Africa rose by 28 percent, to $15 billion, in 2003, but fell short of their 2001 peak of $20 billion (Table 3.4). Thirty-six countries saw a rise in inflows, and 17 a decline. The recovery of FDI in 2003 was led by investment in natural resources and facilitated by the continued liberalization of FDI policies. FDI as a percentage of gross fixed capital formation also grown, from 12 percent in 2002 to 14 percent in 2003, the second highest level in the past decade. This performance was noteworthy for three reasons:

- The growth rate of 28 percent was higher than that of the other groups of countries, developed and developing.
- Several small African economies shared in the growth of FDI. As a result, the distribution of inflows was more broad-based than in any year since 1999, with 22 countries receiving more than $0.1 billion compared to 16 in 2001.
- Oil accounted for the bulk of the increase, especially in Equatorial Guinea.

Among the countries in the league of the top ten recipients, Morocco was the number one recipient: inflows rose from $480 million in 2002 to $2.3 billion in 2003, followed by Equatorial Guinea, Angola, Sudan etc. (figure 3.12).

Table 3.12: AFRICA: top 10 receipts of FDI infolws, 2002, 2003

(Billions of dollar)

country	2002	2003
Morocco	0.5	2.3
Equatorial Guinea	0.3	1.4
Angola	1.6	1.4
Sudan	0.7	1.3
Nigeria	1.3	1.2
Chad	1	0.8
South Africa	0.8	0.8
Libyan Arab Jamahiriya	-0.1	0.7
Algeria	1.1	0.6
Tunisia	0.8	0.6

Figure 3.12: AFRICA : Top 10 recipients of FDI inflows - 2002, 2003 (Billions of dollar)

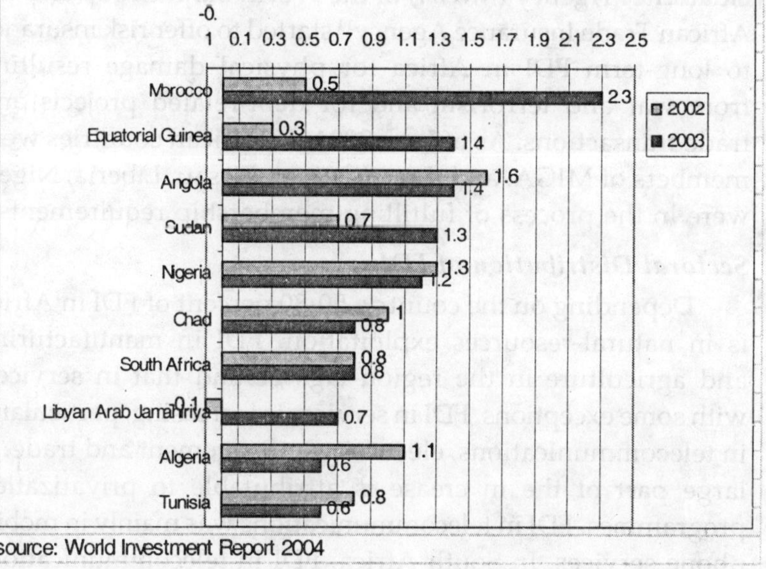

source: World Investment Report 2004

Policies Increasingly Liberal

African countries continued to liberalize their FDI policies, increase their efforts to attract more FDI or initiated action in these respects. Burundi, Kenya, Nigeria and Rwanda resumed economic reforms, privatization and liberalization, further reducing their restrictions on foreign investors. Much of the privatization was related to infrastructure development. The Rwanda Privatization Secretariat, for instance, announced in November 2003 that Rwandatel, the State-owned telecom company, is to be sold, without any restriction on the participation by foreign investors.

Additional measures were also taken to facilitate foreign investment. In September 2003, the Multilateral Investment Guarantee Agency (MIGA) of the World Bank Group and the African Trade Insurance Agency[14] started to offer risk insurance to long-term FDI in Africa for physical damage resulting from war and terrorism and for debt-related projects and trade transactions. As of June 2004, 46 African countries were members of MIGA, and three (Guinea-Bissau, Liberia, Niger) were in the process of fulfilling membership requirements.

Sectoral Distribution of FDI

Depending on the country, 50-80 percent of FDI in Africa is in natural-resources exploitation. FDI in manufacturing and agriculture in the region lags behind that in services, with some exceptions. FDI in services is increasing, particularly in telecommunications, electricity, management and trade. A large part of the in crease is attributable to privatization programmes. FDI in telecommunications was mainly in mobile phone services. In South Africa, FDI in telecommunications and information technology has overtaken that in mining and extraction. The number of Africans subscribing to mobile phone services, mostly offered by TNCs, grew from 1.2 million in 1996 to 51 million in 2003.

Table 3.13

ASIA AND THE PACIFIC: top 10 recipients of FDI inflows - 2002, 2003
(Billions of dollars)

country	2002	2003
China	52.7	53.5
Hong Kong, China	9.7	13.6
Singapore	5.7	11.4
India	3.4	4.3
Korea, Republic of	2.9	3.8
Azerbaijan	1.4	3.3
Malaysia	3.2	2.5
Kazakhstan	2.6	2.1
Brunei Darussalam	1	2
Thailand	1.1	1.8

Figure 3.13 ASIA AND THE PACIFIC : top 10 recipients of FDI inflows - 2002, 2003

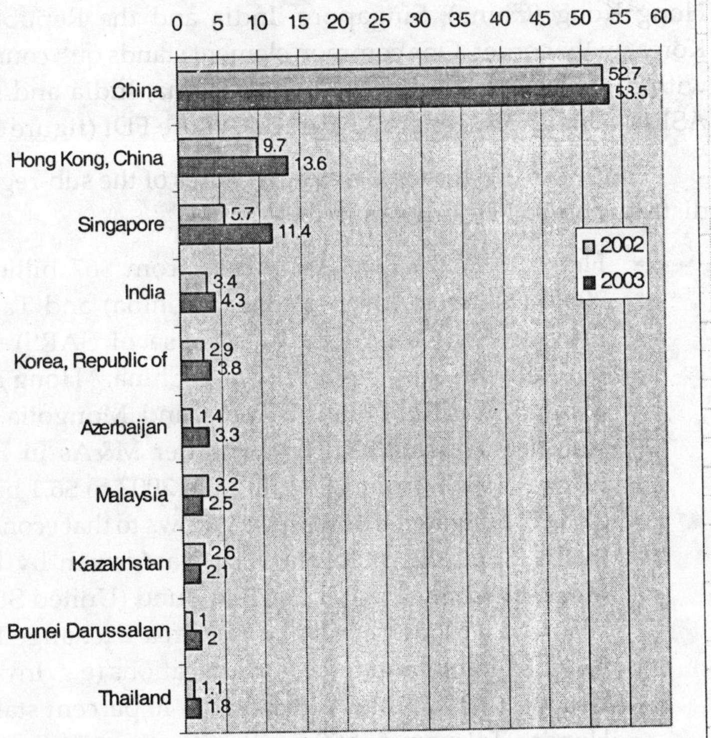

2. *Asia and the Pacific: A Rebound*

FDI flows to the Asia and the Pacific region rebounded in 2003. Total inflows rose from $94 billion in 2002 to $107 billion in 2003, ending the downturn that started in 2001. Out of 55 economies for which data are available, 34 received higher flows than in 2002, and 21 lower inflows.

Asia and the Pacific attracted more FDI than most other regions, thus remaining the largest recipient of FDI in the developing world. FDI inflows as a percentage of gross fixed capital formation rose, from 8 percent in 2002 to 9 percent in 2003. But FDI remained concentrated: ten economies accounted for about 90 percent of all inflows.

The top ten (10) recipients in 2003 were headed by China, Hong Kong (China), Singapore, India and the Republic of Korea, in that order. One common element stands out: countries with high economic growth, such as China, India and some ASEAN countries, generally attracted more FDI (figure 3.13).

The following are some salient features of the sub-regional distribution of FDI inflows in 2003:

- Flows to *North-East Asia*[15] rose from $67 billion in 2003. Falling inflows to Macao (China) and Taiwan Province of China (partly because of SARS) were partially offset by higher flows to China,[16] Hong Kong (China), the Republic of Korea and Mongolia. The significant increase in cross-border M&As in Hong Kong (China), from $1.9 billion in 2002 to $6.1 billion in 2003, mitigated a downturn in flows to that economy. In the Republic of Korea, FDI was driven by large M&As in finance (e.g. Lone Star Fund (United States) acquired a 51 percent stake of Korea Exchange Bank for $1.2 billion) and telecommunications (e.g. Investor Group, United States purchased a 40 percent stake of Hanaro Telecom for $0.5 billion).

- China was the largest FDI recipient in the world, excluding *Luxembourg*,[17] with inflows of $53.5 billion. The number of cross-border M&As in China increased from 107 in 2002 to 214 in 2003,[18] contributing to the surge in FDI flows. Relocation of investment to and expansion of operations in China by TNCs remained strong.
- Regional economic growth and an improved investment environment contributed to a 27 percent increase in FDI flows to *South-East Asia*, which comprises countries of the *Association of South-East Asian Nations (ASEAN)*,[19] from $15 billion in 2002 to $19 billion in 2003. The impact of SARS on FDI flows to the region was limited.[20] Flows to Brunei Darussalam,[21] Singapore, Thailand and Viet Nam rose thanks to improved economic conditions and better investment climates. The successful privatization of a number of State assets in Indonesia (e.g. Bank Danamon, Bank International Indonesia) generated $0.6 billion in FDI (equity flows) in 2003, mitigating an otherwise sizeable decline. Repayments of intra-company loans by foreign affiliates fell in the sub-region.
- *South asia*[22] received $6.1 billion in FDI, up from $4.5 billion in 2002. FDI to India, the dominant host country in this sub-region, grew by 24 percent from $3.45 billion in 2002 to $4.27 billion in 2003, which reflect its strong growth and continued liberalization. The services sector, in particular information and communication technology (ICT) industries, was the most dynamic for FDI inflows. Except for Afghanistan and Bhutan, flows to the other countries rose, and significantly so in Bangladesh, Nepal and Pakistan. In Sri Lanka privatization helped boost FDI flows.[23]

- *Central Asia*[24] also recorded an increase in FDI inflows, from $4.5 billion to $6.1 billion. Resource-rich countries such as Azerbaijan attracted more FDI than others, mostly in oil and gas. Georgia and Kyrgyzstan also received higher flows. Those to Kazakhstan declined by 20 percent, from $2.6 billion in 2002 to $2.1 billion in 2003.
- FDI flows to *West Asia*[25] upturn from $3.6 billion in 2002 to $4.1 billion in 2003. The increase in flows to Bahrain, Jordan, Kuwait, Oman and Saudi Arabia accounted for much of the sub-region's improved performance. However, regional tensions and uncertainty are likely to have held back a higher increase.
- Flows to the *Pacific islands* doubled, from $0.1 billion in 2002 to $0.2 billion in 2003, with most countries benefiting from higher inflows. Papua New Guinea in particular, saw a sharp rise in flows from $21 million in 2002 to $101 million. The increase in M&As in this country, amounting to $82 million (up from $28 million in 2002), was the main explanation.

One common feature is that the countries with high economic growth, such as China, India and some ASEAN countries, generally attracted more FDI.

Privatization has not been a major factor driving FDI in the Asia-Pacific region. Most FDI in Asia is in the form of Greenfield investment.[26] However, some countries – India, Indonesia, the Republic of Korea, Pakistan, Turkey – have increased their efforts to privatize State assets (including through FDI) in order to raise revenue and strengthen industrial development.

• ***Outward Foreign Direct Investment***

Outward FDI from developing countries is becoming important factor. Annual FDI outflows from developing countries have grown faster over the past 15 years than those from developed countries. Negligible until the beginning of the 1990s, outward FDI from developing countries accounted for over one-tenth of the world total stock and some 6 percent of world total flows in 2003 ($0.9 trillion and $36 billion, respectively). FDI from developing countries to other developing countries seems to be growing faster than that from developing countries to developed countries. Some developing countries are now large investors by global

Table 3.14

FDI Outflows as a percentage of Gross Fixed Capital Formation in selected Developing Economies, 2001-2003
(Per cent)

Economy	Value
Singapore	36.3
Hong Kong, China	28.2
Taiwan Province of China	10.5
Chile	7.4
Malaysia	5.3
India	1
China	0.8
Brazil	0.2
Memorandum	
Sweden	27.4
France	22
United Kingdom	19
United States	6.6
Germany	4.1
Japan	3.2
Greece	1.8

source: World Investment Report 2004

standards. In 2003, for instance, Hong Kong (China) had a larger outward FDI stock than Sweden, even if round tripping and indirect FDI is taken into account.[27]

If outflows are viewed in relation to gross fixed capital formation, (Table 3.14), a number of developing economies (Singapore, Hong Kong (China), Taiwan Province of China) rank higher than a number of developed countries (Germany, Japan, the United States). This suggests that a number of developing countries, relatively speaking, are already among top investors.

3. Latin America and the Caribbean

FDI flows to Latin America and the Caribbean (LAC) fell by 3 percent from $51.36 billion in 2002 to $49.72 billion in 2003 – the lowest level since 1996. This was the fourth consecutive year of decline, following a 53 percent drop over the period 1999-2003. Of the region's 40 countries, 19 saw declining inflows. FDI as a percentage of gross fixed capital formation dropped to 11 percent, from a high of 26 percent in 1999.

On the inward side, there was considerable variation within the region. Mexico and Brazil, where services are the most important sector, experienced the sharpest decline in inflows. Mexico, in particular, is faced with a competitive challenge from China, notably in manufacturing. Apart from small island economies (e.g. two offshore centres – Bermuda, the Cayman Islands), other relatively small countries (e.g. Ecuador, Honduras, Nicaragua, Panama, Uruguay) recorded an increase in FDI inflows. Chile and Venezuela recovered a large part of the declines experienced in 2002.

The various factors contributed to the continuing downturn trend, some of which were beyond the control of the host countries are presented below:

Table 3.15

LAC : top 10 Recipients of FDI Inflows - 2002, 2003 (Billions of dollars)		
country	2002	2003
Mexico	14.7	10.8
Brazil	16.6	10.1
Bermuda	2.7	8.5
Cayman Islands	2.5	4.6
Chile	1.9	3
Venezuela	0.8	2.5
Colombia	2.1	1.8
Ecuador	1.3	1.6
Peru	2.2	1.4
Panama	0.1	0.8

Figure 3.14: LAC : top 10 recipients of FDI inflows - 2002, 2003

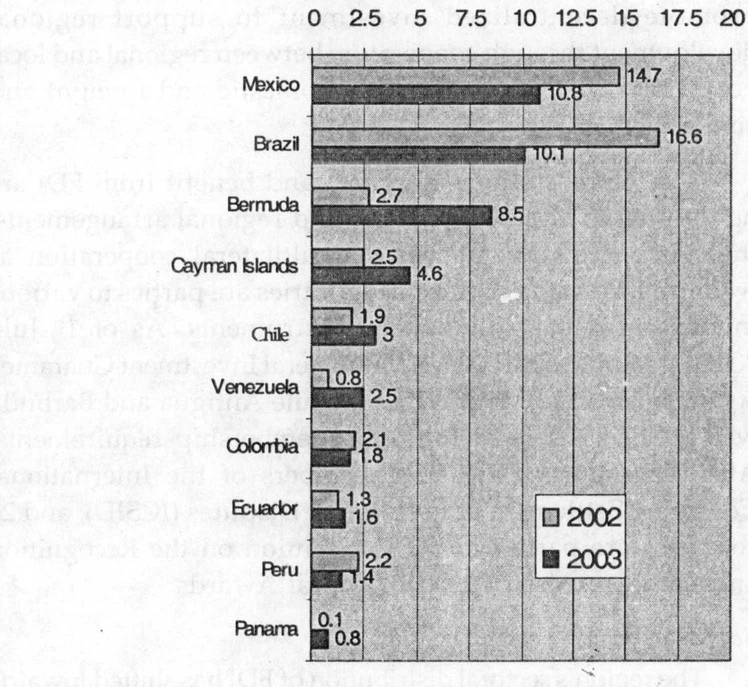

- TNCs from major home countries invested less because of deteriorating economic conditions.
- A steep drop in cross-border M&As in the region, both in number (from 581 in 2000 to 281 in 2003) and value, from a high of $64 billion in 1998 to $12 billion in 2003.

Policy Developments in LAC

At the national level, the trend continued towards greater liberalization and investment facilitation. For instance, Brazil simplified registration procedure by introducing an electronic registration system and initiated an Investment Policy Review. Tax discounts for reinvested earnings were introduced in Mexico, and there are plans to reduce further corporate income taxes. In August 2003, Peru introduced a law seeking to promote decentralized investment to support regional development through cooperation between regional and local governments, private investors (domestic and foreign) and civil society.

The region's efforts to attract and benefit from FDI are not limited to national, bilateral and regional arrangements; there is a growing interest in multilateral cooperation as well. An increasing number of countries are parties to various investment-related multilateral instruments. As of 1st July 2004, 30 countries had joined Multilateral Investment Guarantee Agency (MIGA) of World Bank, while Antigua and Barbuda was in the process of fulfilling membership requirements. Also, 27 countries are now members of the International Centre for Settlement of Investment Disputes (ICSID), and 25 countries are parties to the Convention on the Recognition and Enforcement of Foreign Arbitral Awards.

Sectoral Patterns of FDI

The region's sectoral distribution of FDI has shifted towards services at the expense of manufacturing. This is mainly the result of privatization in the services sector. Resource-seeking FDI has traditionally played an important role in Andean Community countries (Colombia, Ecuador, and Venezuela).

In contrast, the primary sector in the two largest economies of Latin America, Brazil and Mexico, accounts for only a small share of total FDI inflows. Yet, the sectoral structure of FDI differs significantly between these two countries. Almost 70 percent of Brazil's total FDI inflows during 1996-2000 were absorbed by the services sector. The subsequent drop in FDI inflows in 2001-2003 was due to sharply reduced flows to telecommunications and finance. In Mexico, the manufacturing sector accounted for 54 percent of total FDI inflows during 1996-2000. However, unlike in Brazil, this sector's share fell in 2001, mainly because of exceptionally high FDI flows to financial services, but it recovered in 2002 and 2003.

3.10.C. Central and Eastern Europe (CEE) Countries

FDI inflows into CEE declined from a record $31 billion in 2002 to a low of $21 billion in 2003. This decline was almost entirely due to the end of privatization in the Czech Republic and Slovakia. Inward FDI in the rest of the region declined only marginally, from $19 billion to $18 billion. Overall, FDI inflows rose in ten countries and fell in nine, with Poland replacing the Czech Republic as the top recipient.

The share of inward FDI in gross fixed capital formation fell from 17 percent in 2002 to 10 percent in 2003. In contrast, at $7 billion, FDI outflows from CEE reached a new record in 2003, up from $5 billion in 2002.

The decline in FDI inflows into CEE, in 2003 was largely due to a fall in flows to the Czech Republic and Slovakia, two countries that had led the FDI surge in 2002 with large privatization. The winding up of the privatization process contributed to the decline in FDI. Outside the Czech Republic

Figure 3.15

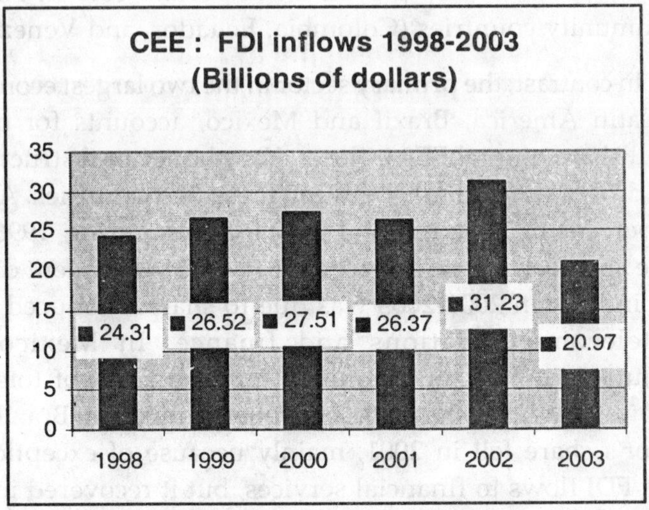

and Slovakia, the decline in FDI inflows was small, leading to the re-establishment of Poland, the Czech Republic and Hungary as the three top locations for inward FDI in region.

The group of eight CEE countries that joined the EU in May 2004 – the Czech Republic, Estonia, Hungary, Latvia, Lithuania, Poland, Slovenia, and Slovakia – witnessed a decline in FDI inflows from $23 billion in 2002 to $11 billion in 2003. However, in the other 11 countries of the region – including Bulgaria and Romania (currently negotiating their entry into the EU) – FDI inflows rose from $8.6 billion in 2002 to $9.5 billion in 2003, representing an increase in their share of total FDI inflows from 28 percent in 2002 to 45 percent in 2003.

FDI outflows from CEE rose by 42 percent in 2003, from $5 billion to $7 billion. The Russian Federation remained the leading source, alone accounting for the bulk (59 percent) of the region's outflows. Non-Russian outward FDI rose faster

Table 3.16: CEE: top 10 Recipients of FDI Infolws - 2002, 2003

(Billions of dollars)

country	2002	2003
Poland	4.1	4.2
Czech Republic	8.5	2.6
Hungary	2.8	2.5
Croatia	1.1	1.7
Romania	1.1	1.6
Ukraine	0.7	1.4
Bulgaria	0.9	1.4
Serbia and Montenegro	0.5	1.4
Russian Federation	3.5	1.1
Estonia	0.3	0.9

Figure 3.16: CEE : top 10 recipients of FDI INFLOWS - 2002, 2003

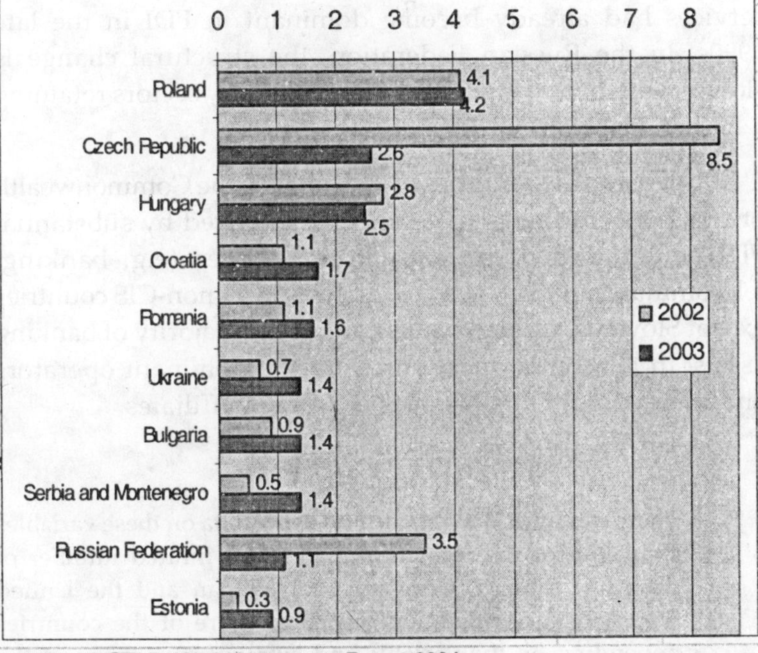

source: UNCTAD, World Investment Report 2004

than that from the Russian Federation: Hungary's outward FDI surged from $0.3 billion in 2002 to $1.6 billion in 2003.

Sectoral Distribution of FDI

Service-related FDI inflows into CEE have followed the trend of growth in services (in GDP, employment, FDI) worldwide and in the region itself. In the CEE region, services had been largely neglected under the centrally planned economic system.

In the largest host countries of the region (the Czech Republic, Hungary, Poland, the Russian Federation), the industry composition of inward FDI is gradually shifting from manufacturing towards services, and within services, from network industries privatized in earlier years towards business services. In the Czech Republic, Hungary and Poland, services had already become dominant in FDI in the late 1990s. In the Russian Federation, the structural change is slower, with both the primary and secondary sectors retaining a higher share of FDI.

In general, the countries of CEE outside the Commonwealth of Independent States (CIS) are characterized by substantial FDI penetration in infrastructure services (e.g. banking, telecommunications, water, electricity). In all non-CIS countries except Slovenia, foreign banks control the majority of banking assets. In telecommunications, both the dominant operators and their competitors are mostly foreign affiliates.

REFERENCES

1. These estimates are obtained by using data on these variables available for the foreign affiliates of a limited number of countries (France, Germany, Italy, Japan and the United States) or a combination of one or more of the countries depending on the variable and extrapolating them on the basis of problems in this methodology. Its use implies the

following assumptions: first, that all TNCs, regardless of nationality, broadly behave in a similar manner no matter where their foreign production takes place, implying that one unit of FDI products the same size of value added, sales and exports everywhere in the world; and second, that the effects of FDI are uniform in all regions as no host-country differences are considered.

2. FDI stock measures the value of share capital and reserves attributable to direct investors, though there are several evaluation methods for deriving the values. It also includes retained dividends and loans, trade credit and debt securities due to direct investors. The OECD recommends that the FDI stock be measured in market value rather than in book value from the balance sheets of investors reported on a historical cost basis (OECD, 1996). Re-valuation of FDI stock by various methods results in different stock figures that may lead to different and sometimes misleading interpretations of FDI situations (for example, see Gray and Rugman, 1994; and Bellak and Cantwell, 1996).
3. The relative variance as measured by the standard deviation divided by the average of the variable is 0.5 for FDI flows, 0.64 for portfolio flows and 5.9 for commercial bank loans between 1990 and 2002.
4. The transnationality index of both developed and developing countries in 1999 was less than 20 percent (WIR –02, p. 21), but it rose to more than 20 percent in 2000 in both groups of economies. Similarly the index for CEE rose by a few percentage points.
5. The lending rate was 4.68 percent in the United States, compared with 6.13 percent in the Euro area in 2002. But during 1997-2001 the lending rate was higher in the United States than in the Euro area, by as much as two percentage points. Lending rates in Japan were very low throughout the period—and FDI outflows from Japan to the United States increased.
6. EU TNCs engaged in far fewer cross-border M & A transactions in the United States: from 400 in 2001 they fell

to 241 deals in 2002. The value of completed cross-border M&As in the United States by EU firms halved in 2001 and halved again in 2002 to only $47 billion, compared with $203 billion in 2000. The value of cross-border M&As by United States firms in the EU rose from $34 billion in 2001 to $39 billion in 2002, however, these levels were about half those in 2000 (data from UNCTAD, cross-border M& A database).

7. Based on 49 markets in 47 countries, the value of stocks traded rose by 13 percent in 2003, but it was still 40 percent lower than the peak level of 2000 (World Federation of Exchanges: www.world-exchanges.org).
8. Many large firms reported higher profits in 2003. For example, Japanese firms listed in stock markets registered record profits in 2003. Profits also rose by 18 percent on average, for United States companies (United States, Department of Commerce 2004a). The market capitalization of Asian firms rose more than twofold in Thailand and by 50 percent in Hong Kong (China), Malaysia and Singapore (World Federation of Exchanges). However, the recovery in profits was concentrated in selected firms in certain industries such as electronics and IT-related companies.
9. For example, the debt-equity ratio for United States non-farm, non-financial companies was 49 percent at the end of 2003, lower than that in 2002, but still higher than in the previous years (United States, Board of Governors of the Federal Reserve System, 2004).
10. Data from United Nations Conference on Trade and Development (UNCTAD) cross-border M&A database (www.unctad.org/fdistatistics).
11. In effect, the Index captures the influence of factors other than market size on FDI flows, assuming, ceteris paribus, that size is the "baseline" for attracting investment. These other factors are diverse, ranging from the business climate, economic and political stability, the presence of natural resources, infrastructure, skills and technologies, to opportunities for participating in privatization or the effectiveness of FDI promotion.

12. About four-fifths of FDI flows are transshipped FDI, i.e. investment that is invested in other countries, World Investment Report 2003.
13. Countries that experienced a fall in the share of services in inward FDI stock were Australia, Canada, Italy, Luxembourg, Portugal, Sweden and Switzerland, while countries that experienced a fall in outward FDI stocks were Australia, Italy, Luxembourg and Portugal.
14. This is the first multilateral export credit and political risk agency in which its member countries directly assume financial liability for political risk-related foreign investment losses that could affect trade within their own countries.
15. Includes China, Hong Kong (China), Democratic People's Republic of Korea, the Republic of Korea, Macao (China), Mongolia and Taiwan Province of China.
16. FDI flows to China slowed down at the initial outbreak of SARS, but surged towards the end of the year, resulting in marginally higher flows than in the previous year.
17. Luxembourg received $88 billion of FDI flows in 2003, most of which was transshipped to other destinations.
18. UNCTAD, cross-border M&A database (www.unctad.org/fdistatistics).
19. Brunei Darussalam, Cambodia, Indonesia, the Lao People's Democratic Republic, Malaysia, Myanmar, the Philippines, Singapore, Thailand and Viet Nam.
20. The initial outbreak of SARS deterred FDI to some countries. But in the second part of the year, flows recovered, averting an overall decline.
21. An increase in investment in the oil industry and construction services contributed to the rise in FDI flows to Brunei Darussalam.
22. Comprises Afghanistan, Bangladesh, Bhutan, India, Maldives, Nepal, Pakistan and Sri Lanka.
23. Privatization proceeds of FDI increased from $5 million in 2002 to $30 million in 2003.
24. Comprises Armenia, Azerbaijan, Georgia, Kazakhstan, Kyrgyzstan, Tajikistan, Turkmenistan and Uzbekistan.

25. Comprises Bahrain, Cyprus, the Islamic Republic of Iran, Iraq, Jordan, Kuwait, Lebanon, Oman, and the occupied Palestinian territory, Qatar, Saudi Arabia, the Syrian Arab Republic, Turkey, the United Arab Emirates and Yemen.
26. Green-field Investment involves the establishment of a wholly new operation in a foreign country.
27. It is assumed that round tripping and indirect FDI accounts for 25-40 per cent of FDI from Hong Kong (China).

4

Aggregate Analysis of FDI in India

4.1. Introduction

Across the world, Foreign Direct Investment (FDI) has been increasing dramatically since the beginning of the Nineties. Most of the countries in the world have recognized the role and relevance of foreign capital for rapid economic and industrial development. Foreign capital contributes in many important ways to the process of economic growth and industrialization. Foreign capital can act as a catalyst for domestic industrial development. Further, it helps in speeding up of economic activity and brings with it other scarce productive factors; such as technical know-how and managerial experience, which are equally essential for economic development.

Foreign Direct Investment plays an important role in the development process of the country. It has the potential for making a contribution to the development through the transfer of financial resources, technology and innovative and improved management techniques. The presence of Foreign Investment in the country could raise the productivity. Developing countries like India needs substantial foreign inflows to achieve the required investment to accelerate economic growth and overall development.

The Foreign Investment includes Official Development

Assistance (ODA), Non-Resident Indian (NRI) Investments, and Commercial Borrowings, in addition to Private Foreign Investment, which together can bridge the resources gap to sustain the targeted growth. The FDI supplements domestic savings to achieve a higher level of investment. The main attraction of FDI is that besides bringing Foreign Exchange, it finances the creation of new manufacturing capacity, new technology, and modern management practices. The Government has always hoped that larger inflows of Foreign Capital will buyout the balance of payments. There has been a fair measure of success in this respect. Net inflow of FDI, which was just $150 millions in 1991-92, has increased to $3,904 millions in 2001-02. The other two objectives have been to encourage some MNC's to use India as an export base and to ask others to invest in high priority and infrastructural areas.

The Indian Government has recognized foreign capital as important supplement to domestic savings for the economic development of the country and for securing scientific, technical, and industrial development. Since the Indian domestic capital is inadequate for rapid economic growth, therefore it is necessary to invite foreign capital. The Government has to ensure that the inflow of financial assets from abroad must be channeled into productive assets in a proper manner, so that the country benefits from their multiplier effect. Therefore, it is necessary to formulate not only a medium term strategy, but also a long-term strategy in this regard to achieve effective utilization of these funds for which they have been mobilized. The structural reform policies initiated in the past two and a half years cover a wide gamut of area of industrial licensing, foreign trade, exchange rate regime, and financial sector and public sector reforms. Under the financial sector reform programme, an effort is being made to inject a greater element of competitiveness in the system.

Full convertibility of rupee on current account and permitting to select Foreign Institutional Investors (FIIs), Merchant Banks and broking firms to come to India have generated a lot of interest among foreign investors. At the same time, Indian companies have been permitted to tap the International Capital Market in the form of issue of shares of Foreign Currency Convertible Bonds (FCCBs) through the Global Depository Receipts (GDRs), American Depository Receipts (ADRs), and American Depository Shares (ADSs) mechanism. Some Indian and foreign financial institutions are trying to mobilize foreign currency funds from institutional and individual investors including NRIs and Corporate bodies in which they have substantial stake, from many countries by floating off-shore funds.

Investment in a country by individuals and organizations from other countries is an important aspect of international finance. This flow of international finance may take the form of *Portfolio Investment* (acquisition of securities) or *Foreign Direct Investment* (creation of productive facilities). In the case of portfolio equity investments, the foreign investor can purchase equity shares of a company. For an investment to qualify as foreign direct investments, the investor has to acquire 10 per cent or more and is usually interested in having at least substantial influence over the operations of the company.

Privatization transactions involving portfolio equity investments are rare, but typically quite large in volume. Hence, this information is generally well documented and easily available. In most cases, however, foreign investors tend to be more interested in direct investments, allowing them to shape the future of the enterprise bought, as independent as possible from interests of local groups, including the state. Information about the participation of foreign buyers in privatization programmes including their share in the purchase is typically not readily available, especially not at a disaggregated level. Hence, in case where no additional information could be obtained, the amount of foreign direct investment resulting from privatizations had to be estimated based on the nationality of the buyer. If no information was at all available regarding the buyers identity, it was assumed that investor was local involving no foreign investment. This respect, the foreign exchange values obtained is a lower bound of actual inflows. On the other hand, inflows are possibly over estimated in case where committed investments were included in the purchasing price.

The involvement of foreign investors in privatization programmes is sought after by the Government, despite after strong – political opposition, fighting against the "selling out" of domestic interests. However, the participation of foreign investments is after essential, particularly for large projects, because the local capital market is too thin and needed technological and managerial expertise is not available. Further more, the sale of such assets promises the receipt of sizeable amounts of foreign exchange needed in a situation of limited access to foreign capital. But in order to attract foreigners, the privatizing authorities first have to prove their political willingness and commitment to an extensive privatization effort, characterised by a reliable and transparent system of rules and regulations. Hence, during the take-off period, most privatization programmes do not show any extensive foreign participation but over time the number of foreign buyers rises quickly, based on the reliability of the project programme.

The present chapter aims at analyzing the role, aggregate flow and the performance of FDI in India. The study is divided into three parts. Part I is devoted to analyse the different routes through which FDI comes in India. Part II presents dimensions and trends of FDI vis-à-vis actual inflows in India.

Part III evaluates the reasons for low FDI in India vis-à-vis some selected Asian countries.

PART I

4.2. Routes of FDI Flows

For a long period India depended too much on foreign aid considering it cheapest source of foreign capital. As we know that aid is nothing but a loan. It is concessional loan as the rate of interest to be paid on aids is slightly lower than other loan and the duration of payment is usually longer, during which it is to be repaid. This practice led to rapidly rising interest burden and the country had to face difficulties in making the interest payments for which foreign exchange was needed. Therefore, to come out from such a situation, the country had to go for allowing on large scale and inflow of foreign direct investment in most of the sectors of economy. It typically takes the form of starting a subsidiary, acquiring a stake in an existing firm or starting joint venture in the foreign country. In India, as per the rules of liberalization, FDI comes through various routes. These are as follows:

RBI (Automatic Route)

Under the liberalized policies and procedures covering foreign technology agreements and FDI, the list of industries/ sectors that are eligible for foreign equity through RBI (Automatic Approval) is summarized in chart 4.1.

Further, under this route, the companies can issue shares up to the limit of foreign equity capital prescribed to the foreign investors and receive remittances. The reporting period for this purpose to the RBI, is thirty days and there is no need of reference to the Government.

CHART 4.I

List of Industries/Sectors Eligible for Foreign Equity Through RBI (Automatic Route)

Sl. No.	*Permissible limit %*	*Industry/Sector*
1.	20-49	Broadcasting (upto 20 per cent in direct to home broadcasting and 49 per cent in an uplinking hub that leases out (facilities)
2.	26	(a) Insurance (automatic, but license from IRDA is must) (b) Defence (prior Government approval is requi red) (c) Print Media
3.	26-100	26 per cent in case of public sector undertakings and 100 per cent in case of private companies.
4.	40	Domestic Airlines.
5.	49	Telecommunications (proposed to hike up to 79 per cent in budget 2004-05).
6.	50	Three industries as mentioned in Annexure III Statement of Industrial Policy 1991 (relating to mining of iron ores or metal ores and non-metallic minerals).
7.	51	(a) pipelines (b) twenty four industries as mentioned in Annexure III Statement of Industrial Policy (relating to manufacturing of food products, cotton textiles, paper and paper products, basic chemicals, rubber products, restaurants and hotels, renting and leasing, market research services, etc.).
8.	51-75	Non-Banking Finance Companies (NBFCs) (for up to 51 per cent $0.5 million to be invested and for up to 75 per cent $5 million to be invested).
9.	51-100	Petroleum (51 per cent in petro products and joint venture in other areas and 100 per cent in exploration).

10.	74	Nine industries as mentioned in Annexure III of Statement of Industrial Policy 1991 (relating to mining services basic metals and alloys industries, electric generation and transmission, etc.).
11.	74-100	(a) Coal and lignite (74 per cent in exploration and mining and 100 per cent in coal processing plants) (b) Air transport (automatic, but beyond 74 per cent, government approval is must) (c) Advertising and film production (74 per cent in case of advertising and 100 per cent in film financing, production and distribution).
12.	100	(a) Housing and Real Estates (b) Trading (only to facilitate export markets) (c) E-Commerce (d) Drugs and Pharmaceuticals (e) Power (including generation, transmission and distribution) (f) Roads and Ports (g) Hotels (h) Mass Rapid Transit System (i) Postal Services (excluding distribution of letters) (j) Tea Industry

Source: (i) Compiled from the SEBI and Corporate Laws, March 1999, p. 350-367.
(ii) Business Today, February 3, 2002 iii) Government of India, Economic Survey 2002-03, p. 146.

(a) Government (SIA/FIPB) Route or Non-Automatic Route

Non-automatic schemes are referred to Foreign Investment Promotion Board (FIPB) which gives clearance on a case by case basis. Once the proposal is put forward to the FIPB, it consults the concerned administrative ministry and depending upon the quantum of investment and other details of the project clearance is given. The Secretariat for Industrial Approvals (SIA) is the servicing Department with an aim of the FIPB and co-ordinates with the apex body while processing proposals.

(b) NRI's Investment

The third route is investment by NRI's. Chart 4.II summarizes the extent of permissible equity by NRI's according to the area of investment.

CHART 4.II

List of Industries/Sectors Eligible for NRI's Investment

Sl. No.	*Permissible limit %*	*Industry/Sector*
1.	24	Small scale industries (repatriable, prior approval by SIA, export obligations)
2.	40	Banking Services
3.	49-51	Telecommunications (up to 49 per cent in basic, cellular mobiles and paging, VSATs and other wireless services and 51 per cent with approval in other value added services)
4.	50	Mining (automatic approval by SIA/FIPB)
5.	51	a) Thirteen priority industries announced in December 1996 (repatriable, automatic approval by RBI)
		b) Entertainment Electronics (automatic approval by RBI)
6.	51-100	NBFCs (up to 51 per cent with no conditions and up to 100 per cent with conditions)
7.	74	Nine high priority industries in metallurgical and infrastructure sectors announced in December 1996 (repatriable, automatic approval by RBI)
8.	100	(a) Thirty five priority industries announced in July, 1991 (repatriable, automatic approval by RBI)
		(b) Export trading/Star trading house

(c) 100 per cent export oriented units (EOUs) and units in free trade zone (FTZ) export processing zone (EPZ), software and hardware technology parks (automatic approval by SIADC EPZ)

(d) sick industries (prior approval by RBI)

(e) Power

(f) Medical clinics, hospitals, shipping, oils exploration, deep-sea fishing industries, (repatriable, prior approval by SIA)

(g) Housing, real estate, business centers, infrastructure facilities (repatriation basis, automatic approval by RBI)

(h) Domestics air taxi operations

Source: Government of India, Economic Survey 2003-04.

(c) Acquisition of Shares

The acquisition of shares has been included as a part of FDI since January 1996 under section 29 of Foreign Exchange Regulation Act, 1973 (at present it is u/s 5 of Foreign Exchange Management Act, 1999). Under this, the FDI proposals for acquisition of shares in existing companies are considered only where the applications are made by Indian company or where the proposals are supported by Board Resolution of Indian Company.

(d)External Commercial Borrowings (ECBs)

Which include American Depository Receipts (ADRs), American Depository Shares (ADSs), Global Depository Receipts (GDRs) and Euro Equities.

However, in view of bringing the foreign direct investment (FDI) compilation of India in line with international best practices, coverage of data on FDI has been expanded from 2000-01 by including certain new items, viz., equity capital of unincorporated bodies, reinvested earnings and inter-corporate debt transactions between the related entities.

PART II

4.3. Dimensions and Trends of FDI

An attempt has been made in this part to analyse the dimensions and trends of FDI in India during the post-liberalization period, i.e. since 1991. The task has been accomplished by analyzing the FDI flows into the following categories:

1. Foreign Direct Investment Approvals: Component-wise Analysis;
2. Foreign Direct Investment Approvals: Country-wise Break-up Analysis;
3. Foreign Direct Investment: Actual inflows Vs. Approvals (year-wise); and
4. Foreign Direct Investment Inflows: Component-wise (category-wise/route-wise) Analysis

4.3.1. Foreign Direct Investment Approvals: Component-wise Analysis

Table 4.1 presents the component-wise amount of flow of Foreign Direct Investment. This data of the table shows the amount of Foreign Direct Investment approved by various agencies such as Secretariat for Industrial Assistance (SIA), Reserve Bank of India (RBI) and Foreign Investment Promotion Board (FIPB). This analysis aims at examining the relative share of each agency in approvals of amount of Foreign Direct Investment and its position during the period January 1991-August 2004 under review.

It is observed from the data of the Table 4.1 that Rs. 2476.9 billions of total Foreign Direct Investment was approved through all the three agencies during the period from 1991 to 31st August 2004 under review. Out of the total approvals, FIPB accounted for Rs. 2170.4 billions, forming 87.8 per cent of total investment and claiming a gaint share. The SIA and

Table 4.1

COMPONENT-WISE AMOUNT OF FOREIGN DIRECT INVESTMENT APPROVALS

(Rupees in Billions)

	1991-95	1996	1997	1998	1999	2000	2001	2002	2003	2004	Total 1991-2004
SIA	15.6 (2.9)	11.8 (3.8)	3.2 (0.6)	7.2 (2.6)	0.1 (0.1)	1.9 (1.1)	7.9 (3.7)	10.1 (9.1)	3.1 (5.7)	0.6 (1.1)	61.5 (2.5)
RBI	26.5 (5.0)	12.5 (4.1)	92.7 (18.4)	1.9 (0.7)	9.9 (3.9)	15.7 (9.1)	23.5 (11.2)	27.8 (25.2)	13.2 (24.3)	16.6 (30.4)	240.3 (9.7)
FIPB	489.1 (92.1)	284.5 (92.1)	408.0 (81.0)	266.8 (96.7)	241.3 (96.0)	154.7 (89.8)	178.0 (85.1)	72.7 (65.7)	37.9 (70.0)	37.4 (68.5)	2170.4 (87.8)
TOTAL	531.2 (100.0)	308.9 (100.0)	503.0 (100.0)	275.9 (100.0)	251.4 (100.0)	172.4 (100.0)	209.4 (100.0)	110.6 (100.0)	54.2 (100.0)	59.9 (100.0)	2476.9 # * (100.0)

Source: SIA, Department of Industrial Policy & Promotion, Ministry of Commerce & Industry (GOI) News Letter- September 2004

Figures in brackets indicate percent to total

\# excludes 100 proposals approved by FIPB for ADRs/GDRs, Foreign Currency Convertible Bonds (FCCBs) involving investment of 490.81 billion.

* The amount of Foreign Direct Investment (FDI) approved US $66.73 billions (approx.)

Note: Figures for 2004 updated upto 31st August, 2004.

RBI route accounted for 2.5 per cent 9.7 per cent respectively. However, the share of SIA route in total investment was 67.9 per cent in 1991, leaving 32.1 per cent to RBI and FIPB route.[1]

A trend of dominance by SIA route in initial years of liberalization and FIPB route in the latter years of liberalization was being observed in the case of amount of total FDI approved. To pinpoint more clearly RBI's approvals of the investment varied from 30.4 per cent to 0.7 per cent as against 67.9 per cent to 0.1 per cent of SIA and 96.7 per cent to 65.7 per cent of FIPB's amount of approvals during the period under review.

Among the three agencies, FIPB route of approvals has gained a lot of significance for approvals of Foreign Direct Investment, since it has accounted for 69 per cent to 96 per cent of the total amount of investment approved from 1991 to 2004. Thus, we conclude that the amount of investment approved by SIA route was prominent in 1991, the first year of liberalization, but then onwards the FIPB route was claimed almost 80 per cent to 90 per cent of total Foreign Direct Investment approvals.

Empirical Analysis

It is proposed to apply the Chi-square test for determining the degree of Association between the aforesaid variables, i.e. of FDI approved through SIA, RBI, and FIPB routes.

Let us take the hypothesis that there is no significant difference in the components of FDI approvals. Applying Chi-square test. The observed frequencies are seen in Table 4.1, whereas the Expected FDI approvals can be obtained below:

The below result of the analysis in Table 4.2 shows that the calculated value of Chi-square value is much greater than the table value. Hence, the hypothesis does not hold good and we, therefore, conclude that the components of FDI are significantly high difference, which means all the components i.e. SIA, RBI, and FIPB routes of FDI approved have not been equally considered. As such, it can be inferred that majority of FDI approvals are through FIPB route only.

TABLE 4.2

Chi-square Test Results

(Rs. In billion)

Route	*1996*	*1997*	*1998*	*1999*	*2000*	*2001*	*2002*	*2003*	*2004*	*Total*
SIA	7.3	11.9	6.5	5.9	4.1	4.9	2.6	1.3	1.4	46
RBI	34.4	55.8	30.6	27.8	19.2	23.2	12.3	6.0	6.7	216
FIPB	268.3	435.3	239	217	149.7	180.1	96.1	46.7	51.9	1685
TOTAL	310	503	276	251	173	209	111	54	60	1947

Chi-Square result:

V = (r-1) (c-1)

= (3-1) 9-1) = 2 x 8 = 16.

Chi-Square (X_2) = 183.4 (calculated value)

For V = 16, Chi-Square ($X^2_{0.05}$) = 26.3 (table value).

Hence, the empirical analysis also strongly support that the FIPB route plays a significant role in the process of approving the proposals of FDI inflows in the country.

4.3.2. Analysis of Country-wise Break-Up of FDI Approvals

It is proposed to analyze the country-wise approvals of Foreign Direct Investment in India during 1991 to 2004 (up to 31.8.2004). The data relevant to the analysis is presented in Table 4.3.

The analysis of country-wise approval of Foreign Direct Investment in India (Table 4.3) indicates that during 1991-2004 total amount of Rs. 2476.9 billions of FDI approved from 113 countries including NRI investments.

India's perception abroad has been changing steadily

TABLE 4.3

Approvals of Country-Wise Foreign Direct Investment During 1991 to 2004

(Excluding ADRs/GDRs)
(Amt. Rs. Million)

Sl. No.	Country Name	1991-1999	2000	2001	2002	2003	2004	TOTAL (1991-2004)	PERCENT TOTOTAL
1.	U.S.A	461845.15	41949.58	49215.30	20511.22	7623.80	6047.79	587192.84	23.7
2.	MAURITIUS	221983.34	72339.82	28925.30	18466.06	13658.94	21426.90	376800.37	15.2
3.	U.K.	159767.18	4112.29	49942.45	18043.58	5001.50	1977.89	238844.89	9.6
4.	JAPAN	91076.79	8275.44	7352.74	7408.49	3429.74	184.90	117728.09	4.8
5.	KOREA (SOUTH)	96900.96	410.79	667.57	290.29	615.14	157.40	99042.16	4.0
6.	NETHERLANDS	46951.68	44.55	36935.71	5523.57	5907.70	1041.71	96404.92	3.9
7.	GERMANY	79027.65	5937.64	4138.91	2531.45	2134.91	1610.61	95381.16	3.8
8.	AUSTRALIA	65552.50	616.95	843.80	772.77	200.20	450.85	68437.07	2.8
9.	FRANCE	50354.30	2020.74	6798.08	6228.72	434.09	256.28	66092.21	2.7
10.	MALAYSIA	55606.24	158.83	1057.96	3726.36	350.81	65.54	60965.73	2.5
11.	SINGAPORE	41597.66	3232.44	3798.70	3721.62	2167.72	3478.40	57996.54	2.3
12.	ITALY	44475.22	1073.12	1714.82	705.45	163.97	587.73	48720.31	2.0
13.	BELGIUM	39186.80	791.33	1621.04	3495.56	769.90	14.48	45879.11	1.9
14.	ISRAEL	42347.48	9.90	86.86	1.18	16.51	57.09	42519.02	1.7
15.	CAYMAN ISLAND	36324.10	998.31	55.22	1487.06	13.74	107.19	38985.62	1.6

16.	SWITZERLAND	27395.27	716.58	1074.97	1450.82	838.09	508.89	31984.61	1.3
17.	CANADA	23818.87	1544.00	537.55	2860.93	41.53	42.70	28845.58	1.2
18.	THAILAND	24588.21	3.75	12.08	0.10	154.21	1684.44	26442.79	1.1
19.	HONGKONG	15417.40	4221.33	429.16	169.79	992.77	48.96	21279.42	0.9
20.	SWEDEN	17012.77	1011.83	2363.99	212.56	48.35	15.35	20664.85	0.8
21.	SOUTH AFRICA	18981.63	59.70	18.88	1.15	60.10	114.37	19235.82	0.77
22.	U.A.E.	6493.29	500.90	622.14	491.73	405.79	3459.11	11972.97	0.48
23.	BERMUDA	7772.25	88.25	824.58	35.35	0.00	1.23	8721.66	0.35
24.	SAUDI ARABIA	8118.74	2.32	0.50	14.54	40.54	1.44	8178.07	0.33
25.	CHINA	7129.36	0.00	0.00	0.10	303.03	2.19	7434.67	0.30
26.	DENMARK	5294.88	263.41	259.34	549.21	426.47	59.11	6852.41	0.28
27.	OMAN	5787.32	37.64	32.80	222.00	46.37	370.09	6496.22	0.26
28.	WEST INDIES	6474.30	0.00	0.00	2.77	0.00	1.40	6478.47	0.26
29.	PANAMA	6405.45	1.30	12.45	9.15	0.00	0.00	6428.35	0.26
30.	KUWAIT	5843.60	7.33	149.45	9.20	1.70	30.00	6041.28	0.24
31.	INDONESIA	3929.80	1.02	0.70	1263.96	73.81	0.00	5269.29	0.21
32.	TAIWAN	1327.54	51.52	5.31	3568.84	1.70	62.15	5017.06	0.20
33.	QATAR	315.30	4300.00	0.00	0.00	7.20	0.00	4622.50	0.19
34.	PHILLIPINES	3839.16	6.58	19.25	0.34	0.05	230.00	4095.38	0.17
35.	NEW ZEALAND	2787.68	2.76	1104.20	5.78	7.31	4.60	3912.33	0.16
36.	SPAIN	3490.32	51.88	1.55	263.22	2.59	89.85	3899.40	0.16
37.	AUSTRIA	2747.40	55.83	77.20	176.71	7.96	5.78	3070.88	0.12

38.	BRITISH VIRGIN ISLAND	760.98	62.05	226.73	1329.50	632.94	8.49	3020.68	0.12
39.	CZECH REPUBLIC	2897.10	0.00	0.30	1.90	0.00	0.00	2899.30	0.12
40.	IRELAND	2431.88	167.05	86.42	7.12	47.31	2.25	2742.04	0.11
41.	FINLAND	2611.07	0.00	174.34	-110.45	36.10	29.77	2740.82	0.11
42.	LUXEMBOURG	2462.84	49.00	7.35	1.75	33.05	30.71	2584.70	0.10
43.	MEXICO	2524.25	0.00	0.00	0.00	0.00	0.00	2524.25	0.10
44.	BAHRAIN	1867.67	165.95	11.16	20.00	176.20	148.32	2389.30	0.09
45.	PORTUGAL	1939.03	15.22	0.00	2.80	0.00	0.00	1957.05	0.08
46.	RUSSIA	1676.18	0.00	2.95	1.19	0.00	7.33	1687.65	0.07
47.	ISLE OF MAN	1569.72	43.09	20.58	0.00	0.00	31.18	1664.57	0.07
48.	NIGERIA	1475.40	30.00	0.10	36.60	27.84	0.00	1569.94	0.06
49.	CHANNEL ISLAND	120.70	10.00	1318.18	80.10	0.22	1.74	1530.94	0.06
50.	NORWAY	950.53	21.84	262.72	24.17	22.98	0.53	1282.76	0.05
51.	GIBRALTAR	989.08	0.00	0.47	0.21	0.00	0.00	989.76	0.04
52.	MORACCO	0.00	0.00	0.00	784.00	0.00	0.00	784.00	0.03
53.	AFGHANISTAN	761.00	0.00	0.00	0.00	0.00	0.00	761.00	0.03
54.	IRAN	711.30	5.85	15.75	5.80	0.00	0.00	738.71	0.03
55.	BANGLADESH	511.57	5.28	0.00	86.36	0.00	0.00	603.20	0.02
56.	CYPRUS	203.85	31.08	182.04	92.38	42.38	10.50	562.22	0.02
57.	BAHMAS	430.72	31.00	3.13	0.50	0.00	0.00	465.35	0.02
58.	SRILANKA	161.80	74.40	48.43	10.48	39.36	32.90	367.37	0.01
59.	KENYA	0.00	4.90	13.37	251.04	0.10	46.20	315.61	0.01

60. NEVIS	0.00	315.00	0.00	0.00	0.00	0.00	315.00	0.01
61. LIECHTENSTEIN	308.74	0.00	0.00	0.00	0.00	0.00	308.74	0.01
62. CUBA	0.00	4.20	0.00	0.00	245.00	0.10	249.29	0.01
63. ARGENTINA	184.00	0.00	0.00	0.00	0.00	0.00	184.00	0.007
64. POLAND	151.63	0.00	0.00	0.00	5.00	0.00	156.63	0.006
65. SCOTLAND	8.30	0.00	79.80	47.00	20.00	1.27	156.37	0.006
66. UKRAINE	89.83	0.00	30.27	0.10	0.10	0.50	120.79	0.005
67. ESTONIA	73.10	0.00	0.00	0.00	0.00	0.00	73.10	0.003
68. SLOVENIA	0.00	0.00	67.74	0.00	0.00	0.00	67.74	0.003
69. HUNGARY	34.26	0.00	0.00	1.00	0.00	20.00	55.26	0.002
70. KOREA (NORTH)	1.60	0.00	0.00	42.12	0.00	0.00	43.72	0.002
71. YOGOSLAVIA	28.90	10.00	0.00	0.00	0.00	0.00	38.90	0.002
72. NEPAL	30.30	0.00	0.00	0.00	0.00	5.98	36.28	0.001
73. TURKEY	0.00	32.17	0.00	0.00	1.44	0.10	33.72	0.001
74. ICE LAND	13.46	0.00	1.80	11.19	0.10	0.00	26.55	0.001
75. VIRGIN ISLANDS	0.00	0.00	0.00	0.00	0.00	26.07	26.07	0.001
76. JORDON	22.56	0.64	0.00	0.00	0.00	0.00	23.20	0.0009
77. ROMANIA	20.00	1.00	0.00	0.00	0.00	0.00	21.00	0.0008
78. GREECE	20.44	0.00	0.00	0.00	0.10	0.05	20.59	0.0008
79. ARMENIA	20.30	0.00	0.00	0.00	0.00	0.00	20.30	0.0008
80. Croatia	0.00	0.00	0.00	19.29	0.00	0.00	19.29	0.0008
81. PAPUA NEW GUINEA	19.20	0.00	0.00	0.00	0.00	0.00	19.20	0.0008

82.	BULGARIA	19.10	0.00	0.00	0.00	0.00	0.00	19.10	0.0008
83.	TUNISIA	0.00	0.00	0.00	0.00	0.00	16.00	16.00	0.0006
84.	KAZAKHSTAN	15.00	0.00	0.00	0.00	0.00	0.00	15.00	0.0006
85.	MALDIVES	12.77	1.50	0.00	0.00	0.00	0.00	14.27	0.0006
86.	JAMICA	10.00	0.00	0.00	0.00	0.00	0.00	10.00	0.0004
87.	SOMALIA	10.00	0.00	0.00	0.00	0.00	0.00	10.00	0.0004
88.	VIETNAM	8.93	0.00	0.00	0.00	0.26	0.00	9.18	0.0004
89.	MONACO	6.71	0.00	0.00	0.00	0.00	0.00	6.71	0.0003
90.	BRAZIL	6.30	0.00	0.10	0.00	0.00	0.00	6.40	0.0003
91.	YEMEN	5.00	0.00	0.00	0.00	0.00	0.35	5.35	0.0002
92.	Tanzania	0.00	0.00	5.28	0.00	0.00	0.00	5.28	0.0002
93.	GUERNSEY	0.00	0.00	5.00	0.00	0.00	0.00	5.00	0.0002
94.	Georgia	0.00	0.00	0.00	5.00	0.00	0.00	5.00	0.0002
95.	ZAMBIA	0.00	0.00	4.63	0.00	0.00	0.00	4.63	0.0002
96.	MAYANMAR	0.00	0.00	2.10	0.00	2.34	0.00	4.44	0.0002
97.	EGYPT	3.15	0.00	0.00	0.00	0.10	0.70	3.95	0.0002
98.	LATVIA	2.60	1.00	0.00	0.00	0.00	0.00	3.60	0.0001
99.	Liberia	0.00	0.00	2.50	0.00	0.00	0.00	2.50	0.0001
100.	Lebanon	0.00	0.00	0.00	1.96	0.05	0.00	2.01	0.0001
101.	SLOVAKIA	1.55	0.00	0.00	0.00	0.00	0.00	1.55	0.00008
102.	BELORUSSIA	0.50	0.00	0.00	0.00	0.00	0.95	1.45	0.00006
103.	MALTA	1.30	0.00	0.00	0.00	0.00	0.00	1.30	0.00005

104. BRITISH ISLES	0.00	0.00	0.00	0.30	0.00	0.91	1.21	0.00004
105. SYRIA	1.20	0.00	0.00	0.00	0.00	0.00	1.20	0.00004
106. PALESTINE AUTHORITY	0.00	0.00	0.50	0.50	0.00	0.00	1.00	0.00004
107. VANUATU	0.00	0.00	0.00	0.9	5 0.00	0.00	0.95	0.00003
108. PERU	0.00	0.00	0.00	0.00	0.00	0.73	0.73	0.00002
109. SUDAN	0.30	0.00	0.00	0.00	0.00	0.00	0.30	0.00001
110. COLUMBIA	0.00	0.00	0.00	0.11	0.10	0.00	0.21	0.00000
111. URUGUAY	0.10	0.00	0.00	0.00	0.00	0.00	0.10	0.00000
112. Costa Rica	0.00	0.00	0.00	0.00	0.00	0.00	0.00	0.00000
113. NRI #	79171.43	16186.36	6079.55	3604.28	4653.81	15168.39	124863.81	5.04
114. TOTAL OF ALL COUNTRIES INCLUDING ABOVE (In Rupees)	1870558.91	172369.69	209397.35	110581.02	54165.85	59860.42	2476933.24	100.00
TOTAL (In Rupees Billions)	1870.56	172.37	209.4	110.6	54.2	59.9	2476.9	

Source: Secretariat for Industrial Assistance (SIA), Department of Industrial Policy & Promotion, Ministry of Commerce & Industry (GOI), News Letter, September, 2004.

Note: i) 1 Million = 10 Lakhs.

ii) * Figures for 2004 updated up to 31/08/2004

iii) Ranking of all countries according to cumulative Total of approvals for the period 1991 to 2004(up to 31/08/2004)

Approval figures.

"#" Represents NRI proposals only.

"+" Excludes proposals for Global Depository Receipts (GDR) & Foreign Currency Convertible Bonds(FCCBs)

Figure 4.1

FOREIGN DIRECT INVESTMENT APPROVED DURING 1991 TO AUG. 2004 – TOP 10 INVESTORS IN INDIA

(Rupees in Billions)

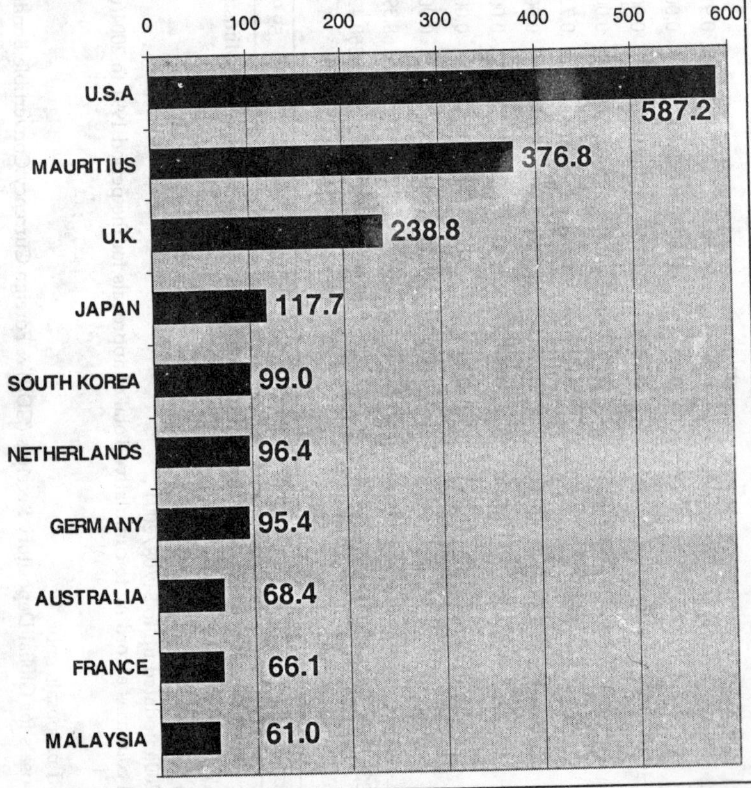

Source: Secretariat for Industrial Assistance, Department of Industrial Policy & Promotion, Ministry of Commerce & Industry, Government of India.

over the years. This is reflected in the ever growing list of countries which are showing interest to invest in India. And as a result, India's over dependence on the US for foreign funds too has declined over the years. The U.S.A. emerged as the most dominant source of inflows with Rs. 587.19 billions, contributing 23.7 per cent of total investment in the country. This country maintained an increasing trend from 1991 to 2001, then it was witnessed a significant decline at 58.32 per cent in 2002 and downturn in the subsequent years. However, among the top 10 investors in India, Mauritius only found increasing trend at 56.9 per cent during the period January-August 2004, as compared to 2003, which placed 2nd position by contributing 15.2 per cent of total approvals during the period under review. U.K. occupied 3rd position with 9.6 per cent, followed by Japan with 4.8 per cent, Korea (South) 4 per cent, Netherlands with 3.9 per cent, Germany 3.8 per cent, Australia (2.8 per cent), France (2.7 per cent), and Malaysia with 2.5 per cent respectively (Figure 4.1 & Figure 4.2).

Figure 4.2

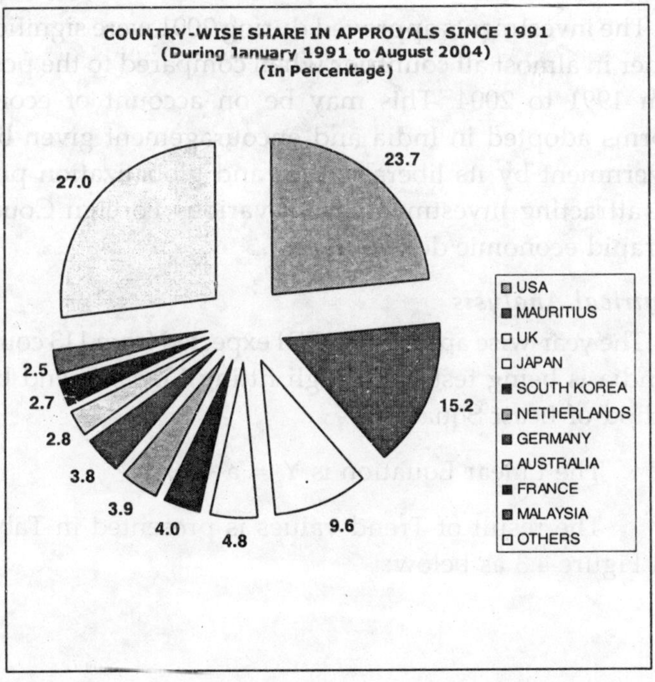

It has been observed that some countries like Israel, Thailand, Hong Kong, South Africa, Oman increasing their share gradually during the period under study, whereas, the share of China declined by 99 per cent during January-August 2004 as compared to 2003, when there was sudden hike of Rs. 303 billion from 0.10 billion in 2002. It is also interesting to note that some of the new countries such as Hungary, Nepal, Virgin Islands, Tunisia, Yemen, Belorussia, Peru are making significant investments in India.

Another contributing factors for Foreign Direct Investment approvals in India are that the investment proposals of NRIs. These stood at Rs. 124.86 billions during the period 1991 to 2004 and accounted for 5 per cent of the total amount of FDI approved. The investment of NRIs have ranked fourth in the list of country-wise break-up of Foreign Direct Investment approved during 1991-04, that is after U.K., NRI's rank fourth highest source of flow of Foreign Direct Investment in India.

The investments approved during 2001 were significantly higher in almost all countries when compared to the position from 1991 to 2004. This may be on account of economic reforms adopted in India and encouragement given by the Government by its liberalization and globalization policies and attracting investments from various Foreign Countries for rapid economic development.

Empirical Analysis

The year-wise approval of FDI expected from 113 countries in India is being tested through fitting Linear Trend by the method of Least Squares.

The Linear Equation is $Y_c = a + bx$

The result of Trend values is presented in Table 4.4 and Figure 4.3 as below:

Table 4.4

TREND VALUES OF YEAR-WISE APPROVALS OF FDI

Year	1991	1992	1993	1994	1995	1996	1997
Trend Values	175.9	176.7	177.6	178.5	179.4	180.3	181.2
Year	1998	1999	2000	2001	2002	2003	2004
Trend Values	182.1	182.9	183.8	184.7	185.6	186.4	187.3

Figure 4.3 LINEAR TREND BY THE METHOD OF LEAST SQUARE

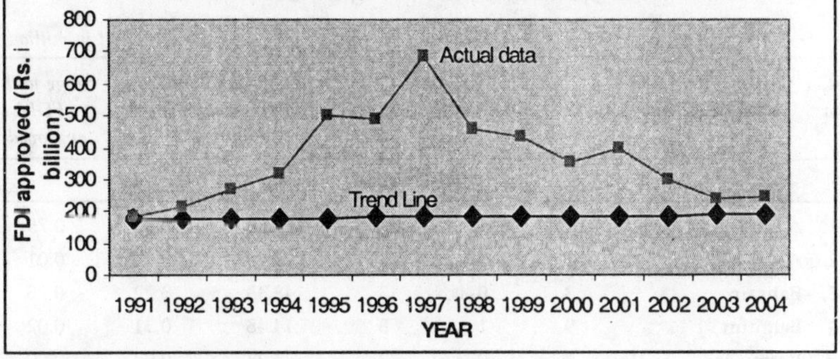

The Linear Equation calculated is given below:

$$Y_c = 181.57 + 0.879x$$

However, the Approvals of FDI for the year 2005 has been projected by using the Linear Equation as below:

For 2005, deviation taken (x) = 7.5

$$Y_{2005} = 181.57 + 0.879(7.5)$$
$$= 188.16$$

Hence, the likely approvals of FDI inflows in 2005 will be Rs. 188.16 billions.

FDI Approvals Rise in 2004 Following Improved Investment Scenario

It is interesting to analyze the amount of FDI approvals during the first 8 months of 2004, between January and August. An amount of Rs. 59.9 billions of foreign direct investment during the first 8 months of 2004, between January and August. An amount of Rs. 59.9 billions of foreign direct investment (FDI) was approved during this period, as against Rs. 54.3 billions in 2003 (Table 4.5).

TABLE 4.5

Country-Wise Foreign Direct Investment (FDI) and Foreign Technology Cases (FTCs) Approved by Government During January 2004 to August 2004

(Amount in million)

Sl. No.	*Name of the Country*	*No. of Approvals*			*Amount of Foreign Direct Investment Approved*		*%age with FDI approved*
		Total	*Technical*	*Financial*	*(In Rs)*	*(In US$)*	
1.	Australia	21	1	20	450.85	9.80	0.75
2.	Austria	7	3	4	5.78	0.13	0.01
3.	Bahrain	3	0	3	148.33	3.22	0.25
4.	Belgium	9	1	8	14.48	0.31	0.02
5.	Bermuda	3	0	3	1.23	0.03	0.00
6.	Canada	18	2	16	42.70	0.93	0.07
7.	Cayman Island	2	0	2	107.19	2.33	0.18
8.	Channel Island	1	0	1	1.74	0.04	0.00
9.	China	5	1	4	2.19	0.05	0.00
10.	Czech Republic	1	1	0	0.00	0.00	0.00
11.	Cyprus	3	0	3	10.50	0.23	0.02
12.	Denmark	6	0	6	59.11	1.28	0.10
13.	Finland	4	0	4	29.77	0.65	0.05
14.	France	27	4	23	256.28	5.57	0.43
15.	Greece	2	0	2	0.05	0.00	0.00
16.	Germany	64	6	58	1610.61	35.01	2.69
17.	Hong Kong	16	1	15	48.96	1.06	0.08
18.	Hungary	1	0	1	20.00	0.43	0.03
19.	Indonesia	1	0	1	0.00	0.00	0.00
20.	Ireland	4	0	4	2.25	0.05	0.00
21.	Isle of Man	2	0	2	31.18	0.68	0.05
22.	Israel	15	0	15	57.09	1.24	0.10
23.	Italy	27	5	22	587.73	12.78	0.98
24.	Japan	47	18	29	184.90	4.02	0.31
25.	Korea(South)	17	2	15	157.40	3.42	0.26
26.	Kuwait	2	0	2	30.00	0.65	0.05

27.	Luxembourg	3	0	3	30.71	0.67	0.05
28.	Malaysia	10	0	10	65.54	1.42	0.11
29.	Mauritius	93	0	93	21426.90	465.80	35.80
30.	NRI	70	0	70	15168.39	329.75	25.34
31.	Nepal	2	0	2	5.98	0.13	0.01
32.	Netherlands	40	0	40	1041.71	22.65	1.74
33.	New Zealand	2	0	2	4.60	0.10	0.01
34.	Norway	3	0	3	0.53	0.01	0.00
35.	Oman	4	0	4	370.09	8.05	0.62
36.	Philippines	1	0	1	230.00	5.00	0.38
37.	Russia	4	1	3	7.33	0.16	0.01
38.	Saudi Arabia	2	0	2	1.44	0.03	0.00
39.	Singapore	66	0	66	3478.40	75.62	5.81
40.	Scotland	1	0	1	1.27	0.03	0.00
41.	South Africa	4	0	4	114.37	2.49	0.19
42.	Spain	6	2	4	89.85	1.95	0.15
43.	Sri Lanka	2	0	2	32.90	0.72	0.05
44.	Sweden	8	0	8	15.35	0.33	0.03
45.	Switzerland	21	2	19	508.89	11.06	0.85
46.	Taiwan	8	0	8	62.15	1.35	0.10
47.	Thailand	11	1	10	1684.44	36.62	2.81
48.	Turkey	1	0	1	0.10	0.00	0.00
49.	U.A.E.	39	0	39	3459.11	75.20	5.78
50.	U.K.	99	8	91	1977.89	43.0	03.30
51.	U.S.A.	362	26	336	6047.79	131.47	10.10
52.	Ukraine	1	0	1	0.50	0.01	0.00
53.	British Virginia	12	0	12	8.49	0.18	0.01
54.	West Indies	3	0	3	1.40	0.03	0.00
55.	Unindicated Country	6	1	5	72.00	1.57	0.12
56.	Kenya	1	0	1	46.20	1.00	0.08
57.	Egypt	1	0	1	0.70	0.02	0.00
58.	Yaman	1	0	1	0.36	0.01	0.00
59.	Cuba	1	0	1	0.10	0.00	0.00
60.	BRITISH ISLES	2	0	2	0.91	0.02	0.00
61.	VIRGIN ISLANDS	2	0	2	26.07	0.57	0.04
62.	PERU	1	0	1	0.73	0.02	0.00
63.	TUNISIA	1	0	1	16.00	0.35	0.03
Grand Total120286111659859.471301.29							

Note: The Statement excludes ADR/GDR amounts

Source: Secretariat for Industrial Assistance (SIA), Ministry of Commerce & Industry, Govt. of India – NEWS LETTER, September 2004.

This may look less impressive when considered against the figures of the nineties – for five consecutive years from 1994 to 1999 the FDI approval was more than Rs.250 billions a year – but when compared against the figure of 2003 it would indicate a sharp rise. In fact, the FDI approvals during the first eight months of 2004 were 96 per cent of the total FDI approved during the full year of 2003.

Country-wise break-up of Foreign Direct Investment approved during the period of 8 month shows that (Table 4.3) Mauritius stood top 1 position with 35.8 per cent of total FDI approved. U.S.A. downturn to 2nd position which was occupied 1st position during 1991-2004. Singapore placed in 3rd position, followed by U.A.E., U.K., Thailand, and Germany. NRI's amount of FDI approved again found significant amount at 25.3 per cent of total, next to that of Mauritius.

4.3.3. Analysis of Approval of FDI vis-a-vis Actual Inflows

In response to the liberalized policy measures introduced by the Government since 1991, foreign direct investment in India has increased progressively in the post reform period both in terms of approvals and actual inflows. Table 4.6 shows the trends in approvals of FDI proposals vis-à-vis inflows; and examines the actual Inflows of Foreign Direct Investment (FDI) as percentage to the total Approvals from the period 1991 to 2004 (up to 31st August 2004).

Analysis of the data in Table 4.6 discloses that the approvals of foreign investment increased from Rs. 5.30 billions in 1991 to Rs. 59.90 billions in 2004. These have increased significantly from 1992 onwards, the second year of economic reforms, and reached to Rs. 38.90 billion, which accounts for 633.9 per cent increase over 1991. They aggregated to a total of Rs. 2476.90 billions (US $ 66.73 billions) in the post-liberalization period, i.e. 1991 to 2004.

TABLE 4.6

Foreign Direct Investment in India: Approvals and Actual Inflows: 1991-2004

(Rupees in Billions and Annual rate of growth in percentage)

	1991	*1992*	*1993*	*1994*	*1995*	*1996*	*1997*	*1998*	*1999*	*2000*	*2001*	*2002*	*2003*	*2004**	*1991-2004*
Approvals	5.30	38.90	88.60	141.90	320.70	308.90	503.90	275.90	251.40	172.40	209.40	110.60	54.20	59.90	2476.9 (US$
(Rs. Billions)		(633.9)	(127.8)	(60.2)	(126.0)	(-3.7)	(63.1)	(-45)	(-8.9)	(-31)	(21.3)	(-47)	(-51)	(10.5)	66.73Billions)
Actual Inflows	3.51	6.75	17.87	29.82	63.70	87.44	129.89	132.69	101.67	123.54	167.78	181.96	116.17	120.95	1283.74(US $
(Rs. Billions)	(92.3)	(164.7)	(66.8)	(113.6)	(37.3)	(48.5)	(2.2)	(-23)	(21.5)	(35.8)	(8.5)	(-36)	(4.1)		31.45 Billions)
Inflows as percentage of Approvals (percentage)	66.1	17.4	20.2	21.0	19.9	23.3	25.8	48.1	40.4	71.7	80.1	164.5	214.7	201.9	51.83

Source: Secretariat for Industrial Assistance, Dept. of Industrial Policy Promotion, Ministry of Commerce & Industry, Govt. of India- News Letter September 2004.

* Figures for 2004 were updated up to 31st August 2004; Figures in brackets indicate annual growth rate over the previous year.

A close observation of actual inflow of Foreign Direct Investment reveals that they increased from Rs. 3.51 billion in 1991 to Rs. 120.95 billion in 2004. Cumulative inflows during 1991 to August 2004 amounted to Rs. 1283.74 billions (US $ 31.45 billions).

However, by comparing the actual inflows of FDI to that of the approved amount, we find that a significant increase in the ratio was at 66.1 per cent in 1991 due to implementation of reforms in foreign investment. A notable feature is that the inflow as percentage of total approvals has declined in the subsequent year, i.e. 1992. Further, an interesting aspect is that, there was an increasing trend in the ratio of inflows to approvals from 1995, which found at 164.5 per cent in 2002. As the coverage of FDI revised by the Government during 2000-01 on par with the international best practices, by including Re-invested Earnings and Other capital flows, 214.7 percentage of approved FDI realized in 2003. Similarly, a steep increase in the ratio at 201.9 percentage of actual inflows of approvals observed during the period January – August, 2004. However, the actual FDI inflow is expected to surpass last year's figure – during the first eight months of 2004 actual FDI inflow at Rs. 120.95 billion was more than 80 per cent of what the country received at Rs. 116.17 billion in 2003. This is significant, for, after a steady rise for three consecutive years up to 2002, the actual inflow of FDI had declined in 2003. The reversal of the trend now will not only raise industrial investment but will also indicate a revival of the confidence of foreign investors in Indian industry.

The data of the Table 4.6 clearly indicates that the post-reform period has witnessed a rapid increase in FDI approvals, where as the actual inflows have been much less. FDI approvals over the period January 1991 to August 2004 amounted to Rs.2476.90 billions, while actual FDI inflow was only Rs.1283.74 billions. Thus, the aggregated actual FDI inflows were only about 51.83 per cent of FDI approvals during the period under review. In other words, almost 48.17 per cent of FDI approved has not been materialized.

In this context, it is observed that, if inflows are far lower than that of the approvals, may indicate two things. Firstly, it is possible that approvals are sought in haste making in order to use liberalized atmosphere while the actual decision to invest is taken at much later stage. Secondly, non-implementation of approved projects for establishing industrial activities due to procedural delays, political instability, non availability of infrastructural facilities, etc. and causing for a slow rate of growth in industrial activity than compared with the expected growth rate.

Empirical Analysis

To analyse the Approvals and Actual Inflows of FDI, Correlation and Regression Techniques have been applied.

Correlation Co-efficient is a measure of degree of co-variability between X and Y, whereas the objective of Regression Analysis is to study the nature of relationship between the variables so that we may be able to predict the value of one on the basis of another. As such, the amount of actual inflows is being predicted based on the projected approvals for the year 2005.

The Correlation between Approvals and Actuals during the period 1991 to 2004 is presented below:

$$r = 0.359$$

$$r^2 = 0.129$$

Hence, a low degree of positive correlation is found between the two above said variables.

Further, the Regression Technique has been applied to

derive the Regression equation so as to calculate the Actual Inflows based on estimated approvals for the period 2005.

Regression result:

Independent Variable = Approvals of FDI (x)

Dependent Variable = Actual Inflows of FDI (Y)

Period = 1991-2004

Method = Least Square Method

Equation = Y on X

Therefore, the Regression Equation is Y = 64.44 + 0.151x

Estimation of Actual Inflows in 2005 when assumed Approvals amount is Rs. 188.16 billion by using the Regression equation:

$$Y_{188.2} = 64.44 + 0.151(188.2)$$
$$= 92.85.$$

Hence, the Empirical Analysis gives the following result for the year 2005:

Likely Approvals of FDI = Rs. 188.16 billion

Likely Actuals of FDI = Rs. 92.85 billion

Rate of Actuals to Approvals = 49.3 per cent.

Hence, it can be inferred that even during the coming years in future, the actual inflows ratio is found at on 49.3 per cent. Further, it is suggested that the Government has to take initiation and further liberalized steps as to improve the percentage of Actual Inflows over the Approvals.

4.3.4. *FDI Inflows: Component-Wise (Category-wise/ Route-wise) Analysis*

FDI is the most important source of foreign investment inflows in developing countries like India. Before 1991, the inflows of FDI in India were not all satisfactory. But after the

TABLE 4.7

Year-wise (Route-wise Inflows of Foreign Direct Investment (FDI/NRI) During January 1991 to August 2004 (Excluding ADRs/GDRs)

(Amount Rupees / US $ in million)

	ACTUAL INFLOW OF FOREIGN DIRECT INVESTMENT IN THE FOLLOWING ROUTES							
Year (Jan-Dec)	*I Govt's approval (FIPB, SIA routes)*	*II RBI's Automatic approval (under delegated power)*	*III Amount of Inflows on acquisition of existing shares #*	*IV RBI's - Various NRI's schemes Ø*	*TOTAL (I to IV)*	*V Stock Swapped*	*VI Closing balance of advance*	*Grand Total (I to VI) in Rupees (in US $)*
1991	1,911.8 (54.3)	—	—	1,602.5 (45.7)	3,514.3	—	—	3,514.3 (100.0)
1992	4,779.5 (70.6)	475.4 (7.3)	— —	1,496.9 (22.1)	6,751.8	—	—	6,751.8 (100)
1993	9,851.6 (55.3)	2,411.0 (13.4)	—	5,604.5 (31.3)	17,867.1	—	--	17,867.1 (100)
1994	15,007.6 (50.3)	3,625.8 (12.1)	—	11,185.1 (37.6)	29,818.5	—	—	29,818.5 (100)
1995	38,694.4 (60.8)	5,301.6 (8.3)	—	19,705.6 (30.9)	63,701.6	—	—	63,701.6 (100)
1996	57,589.1 (65.9)	6,196.2 (7.1)	3,038.0 (3.4)	20,620.4 (23.6)	87,443.7	—	—	87,443.7 (100)
1997	101,284.0 (78.0)	8,672.2 (6.7)	9,540.3 (7.3)	10,396.2 (8.0)	129,892.7	—	—	129,892.7 (100)

1998	82,397.3 (62.1)	6,106.5 (4.6)	40,593.5 (30.6)	3,594.8 (2.7)	132,692.1	—	—	132,692.1 (100)
1999	61,894.3 (60.9)	7,608.1 (7.5)	19,608.3** (19.3)	3,488.3 (3.4)	92,599.0	—	9,067.8 (8.9)	101,666.8 (100)
2000	63,425.3 (51.3)	16,918.0 (13.7)	20,580.5 (16.7)	3,488.2 (2.8)	104,412.0	—	19,125.8 (15.5)	123,537.8 (100)
2001	96,385.9 (57.4)	32,410.4 (19.3)	29,621.7 (17.6)	2,292.5 (1.4)	160,710.5	—	7,066.0 (4.3)	167,776.5 (100)
2002	69,577.2 ¥ (38.2)	39,030.5 (21.4)	52,625.9~ (28.9)	110.8 (0.1)	161,344.4	840.0 £ (0.5)	19,771.3 (10.9)	181,955.7 (100)
2003	42,956.8 (37.0)	23,399.7 (20.1)	29,283.9 (25.2)	—	95,640.4	1,725.0 (1.5)	18,807.6 (16.2)	116,173.0 (100)
2004 (Jan-Aug.)	38,981.1 (32.2)	33,481.3 (27.7)	31,170.3 (25.8)	—	103,632.7	—	17,312.7 (14.3)	120,945.4 (100)
Total @ (as on 31.08.04)	684,735.9 (53.3)	185,636.7 (14.5)	236,062.4 (18.4)	83,585.8 (6.5)	1,190,020.8	2,565.0 (0.2)	91,151.2 (7.1)	1,283,737.0 (100.0) (US $ 31,454.1)

Source: RBI, (FED) Central Office, Mumbai

Total: Rs. 1,283.74 (US $ 31.45) billion (1991 to August 2004)

Note: (i) @ Provisional subject to reconciliation with RBI, Mumbai

(ii) Figures for 2004 updated up to 31.08.2004.

(iii) The amount of inflows raised through ADRs/GDRs/FCCBs against the FDI approvals accorded by FIPB during the period from August 1994 to August 2004, has not been included in the above table.

(iv) # Reported by RBI, Mumbai- transfer of existing shares from Resident to Non-resident under FEMA during January 1996 to August 2004.

(v) Ø Special NRI Schemes Administered by RBI from 01.01.1991 to 31.08.2004; (Scheme i.e. 40%, 100%, 24%, Air Taxi, Housing & Real Estate Development & Sick Unit).

(vi) ** An amount of Rs. 69.4 million as final amount reported by RBI, on account of acquisition of existing shares for the years of 1996 to 1998.

(vii) © Including an amount of Rs.194.8 million as reported later on by RBI on a/c of ADRs/GDRs for the year 1998.

(viii) The advance of inflows received during October to December for the years from 1999 to 2003 has already been adjusted in the following year during January to March every year.

(ix) ~ Includes an amount of Rs. 10,000.0 million being control premium paid to Government by Suzuki Motor Corporation, Japan towards shares issued to them on renouncing of rights by GOI (as per Government of India letter dated 9.08.2002).

(x) ¥ Includes an amount of Rs. 3,961.4 (US $ 82.5) million received by M/s. Bharti Televentures under private placement made with FIPB approval.

(xi) £ The figures pertain to the period from January to November 2002

announcement of New Industrial Policy in July 1991, India has experienced acceleration in the inflows of FDI into the country.

Table 4.7 presents the component-wise (category-wise) inflows of Foreign Direct Investment from the period 1991 to 2004. This data shows the amount of Foreign Direct Investment received through various agencies/routes, such as Government's approval (FIPB/SIA routes); RBI's automatic approval; Acquisition of shares; NRI's schemes; Re-invested earnings; and Other Capital flows.

The data of Table 4.7 shows that the total amount of actual inflows of FDI during 1991-2004 accounted for Rs. 1283.7 billion (US $ 31.45 billion), out of which, inflows of Government's FIPB/SIA approval had a significant share of 53.3 per cent; RBI's automatic approval accounted for 14.5 per cent; NRI's share at 6.5 per cent; and remaining 25.7 per cent shared by acquisition of shares, reinvested earnings and other capital flows.

Among the categories of FDI inflows, Government (SIA/FIPB) route has gained a lot of significance for inflow of Foreign Direct Investment, since it has accounted for 51 per cent to 78 per cent of the total inflow of FDI from 1991 to 2004. The investment through NRI's route was prominent in 1991-92, the first year of liberalization, but then onwards the SIA/FIPB route was claimed a major proportion. The proportion of Reinvested earnings contributed a major share in 2002, 2003 and in the first eight months of 2004 (up to August 2004). The total FDI inflows accounted during January-August 2004 for Rs. 120.95 billion with a growth rate of 4.1 per cent over 2003. Thus, it has been observed that in response to the policy of liberalization introduced in India, the inflows of FDI have been encouraging.

Interpretation of the above Table 4.7 also gives the following results:

(a) There has been continuous increase in FDI inflows through Government (SIA/FIPB) and RBI route during 1991 to 1997. The increase has been largely on account of expanded list of industries/sectors which are permitted for foreign equity (Chart 4.I). Besides this, there are several investors' friendly policies introduced by Government to promote FDI. These are as given below:

(i) India has signed the Multilateral Investment Guarantee Agency Protocol for the protection of foreign investment on April 13, 1992.

(ii) Provisions of the Foreign Exchange Regulation Act (FERA) have been liberalized through an ordinance dated January 9, 1993 as a result of which companies with more than 40 per cent of foreign equity are also now treated on par with fully Indian owned companies.

(iii) Foreign companies have been allowed to use their trade marks on domestic sales from May 14, 1992.

(iv) Foreign Investment Promotion Council (FIPC) has been constituted to prepare project reports in selected thrust areas and there by to facilitate the flow of foreign investment in the country.

(v) In August 1991, Foreign Investment Implementation Act (FIIA) was established with in the Ministry of Industry to quicken the translation of foreign investment proposals into actual investment inflows. Further, where the clearance of FIPB is needed, approval line has been reduced to thirty days.

(b) The inflows of FDI declined to Rs. 101.67 billions in 1999 by 23.3 per cent as compared to 1998. Several restrictions imposed on India by United States on account of nuclear test at Pokharn, slow down of economy, political instability, restrictions imposed on FDI regarding TRIMS (Trade Related Investment Measures), etc. are some of the contributing factors for this declining trend. There was also declining trend in NRI's investment since 1998-99 and found nil with effect from 2002-03 because of the depressing stock market conditions, as such FDI inflows during 2002-04 rush declined.

(c) The inflows of FDI has been increased to Rs. 167.78 billion in 2001 and further to Rs. 181.96 billions in 2002 in spite of facing exogenous factors like Gujarat Earthquake (January 2001), terrorist attack on Indian Parliament (December 2001), terrorist attack on World Trade Center (September 11, 2001), etc. This is due to liberalization of foreign investment policies such as:

   (i) On January 5, 1999, Government of India has notified that RBI automatic route would be available for foreign investors seeking to invest up to 100 per cent in the roads and port sectors including projects for construction and maintenance of roads, highways, vehicular bridges, vehicular tunnels, ports and harbours, (ET, January 6, 1999, p6).

   (ii) On June 11, 2000, 100 per cent FDI has been allowed by Ministry of Commerce and Industry to E-Commerce ventures, oil and petroleum refinery including power generation, transmission and distribution (ET, June 12, 2000, p.1).

   (iii) 100 per cent FDI has been allowed in integrated

town ships. Under this policy, the developer would be required to build up commercial premises i.e. hotels, roads, bridges and Mass Rapid Transit (MRT) System besides setting up residential units.

(iv) More recently, 26 per cent FDI was allowed in print media and 100 per cent in tea sector (including tea plantation).

(v) The coverage of FDI since 2000-01 includes, besides equity capital (i.e. RBI automatic route, SIA/FIPB route, NRI and acquisition of shares), "Reinvested earnings" and "Other Direct Capital". As a result of this revision, while FDI in 2000-01 according to earlier definition was US $ 2,339 million, it is now estimated at US $ 4,029 million. Similarly, estimate of FDI in 2001-02 has increased from US $ 3,904 million to US $ 6,131 million.

PART III

This part of the chapter presents the India's position in Global Context as well as in Developing Economies, and also the comparison of FDI inflows to India vis-à-vis some selected Asian countries.

4.4. India's Position in Global FDI Flows

On the eve of Independence in 1947, India was a country at a low level of development with high incidence of poverty and inequality. The land-labour ratio was quite adverse. The economy was stagnant because of lack of capital. During the century long direct British rule the inflow of capital was not commensurate with the poor capital endowment of the country when there were apparently no political constraints on inflow to India. The low per capita income restricted the market.

Foreign Investment did take place but mainly to export oriented industries such as tea, jute, coal etc. Most of the profits were repatriated and not reinvested. Such investment could not have led to growth as the objective was exploitation of the natural resources.

Since the inception of centralized planning in 1951 till 1980, India followed a preventive policy regime with restrictions on investment of capital and import of capital goods by local as well as foreign firms. The policy restrictions persisting till mid-80s consisted mainly of the restrictions on new and existing Foreign Direct Investment through screening and preventive measures. This trend of restricted Foreign Direct Investment continued till late 1980s.

Since 1991, the Government of India has embarked on liberalization and economic reforms programme with a view to bring about rapid and substantial economic growth and move towards globalization of the economy. The new policies have substantially relaxed restrictions on foreign investment, industrial licensing and foreign exchange. Capital market has been opened to foreign investment and banking sector controls have been eased.

As a part of major initiatives to attract foreign investment, measures have been initiated to enter into agreements to provide for promotion and protection of investment. India has become a Member of Multilateral Investment Guarantee Agency (MIGA). Full subscription and membership rights have become operative from January, 1994. As a consequence, all investments approved by Government are insured against expropriation/nationalization by MIGA. Bilateral Investment Promotion and Protection Agreements have been signed with 46 countries including principal FDI investors such as the UK, Germany, Malaysia and Denmark. Others are in the process of being finalized.

India's Share in FDI Flows to Developing Countries

It is evident from the available data in Table 4.8 that the share of India in FDI flows to developing countries is meager, as such it is no way comparable to that of some selected Asian countries such as China, Singapore, etc. In 1993, India

TABLE 4.8

FDI Inflows in Selected Asian Countries

(Millions of Dollars)

Country	*1992-97*	*1998*	*1999*	*2000*	*2001*	*2002*	*2003*
Developing Countries Total	118 596	194 055	231 880	252 459	219 721	157 612	172 033
China	32 799	45 463	40 319	40 715	46 878	52 743	53 505
India	1 676	2 633	2 168	2 319	3 403	3 449	4 269
Indonesia	3 518	-241	-1 866	-4 550	-2 977	145	-597
Korea Republic of	1 298	5 039	9 436	8 572	3 683	2 941	3 752
Malaysia	5 816	2 714	3 895	3 788	554	3 203	2 474
Philippines	1 343	2 212	1 725	1 345	982	1 792	319
Singapore	8 295	7 690	16 067	17 2117	15 038	5 730	11 409
Thailand	2 269	7 491	6 091	3 350	3 813	1 068	1 802
Share of China in Developing Countries (Percentage)	27.7	23.4	17.4	16.1	21.3	33.5	31.1
Share of India in Developing Countries (Percentage)	1.4	1.4	0.9	0.9	1.5	2.2	2.5

Source: *UNCTAD, World Investment Report 2004.* The data in Table 4.8 also shows that the share of FDI inflows to India and China varied from a minimum of 0.9 per cent and 16.1 per cent to a maximum of 2.5 per cent and 33.5 per cent respectively during 1992 to 2003. Thus, China is very much successful in attracting FDI for the benefit of her economy whereas India failed in attracting FDI. There are various factors responsible for such a trend as mentioned below:

accounted for 2.5 per cent (US $ 4269 million out of US $ 172033 million) of total FDI flows to developing countries. However, China gained a significant share of 31.1 percentage of total FDI flows.

In terms of aggregate annual inflows, FDI maintained its declining trend for the second successive year after 1998. FDI inflows in India for the year 1999 and 2000 were lower than the previous year. The share in total FDI flows to developing countries has increased by one percentage point from 1.5 per cent in 2001 to 2.5 per cent in 2003. However, India's share in FDI inflows too low as compared to China.

- Procedural disputes regarding land availability, environmental clearance, delays at State level in getting power and other infrastructural back up. These bottlenecks result in delays in the commencement of many projects.
- Non-implementation of approved projects for establishing industrial activities, resulting slow industrial growth rate both in domestic and export industries. It is also observed that the exports from developing countries are associated with international firms choosing to use a country as a target for FDI and for production destined for global markets;
- Sizeable investment flows are concentrated in the infrastructure industries, like power, refineries, telecom etc. where gestation period is long and projects take time to materialize;
- High fiscal deficit because of high government expenditures, Geneva based World Economic Forum (1998) observed that in overall burden of Governments expenditure, India ranked 50th where as China, Korea, Malaysia, Philippines and Thailand are ranked 11th, 13th, 3rd, 10th, and 4th respectively;
- Political instability;
- Anti FDI lobby;
- Social tensions;
- Non-availability of infrastructure facilities;

- Corruption, red-tapism in government departments; and
- Inefficiency of labour.

India's Foreign Direct Investment to GDP ratio continues to be dismal at GDP ratio of 0.8 per cent despite efforts by successive government's to boost FDI inflows. FDI inflows in China is 4.3 per cent, 4.7 per cent in UK, 4 per cent in Brazil, 3.7 per cent in Thailand, 3 per cent in Mexico and 1.8 per cent in Philippines. Hong Kong emerges as the No.1 economy with its FDI inflow – GDP ratio of 16.8 per cent, while Singapore has an impressive figure of 12.2 per cent and India was at the bottom of the table with 0.8 per cent by the end of November 2004.*

Hence, it is concluded that India is a strategic location with access to a vast domestic and South Asian market, its share in world's total flow of direct investment to developing countries is a meager 2.5 per cent in 2003. This calls for further liberalization of norms for investment by present and prospective foreign entrepreneurs. Attracting foreign capital requires an investor-friendly environment. It underlines the need for efficient and adequate infrastructural facilities, availability of skilled and semi-skilled labour force, business-friendly public administration and moderate rates of taxation.

REFERENCE

1. Total approvals of FDI during 1991, initial year of liberalization was Rs. 5.30 billions, of which Rs. 3.60 billions approved through Secretariat for Industrial Assistance (SIA), accounting for 67.9 per cent of total.

---

* A study conducted by Associated Chambers of Commerce and Industry of India, 31st January 2005, The Hindu.

5

State and Industry-wise Analysis of FDI

5.1. Introduction

Economic Policy reforms have played vital role in the performance of the Indian economy since 1991. Among other things, the reforms have involved opening up the economy, making it more competitive, getting the Government out of the regulations, empowering the States to take more responsibility for economic management, and thereby creating a kind of competition among them for foreign investment. The positive trends are being seen in most sectors had the capability to more than neutralize the debilitating effects of two general elections in two years, the crisis in East Asia, Kargil war, the nuclear explosions, and the U.S. sanctions that followed.

Significantly, India went through a near disaster in 1991, which was among other causes, based on short-term borrowing. Of course, at that time it was short-term borrowing from non-resident Indians (NRIs), but it was the same kind of phenomenon – lots of short-term capital had come in and lots had moved out and created a severe payments crisis. In terms of foreign investment, it is the direct investment that should be actively sought for. FDI brings several advantages (new capital, technology, managerial expertise, and access to foreign markets) with little or no downside.

There are lots of international investors who would flock to India, especially now that they see that India has a lot of safety for them. The Government also set an ambitious target of achieving actual FDI inflows at a greater task. As such it is decided to implement some of the most critical reform actions necessary for making India an attractive investment destination, then India may not only be able to meet the target, but in fact do much better than that. Of course, additionally, availability of infrastructure services such as uninterrupted power, good roads, and adequate port and telecom and other facilities are essential.

Most of the States have been more reform-oriented, such as Andhra Pradesh, Gujarat, Karnataka, Maharashtra, Tamil Nadu, etc. However, Haryana, Kerala, Orissa, Madhya Pradesh, Punjab, Rajasthan and West Bengal have a lot of catching up to do.

The present chapter has been devoted to study and aimed at analyzing state/region-wise approvals of FDI; sectoral analysis of approvals and actual inflows of FDI as to find out the top sectors, which attract major portion of inflow of FDI; and presents sector-wise Prospects and Opportunities of Foreign Direct Investment in India.

5.2. State-wise Approvals of FDI

It is aimed at analyzing state-wise approvals of Foreign Direct Investment (FDI) during the period August 1991 to August 2004. Table 5.1 presents the relevant data.

A close examination of the data in Table 5.1 pertaining to approval of Foreign Direct Investments reveals that about half of the total FDI approved, aggregating 48.5 percent of total FDI approved, concentrated in top five States, namely, Maharashtra (14.78 percent), Delhi (12.24 percent), Tamil Nadu (9.2 percent), Karnataka (7.6 percent), and Andhra Pradesh (4.69 percent). However, the other states in the country covered remaining 51.5 percent of the total amount of FDI approved (Figure 5.1).

TABLE 5.1

State-wise Foreign Direct Investment (FDI) Approval During August 1991 to August 2004

Sl. No.	*Name of the State*	*No. of Approvals*			*Amount of Foreign Direct Investment Approved*	
		Total	*Technical*	*Financial*	*Rs. in Million*	*% to Total*
	States Not Indicated	6033 (23.1)	2518	3515	701362.84	28.32
1.	MAHARASHTRA	4972 (19.0)	1317	3655	366024.15	14.78
2.	DELHI	2763 (10.6)	306	2457	303037.96	12.24
3.	TAMIL NADU	2656 (10.2)	615	2041	225826.40	9.12
4.	KARNATAKA	2586 (9.9)	501	2085	188184.32	7.60
5.	ANDHRA PRADESH	1276 (4.9)	266	1010	116091.37	4.69
6.	GUJARAT	1224 (4.7)	566	658	111765.07	4.51
7.	MADHYA PRADESH	243 (0.9)	73	170	92714.08	3.74
8.	ORISSA	141 (0.5)	50	91	82293.13	3.32
9.	WEST BENGAL	679 (2.6)	198	481	77898.35	3.15
10.	UTTAR PRADESH	811 (3.1)	277	534	48266.92	1.95
11.	HARYANA	874 (3.3)	322	552	38751.56	1.56
12.	RAJASTHAN	343 (1.3)	103	240	29112.04	1.18
13.	PUNJAB	201 (0.8)	62	139	21241.53	0.86
14.	KERALA	332 (1.3)	70	262	17806.31	0.72
15.	PONDICHERRY	130 (0.5)	42	88	12861.53	0.52
16.	HIMACHAL PRADESH	99 (0.4)	57	42	11741.45	0.47
17.	GOA	276 (1.1)	66	210	9977.32	0.40
18.	BIHAR	49 (0.2)	22	27	7397.05	0.30
19.	CHATTISGARH	48 (0.2)	31	17	6363.03	0.26
20.	CHANDIGARH	84 (0.3)	12	72	2413.60	0.10
21.	JHARKHAND	81 (0.3)	54	27	1465.15	0.06
22.	UTTARANCHAL	52 (0.2)	24	28	1256.49	0.05
23.	DADRA & NAGAR HAVELI	72 (0.3)	48	24	1239.80	0.05
24.	DAMAN & DIU	43 (0.2)	15	28	554.64	0.02

25. MEGHALAYA	5 (0.02)	0	5	529.60	0.02
26. ANDAMAN & NICOBAR	8 (0.03)	0	8	137.87	0.01
27. ARUNACHAL PRADESH	2 (0.008)	0	2	110.60	0.00
28. JAMMU AND KASHMIR	5 (0.02)	3	2	84.10	0.00
29. NAGALAND	2 (0.008)	1	1	36.80	0.00
30. MANIPUR	2 (0.008)	0	2	31.85	0.00
31. TRIPURA	4 (0.02)	1	3	30.88	0.00
32. MIZORAM	1 (0.004)	0	1	15.22	0.00
33. ASSAM	19 (0.07)	15	41	4.95	0.00
34. LAKSHADWEEP	1 (0.004)	0	1	5.00	0.00
Grand Total	**26117(100.0)**	**7635**	**18482**	**2476642.96**	**100.00**

Note: The Statement excludes ADR/GDR amounts.

Source: Secretariat for Industrial Assistance (SIA), Department of Industrial Policy Promotion, Ministry of Commerce & Industry, Govt. of India, New Delhi – News Letter September 2004.

* Figures in brackets indicate percent to total.

Figure 5.1: STATE-WISE APPROVALS OF FDI SINCE 1991 (in percentage)

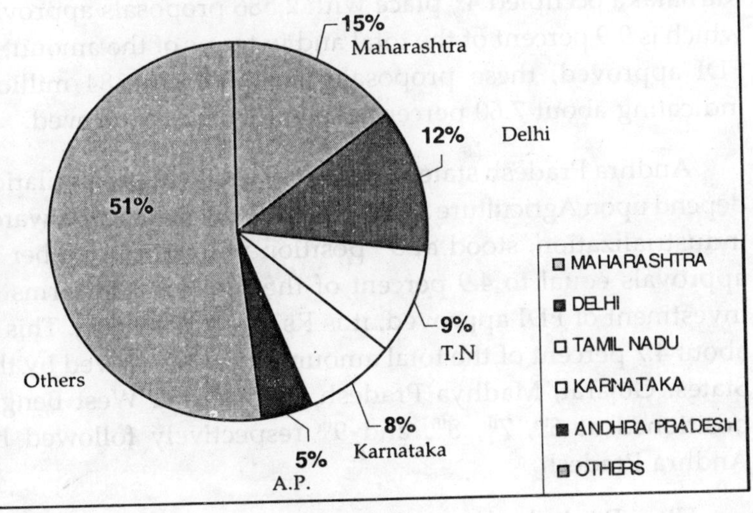

The table shows that largest number of FDI proposals approved is by the State of Maharashtra, which in terms of percentage of total is 19.0 percent. This figure is highest among all the states. However, in terms of the amount of Investment approved, Maharashtra stood at top one with FDI approved of Rs.366 024 million, which is 14.78 percent of total FDI approved in the country. Delhi state is at second place in terms of the amount of investment with Rs. 303 037 million and its share in the total also with 12.24 percent. But in terms of number of proposals approved, Maharashtra has 4,972 and Delhi has only 2,763, which is about 56 percent as to number of approvals of Maharashtra. It is indicated that heavy investment proposals should come to Delhi state, as it is the Capital city of the country.

In terms of the number of proposals approved as well as the total FDI approved by the States, Tamil Nadu is at 3rd position with 2,656 proposals, which is 10.2 percent of the total, and in terms of amount of investment it is Rs. 225 826 million, accounting for 9.12 percent of the total FDI approved. Karnataka occupied 4th place with 2,586 proposals approved which is 9.9 percent of the total and in terms of the amount of FDI approved, these proposals have Rs. 188 184 million, indicating about 7.60 percent of the total FDI approved.

Andhra Pradesh state, where 70-80 percent of population depend upon Agriculture Sector and recently marching towards industrialization, stood at 5th position with 1,276 number of approvals equal to 4.9 percent of the total, and in terms of investment of FDI approved, it is Rs. 116 091 million. This is about 4.7 percent of the total amount of FDI approved by the States. Gujarat, Madhya Pradesh, Orissa, and West Bengal positioned at 6th, 7th, 8th, and 9th respectively followed by Andhra Pradesh.

Uttar Pradesh, despite being the largest state of India in

terms of population and has large number of industrially developed cities, which are capable of absorbing highest number of FDI approvals in the state, has failed miserably in this aspect. It has only 811 proposals approved, accounting for 3.1 percent of the total and stood at 10th place. This state attracted FDI approvals amounting to Rs. 48 266 million, which is 1.95 percent of the total FDI approved. Likewise, there are other states, which have capability to absorb FDI in different areas, but the approval rate is below 1 percent. States like Punjab, Kerala, Pondicherry, Himachal Pradesh, Goa, Bihar etc. have the infrastructural facilities comparable to other states who have done well as this front, and have reasonably good industrial base, but have been found wanting in giving required encouragement and attention to this area. It is clear from the table that out of 35 states/Union Territories under review, 22 have approval of FDI less than 1 percent of the total amount of FDI approved. This indicates a clear case of uneven flow of Foreign Direct Investments.

There are rather significant differences in reform interest and economic performance between a large part of northern India and Southern India where Karnataka, Tamil Nadu and Andhra Pradesh are quite dynamic now in trying to get the infrastructure, and the policy regime right to attract FDI. In Uttar Pradesh and Bihar, one does not see the same kind of reform dynamism and the results are therefore poor in terms of economic growth. These differences will be noticed politically sooner rather than later, (as inequalities will become glaring) and the States that are ahead will be rewarded with better performance and those that are behind will face a demand to catch up. That will spur a kind of competition among the States and make the reform process go much faster. Hence, it is further required wide scope for increasing FDI in India.

5.3. Industry-wise Analysis of Approvals of FDI

It is proposed to assess the sector-wise Foreign Direct

Investment approvals with a view to identify which sector of Indian economy has attracted maximum amount of FDI approvals and which sector has lost its importance during the era of liberalization and globalization since 1991 to August 2004. For the purpose of sector-wise analysis of FDI, the Indian Economy has been broadly classified into the following sectors, where FDI has been permitted:

(i) Metallurgical Industries
(ii) Fuels (Power & Oil Refinery)
(iii) Electrical Equipments
(iv) Telecommunications
(v) Transportation Industry
(vi) Industrial Machinery & Tools
(vii) Chemicals & Fertilizers
(viii) Drugs and Pharmaceuticals
(ix) Textiles
(x) Paper and Pulp including Paper Products
(xi) Food Processing Industries
(xii) Rubber & Leather goods
(xiii) Consultancy Services
(xiv) Service Sector (including Banking & Insurance)
(xv) Hotel & Tourism
(xvi) Trading (including E-Commerce)
(xvii) Miscellaneous Industries.

The main objective of the new policy was to attract foreign investment in high priority industries and seeking to inflow of Foreign Capital and Technology in critical areas of the industrial economy has met with encouraging response from Multinationals, Non-Resident Indians and other foreign affiliates.

However, FDI is not permitted only in few sectors which are:

(i) Agriculture and plantations excluding tea plantation;

(ii) Real estate business, excluding integrated township development. However, NRI/OCB investment is allowed for real estate business;

(iii) Retail trade in any form;

(iv) Lottery, betting and gambling business;

(v) Security services; and

(vi) Atomic Energy.

Table 5.2 shows the data of Foreign Direct Investment approvals from August 1991 to August 2004 in various industrial sectors in India.

TABLE 5.2

Sector-wise Foreign Direct Investment (FDI) & Foreign Technology Cases (FTCs) Approved during August 1991 to August 2004

Sl. No.	Name of the Sector Industry	No. of Approvals			Amount of Foreign Direct Investment Approved	
		Total	Technical	Financial	Rs. in Million	% to Total
1.	**METALLURGICAL INDUSTRIES**					
i)	Ferrous	377	216	161	71033.21	2.87
ii)	Non-Ferrous	75	34	41	7824.20	0.32
iii)	Special Alloys	131	59	72	19472.13	0.79
iv)	Mining Service	101	15	86	43060.38	1.74
v)	Misc. (other Items)-Metallurgy	105	41	64	12660.41	0.51
	Sector Total	**789**	**365**	**424**	**154050.32**	**6.22**
2.	Fuels (Power and Oil Refinery)					
i)	Power	296	22	274	381907.23	15.42
ii)	Oil Refinery	267	112	155	182442.49	7.37
iii)	Power (Other)	110	15	95	54782.15	2.21
iv)	Oil Refinery (Other)	138	76	62	44397.88	1.79
v)	Others(Fuels)	191	71	120	33941.71	1.37

	Sector Total	**1002**	**296**	**706**	**697471.46**	**28.16**
3.	BOILERS AND STEAM GENERATING PLANTS	87	50	37	1471.58	0.06
4.	PRIME MOVERS OTHER THAN ELECTRICAL	61	38	23	917.24	0.04
5.	**ELECTRICALS EQUIPMENT (INCL S/W & ELEC)**					
i)	Electrical Equipment	1813	959	854	57453.81	2.32
ii)	Computer Software Industry	3355	92	3263	92711.24	3.74
iii)	Electronics	615	165	450	31520.10	1.27
iv)	Computer Hardware	34	4	30	3815.52	0.15
v)	Others(S/W)	87	24	63	1760.47	0.07
	Sector Total	5904	1244	4660	187261.13	7.56
6.	**TELECOMMUNICATIONS**					
i)	Telecommunications	463	103	360	127590.00	5.15
ii)	Radio Paging	51	4	47	12488.95	0.50
iii)	Cellular Mobile/Basic Telephone Service	206	12	194	233713.98	9.44
iv)	Telecommunication (I&B)	140	5	135	31405.82	1.27
v)	Others (Telecommunications)	66	5	61	8484.01	0.34
	Sector Total	**926**	**129**	**797**	**413682.76**	**16.70**
7.	**TRANSPORTATION INDUSTRY**					
i)	Automobile Industry	831	425	406	51229.57	2.07
ii)	Air/Sea Transport	267	20	247	17327.80	0.70
iii)	Passenger Cars	85	6	79	83171.05	3.36
iv)	Auto Ancillaries/Parts	384	183	201	26007.23	1.05
v)	Ports	33	0	33	15588.42	0.63
vi)	Others(Transport)	177	53	124	14345.77	0.58
	Sector Total	**1777**	**687**	**1090**	**207669.83**	**8.39**
8.	INDUSTRIAL MACHINERY	1527	858	669	15873.49	0.64
9.	MACHINE TOOLS	234	91	143	4137.55	0.17
10.	AGRICULTURAL MACHINERY	50	32	18	4577.85	0.18
11.	EARTH-MOVING MACHINERY	81	47	34	2489.25	0.10
12.	MISCELLANEOUS MECHANICAL & ENGINEERING	1079	432	647	18607.21	0.75
13.	COMMERCIAL, OFFICE & HOUSEHOLD EQUIPMENT	119	40	79	11654.41	0.47
14.	MEDICAL AND SURGICAL APPLIANCES	143	36	107	3897.08	0.16

15.	INDUSTRIAL INSTRUMENTS	226	120	106	1673.56	0.07
16.	SCIENTIFIC INSTRUMENTS	48	17	31	658.09	0.03
17.	MATHEMATICAL, SURVEYING AND DRAWING	6	2	4	383.70	0.02
18.	FERTILIZERS	72	59	13	1476.53	0.06
19.	CHEMICALS (OTHER THAN FERTILIZERS)	1923	855	1068	117129.36	4.73
20.	PHOTOGRAPHIC RAW FILM AND PAPER	33	12	21	2382.49	0.10
21.	DYE-STUFFS	24	5	19	1233.50	0.05
22.	DRUGS & PHARMACEUTICALS	622	263	359	27530.67	1.11
23.	TEXTILES (INCLUD DYED, PRINTED)	813	168	645	29374.57	1.19
24.	PAPER AND PULP INCLUDING PAPER PRODUCT	201	65	136	31131.26	1.26
25.	SUGAR	16	1	15	10634.28	0.43
26.	FERMENTATION INDUSTRIES	87	25	62	15366.19	0.62
27.	**FOOD PROCESSING INDUSTRIES**					
i)	Food products	814	140	674	93439.87	3.77
ii)	Marine products	101	22	79	989.27	0.04
iii)	Miscellaneous (Food prod)	28	2	26	1028.24	0.04
	Sector Total	**943**	**164**	**779**	**95457.38**	**3.85**
28.	VEGETABLE OILS AND VANASPATI	64	4	60	3081.68	0.12
29.	SOAPS, COSMETICS AND TOILET PREPARATIONS	70	24	46	3817.90	0.15
30.	RUBBER GOODS	251	114	137	14200.86	0.57
31.	LEATHER, LEATHER GOODS AND PICKERS	225	44	181	5760.03	0.23
32.	GLUE AND GELATIN	5	1	4	19.33	0.00
33.	GLASS	155	44	111	25223.03	1.02
34.	CERAMICS	243	61	182	6376.54	0.26
35.	CEMENT AND GYPSUM PRODUCTS	119	43	76	19571.36	0.79
36.	TIMBER PRODUCTS	23	3	20	364.44	0.01
37.	DEFENCE INDUSTRIES	9	9	0	0.00	0.00
38.	**CONSULTANCY SERVICES**					
i)	Design & Eng. Services	417	70	347	12654.46	0.51
ii)	Management Services	371	27	344	9105.00	0.37
iii)	Marketing	71	9	62	587.62	0.02

iv) Construction	20	2	18	575.10	0.02
v) Others(CONSULTANCY SERVICE)	71	12	59	1606.91	0.06
Sector Total	**950**	**120**	**830**	**24529.09**	**0.99**
39. SERVICE SECTOR					
i) Financial	477	9	468	76083.46	3.07
ii) Non-Financial Services	385	26	359	34833.64	1.41
iii) Banking Services	38	0	38	5908.90	0.24
iv) Insurance	33	0	33	4803.58	0.19
v) Hospital & Diagnostic Centers	169	17	152	12371.29	0.50
vi) Outsourcing	22	0	22	1788.75	0.07
vii) Research & Development	50	4	46	8200.94	0.33
viii) Education	103	0	103	12497.29	0.50
ix) Other Services	101	13	88	9332.93	0.38
Sector Total	**1378**	**69**	**1309**	**165820.76**	**6.70**
40. HOTEL & TOURISM					
i) Hotel & Restaurants	522181	341	37827.76	1.53	
ii) Tourism	179	27	152	8549.41	0.35
iii) Others(Hotel & Tourism)	48	10	38	2704.99	0.11
Sector Total	**749**	**218**	**531**	**49082.15**	**1.98**
41. TRADING					
i) TRADING	265	7	258	4696.58	0.19
ii) Trading (For Exports)	256	4	252	4015.35	0.16
iii) Trading(Activities)	243	9	234	21854.35	0.88
iv) E-COMMERCE	44	0	44	2114.93	0.09
Sector Total	**808**	**20**	**788**	**32681.21**	**1.32**
42. MISCELLANEOUS INDUSTRIES					
i) Horticulture	118	38	80	1568.66	0.06
ii) Agriculture (Hybrid Seeds & Plantation)	189	67	122	4371.98	0.18
iii) Floriculture	185	70	115	2909.96	0.12
iv) Diamond	20	1	19	1519.70	0.06
v) Ornament & Gold	34	2	32	1270.94	0.05
vi) Construction Activities & Real Estate	181	9	172	23188.29	0.94
vii) Tea/Coffee	11	2	9	720.70	0.03
viii) Cigarettes	6	3	3	127.30	0.01
ix) Printing of Books etc.	23	2	21	355.82	0.01

x)	COIR	11	2	9	49.69	0.00
xi)	Others (Misc. Industries)	1497	564	933	31838.84	1.29
	Sector Total	**2275**	**760**	**1515**	**67921.87**	**2.74**
	Grand Total	**26117**	**7635**	**18482**	**2476642.96**	**100.00**

Source: Secretariat for Industrial Assistance (SIA), Department of Industrial Policy Promotion, Ministry of Commerce & Industry, Govt. of India, New Delhi – News Letter September 2004.

Note: The Statement excludes ADR/GDR amounts

Figure 5.2: SECTOR-WISE SHARE IN APPROVALS OF FDI DURING 1991 TO AUGUST 2004 (in percentage)

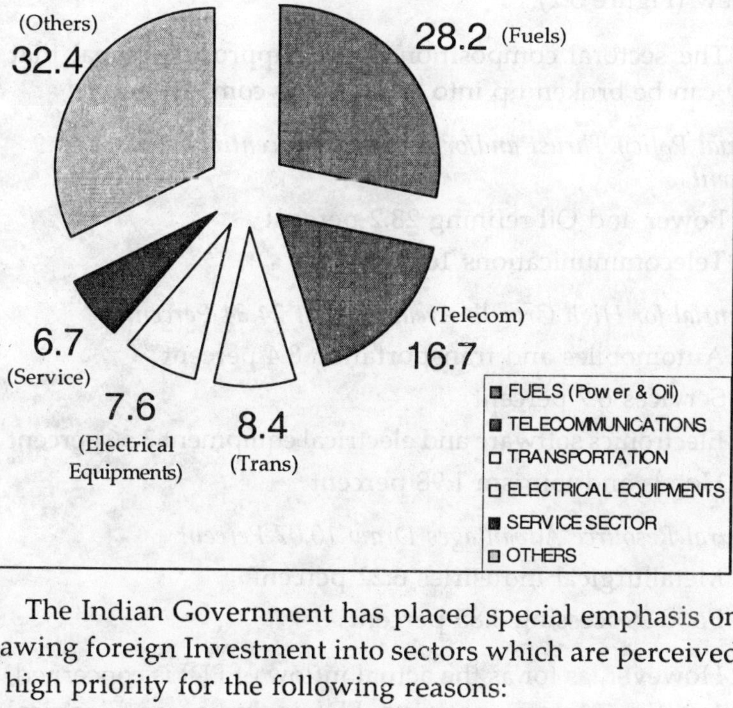

The Indian Government has placed special emphasis on drawing foreign Investment into sectors which are perceived of high priority for the following reasons:

1. Need for rapid development.
2. Volume of investment required.

3. Importance for overall economic growth and employment.
4. Comparative advantages in terms of human or natural resources.

In terms of the industries, where amount of FDI approvals has come to India, Table 5.2 shows that the most important top 5 sectors are Fuels (Power & Oil) (28.2 percent), Telecommunications (16.7 percent), Transportation (8.4 percent), Electrical Equipments (7.6 percent), and Service Sector (6.7 percent). These sectors have combinely accounted for 67.6 percent of the total amount of FDI approved (i.e., more than half of the total FDI approved), whereas the other sectors attracted remaining 32.4 percent during the period under review (Figure 5.2).

The sectoral composition of FDI approvals reveal that they can be broken up into three major compartments:

Special Policy Thrust and/or Attractive Incentives Attract 44.9 Percent

Power and Oil refining 28.2 percent

Telecommunications 16.70

Potential for High Growth Areas Attract 24.64 Percent

Automobiles and transportation 8.4 percent

Services 6.7 percent

Electronics software and electrical equipment 7.56 percent

Hotels and tourism 1.98 percent

Natural Resource Advantages Draw 10.07 Percent

Metallurgical Industries 6.22 percent

Food Processing 3.85 percent

However, as for as the actual inflow of FDI is concerned, the top five sectors receiving FDI in India are Electrical Equipment $ 373 million (accounting for 18 percent inflow),

Drugs and Pharmaceuticals $ 286 million (14.43 percent), Consultancy Services $ 214 million (10.76 percent), Fuel including Power and Oil $ 190 million (9.55 per cent), and Metallurgy $ 164 million dollar (8.27 per cent) respectively.*

The particular industrial sectors, which have been identified as presenting tremendous opportunities for foreign investments are: Power, Telecommunications, Transportation Industry, Electrica' Equipments, Service Sector, Metallurgical Industries, etc.

1. Power Sector

The Power sector is India's top infrastructure priority area. Shortage of power has been cited as one of the main problems of the economy and it is realized that the future is bleak unless enough power is generated for industrial and consumer use. That is precisely why the government accords top priority to foreign investment in this capital-intensive sector.

The main elements of the policy of the Government regarding private investment in the power sector are the following:

(i) Foreign Investment in the power sector is actively encouraged and can take place either in the form of a joint venture with an Indian partner or as a fully-owned operation with 100 percent foreign equity. According to the new liberalized policy, Foreign Direct Investment up to 100 percent is allowed in respect of projects relating to electricity generation, transmission and distribution, other than atomic reactor power plants. There is no limit on the project cost and quantum of foreign direct investment.[1]

* The study on Foreign Direct Investment conducted by the Associated Chambers of Commerce and Industry of India (ASSOCHAM), January 31, 2005, *The Hindu*.

(ii) Companies may operate either as power distribution or generator companies.

(iii) Power generation companies are required to supply to State Electricity Boards (SEBs) who in turn will distribute the power.

(iv) Since the entry of private sector in the power generation, Central Electricity Authority (CEA) has accorded techno-economic clearance (TEC) to 56 private sector power projects with a capacity generate 28,849MW.

(v) The Accelerated Power Development and Reforms Programme (APDRP), which has an outlay of Rs. 3500 crore, has been designed to assist reforms in the distribution sector. It seeks to target 63 distribution centers, and develop them as "centers of excellence". It seeks to obtain 100 percent metering, energy audit, better HT/LT ratio, replacement of distribution transformers, and IT solutions relating to power flow at critical points to ensure accountability at all levels. During 2002-03, 332 projects covering concentrated load centers with capital cost of Rs. 13,703 crore have been cleared till December 2002.[2]

(vi) A series of approvals are required for power projects. These include 'in principle' endorsement of a project followed by approvals of techno-feasibility reports, funding plans, clearance by environmental authorities, Foreign Investment Promotion Board, etc.

Prospects and Opportunities: This sector offers the following prospects and opportunities to the potential investors:

(i) 100 percent foreign equity is permitted in this sector

(ii) Private power projects are based on a 16-18 percent return on equity, so their costs are high. Since they have to sell their power to the financially weak State

Electricity Boards, there were concerns about whether the foreign investors would get their money back. To allay these fears, the Government provides guarantees to foreign investors in projects found viable.

(iii) The World Bank has advised that the State Electricity Boards be restructured into smaller units. The bank has also recommended creation of smaller units for privatization. This has been done in Greater Noida in north Indian state of Uttar Pradesh and the general mood is to do the same in other parts of the country. Accordingly, power distribution by the Delhi Vidyut Board was privatized in July 2002. These developments have made foreign investors confident of investing in India.

(iv) Special incentive package including tax holiday, rationalized depreciation, reduced customs duty on equipment etc. has been devised. Further, the power sector could work in a reliable manner to increase the efficiency of capital utilization in the country. The government has drawn up an ambitious programme, which entails new generation capacity of 1, 00,000 MW (which would roughly double the existing generation capacity), and substantial investments in transmission and distribution. It is estimated that these efforts would require investments of Rs. 8,00,000 crore, of this, about 40 percent of the new generation capacity is envisaged in the Xth plan, and the remainder in the XIth plan.[3]

(v) A blend of thermal, hyudel and nuclear sources of energy are available. Non-conventional energy from solar, wind and tidal sources are also encouraged.

These directions for development of the power sector involve enormous requirements of capital, and motivate the quest for private and foreign investment. In early 1990s, there was a concerted effort to attract foreign direct investment into the power sector.

The Table 5.2 shows that the Power Sector including Oil Refinery attracted 1002 number of Approvals. In terms of amount of Foreign Direct Investment approved, this sector gained top 1 position with Rs. 697.47 billions, accounting for 28.16 percent of total FDI approved during the period August 1991 to August 2004 under review.

2. *Telecommunications*

Telecommunications is a prime support service needed for rapid growth and modernization. It is also one of the fastest growing sectors in India and has immense potential for growth. Abundant investment opportunities exist in areas of basic and cellular communication infrastructure, optic fibre cable, gateways, satellite based communications, etc. The telecom sector has witnessed the presence of many leading foreign companies including US companies: AT&T, Motorola, US West, Hughes, Harris, Qualcomm, Sprint, Telstra, NTT, Singapore Telecom, Philippine Telecom, Bezeq, Siemens, Ericsson, Nokia, Fujitsu, Alcatel, and Bell Canada among others.

In order to modernize the telecom facilities in the country, the Government has announced a comprehensive policy for attracting private, including foreign investment in Value Added and Basic Services.

Value Added Services: The Value Added Services were thrown open to private sector in 1992. The value added services, where private, including foreign investment is encouraged with electronic mail, voice mail, data services, audio text services, video text services, etc.

In view of the constraints in the number of companies that can be allowed to operate, a policy of selection through a system of tendering is adopted, for the following value added services: Ratio Paging, Cellular Mobile Telephone, and Global Mobile Personal Communications by Satellite (GMPCs).

All foreign investment proposals in the above telecom services require license from Department of Telecommunications (DOT) and approval of FIPB.

Basic Services: The private sector participation in the basic telecom services is guided by the National Telecom Policy, 1994. Basic services were opened to private participation in 1994 by dividing the country into 21 Telecom Circles and allowing one private operator per Circle to compete with DoT. Only companies registered in India will be permitted to participate in providing basic voice telephone services. In the case of a joint venture, foreign equity up to 49 percent would be permitted. However, there will be no limit of foreign equity in the manufacturing sector. Six licenses for basic services have been granted for six States. Two operators M/s. Bharati Telenet Ltd. in Madhya Pradesh, and Hughes Ispat Ltd. in Maharashtra have started providing services.[4]

Prospects and Opportunities

(i) The two important goals of the telecom sector are: delivering low-cost voice telephony to the largest possible number of individuals, and delivering low-cost high speed computer networking to the largest number of firms. The number of phone lines per 100 persons of the population, which is called teledensity, has improved rapidly, from 3.6 in March 2001 to 4.9 in December 2002.[5] This is way below international standards and is not becoming of a country aspiring to be a major player in the global economy of the 21st century. This means that opportunities for investment in this sector are immense.

(ii) The Government cannot make investments of this

magnitude because of resource limitations. The private sector and foreign companies are therefore welcomed into this sector, both as direct investors and exporters of equipment and technology. With a view to supplementing the efforts of public sector service providers, and to ensure greater competition in providing basic telephone services, private companies are being licensed to offer basic services. Presently, these services are being provided in the states of Andhra Pradesh, Gujarat, Haryana, Karnataka, Maharashtra, Madhya Pradesh, Rajasthan, Punjab, Tamil Nadu and Delhi.[6]

(iii) Provision of Internet Services has been thrown open to domestic and foreign investors with effect from October 7, 1998. In 2002-03, some major initiatives in telecom policy came out, such as opening up of international long distance traffic, permitting internet telephony, setting up a mechanism for Universal Social Obligation (USO), permitting a fourth operator in the cellular mobile segment, and the commissioning of National Internet Backbone (NIB).

(iv) A new policy for Internet Service Providers (ISPs) was announced in 1998 allowing independent service providers to enter the sector, as the monopoly of VSNL over International Long Distance (ILD) service was ended, and VSNL was privatized. The International long distance business was opened up for unrestricted entry of foreign investors.

In response to the policy changes in the Indian Telecom Sector, data of Table 5.2 shows that the Telecom Sector is a major recipient of foreign direct investment (FDI) flows. During the period August 1991 to August 2004, 926 proposals for FDI of Rs. 413.68 billion, accounting for 16.7 percent of total

FDI approved. In terms of approval of FDI, the telecom sector, is the second largest, after the Power & Oil Refinery Sector.

3. Transportation Industry

The transportation industry includes the automobile industry, air and sea transport, passenger cars, auto ancillaries/ parts, ports etc. This sector occupies 3rd largest approval of FDI with 1777 proposals for FDI of Rs. 207.67 billion indicating 8.39 percent of total approvals during August 1991 to August 2004.

3.1 Automobile Industry: India's automotive components industry is the most lucrative sector for foreign direct investments. Hundreds of collaborations foreign direct investments have been made in recent years and there is tremendous potential for more. Markets are huge and growing both within India and overseas. The Automotive Components Manufacturers Association (ACMA) represents this sector in India.

Prospects and Opportunities

(i) India offers a relatively low cost production base and is strategically positioned as a launching base for third country export to Asia-Pacific and European markets.

(ii) Growth in road transport, increasing urbanization and privatization of public transport will translate into growing demand for commercial vehicles. During 2003-04, automobile production grew by 15.1 percent. This was on top of a growth of 18.6 percent during the previous year. Commercial vehicles witnessed a sharp growth of 35.1 percent, while passenger cars grew at 38.3 percent. A major development in Indian manufacturing has been the success in exports of automobile components and finished vehicles. The export of vehicles grew by 56 percent in 2003-04.[7]

(iii) The growth of commercial vehicles and passengers cars segments was assisted by the reduction in excise duty on passenger cars from 32 percent to 24 percent, reductions in tariffs, and improvements in the availability of retail credit. The liberalization of the norms for foreign investment and import of technology for manufacturing of vehicles, permission of 100 percent Foreign Direct Investment under automatic route in this sector have helped it to restructure, absorb new technologies, and get integrated into global production chains.

(iv) Automobile exports have increased to 4.8 lakhs units and registered robust growth of 55.9 percent during 2003-04. Over the last four years, the exports of automobiles (of all kinds) have grown by roughly three and a half times. Alongside the hectic growth in export of finished automobiles, there has also been a major upswing in the export of automobile components which grew by 26 percent from Rs.2,775 crore in 2001-02 to Rs. 3,496 crore in 2002-03 and further grew by 30.1 percent in the year 2003-04 to Rs. 4,550 crore. A host of major international automobile companies, increasingly harnessing India as a production base, either directly through FDI, or indirectly by contracting with firms operating in India.[8]

(v) Growth of consumer finance, leasing and hire-purchase options for vehicle dealers and buyers also increased demand.

(vi) A well developed components industry offers opportunities for sourcing. The scope is vast for foreign collaborations to produce branded models stressing on emission standards, fuel efficiency, advanced features and contemporary styles.

(vii) Automotive components manufactured in India are

of top quality and used as original components for vehicles made by such top international companies as General Motors, Mercedes, and Daewoo among others.

(viii) Japanese and British component manufacturers are already operating joint-ventures in India. American companies which have, or are planning to, set up plants in India include Delphi (an automotive components division of General Motors, USA), Delco Electronics, Textron and Magna International of Canada.

3.2 ***Roads and Highways:*** Massive investments are envisaged in widening and strengthening existing highways, reconstructing bridges, constructing expressways, upgradation initiatives especially in high density corridors. The following points are noteworthy regarding the policy of the Government:

(i) The National Highway Act, 1956 was amended in June 1995 to provide for a legal framework for private sector participation in road development.[9]

(ii) Private sector including foreign equity participation up to 100 percent in the highways is envisaged under Build Operate and Transfer (BOT) concept. As on November 30, 2002, over 20 projects costing around Rs. 6,822 crore have already been taken under BOT Scheme. This includes an agreement between the National Highways Authority of India (NHAI) and Construction Industry Development Board (CIDB) Inventure.

(iii) Automatic approval of foreign equity up to 74 percent for construction and maintenance of rail bridges, non-vehicular bridges, non-vehicular tunnels, rope ways and run ways and up to 100 percent for construction and maintenance of roads, highways, vehicular bridges, Government roads, vehicular tunnels, subject to foreign equity not exceeding Rs. 15 billion.

Prospects and Opportunities

(i) Investments worth US $ 34 billion is needed till 2005-06 for the development of National and State Highways. Out of this, the requirement of private sector investment is US $ 8.3 billion.

(ii) To encourage private sector participation, a Model Concession Agreement for major projects costing more than Rs. 100 crore has been finalized to undertake under BOT Scheme.

(iii) Projects relating to bypasses, bridges, and four laning of existing sections of National Highways, which on the basis of traffic density are financially viable and bankable, would be taken up through private sector participation.

(iv) Land acquisition, preliminary project preparation and operation of facilities will be undertaken by government at free of cost and free of encumbrances.

(v) Incentives offered include tax holidays, reduced custom duties on construction equipment etc.

3.3 *Ports and Shipping:* Ports are a key component of infrastructure sectors of the country, where the government has initiated various steps to expand the infrastructural and management innovations. In order to encourage private sector including foreign equity participation in development of port facilities, policies and procedures have been significantly liberalized.

Following areas have been identified for private sector participation and foreign investment:

1. Leasing out existing assets of the port,

2. Construction/creation of additional assets, such as:
   (a) Construction and operation of container terminals.
   (b) Construction and operation of bulk, break bulk, multipurpose and specialized cargo berths.
   (c) Warehousing, container freight stations, storage facilities and tank farms.
   (d) Carnage/handling equipment.
   (e) Setting up of captive power plants.
   (f) Dry docking and ship repair facilities.
3. Leasing of equipment for port handling and leasing of floating crafts from the private sector.
4. Pilotage.
5. Captive facilities for port based industries.[10]

Foreign equity participation up to 100 percent is allowed for BOT PROJECTS. Automatic approval up to 74 percent foreign equity for construction and maintenance of ports and harbors has been allowed.

The shipping, ship building and ship repair sectors offer a number of incentives and opportunities to investors. Facilities at par with 100 percent Export Oriented Units (EOUs) are also available for the ship repair industry.

Prospects and Opportunities

(i) Significant potential exists for expansion of infrastructural and management base of key ports. As against a total capacity of about 344 million tonnes on March 31, 2002, major ports handled about 288 million tones of cargo during 2001-02. Capacity addition is being planned according to projected traffic requirements. It is expected that by the end of the 10th Five Year Plan, total capacity of major ports would be 470 million tones.[11]

(ii) Considerable scope exists for construction, operation and maintenance of container terminals, cargo handling terminals, dry docking and ship repair facilities.

(iii) Opportunities also in areas of warehousing and storage, floating crafts, carnage services, dredging and general maintenance.

(iv) Options available for private participation include lease of assets and equipments; management contract for running port facilities or providing services; leasing of well-defined services; transfer of ownership to private parties. Under the scheme for private sector participation in major ports, 41 projects involving capacity addition of about 161 MTPA and an investment of about Rs. 10,810 crore by the private sector are at various stages of evaluation and implementation.

(v) The Government has already awarded the project for construction, management, and maintenance of two berths container terminal on BOT basis at Jawaharlal Nehru Port (JNPT) to a consortium headed by an Australian firm. Jawaharlal Nehru Port Trust, Navy Mumbai, signed an agreement with P&O Australia, for the development of a two berth container terminal of 600 meter quay length on "Build, Operate and Transfer" (BOT) basis for a period of 30 years in July 1997. The total investment on this project was about Rs. 900 crores. The new terminal was named as Nhava Sheva International Container Terminal (NSICT).[12]

3.4 Air Taxi Operation: The policy envisages encouraging private sector participation in air taxi operations. Foreign equity participation up to 40 percent and 100 percent NRI equity are allowed subject to the approval of FIPB. No direct or indirect equity participation by foreign airlines is allowed.

However, foreign equity up to 74 percent has been allowed in the airport infrastructure under the automatic approval route.

Following are guidelines for air taxi operations:

1. Air taxi operators shall be air carriers engaged in air transportation of persons, their baggage, and cargo.
2. Operations by the air taxi operators shall, except on routes not covered by any scheduled operator where an air taxi operator shall have the option to sell tickets to individual passengers and where prior permission of DGCA for each flight will not be necessary, be charter and non-scheduled operations. It shall be necessary to obtain authorization from the Director General of Civil Aviation (DGCA) for each individual flight and tickets will be sold to individual passengers.
3. Air taxi operations shall not be permitted to destinations outside India.

4. Electrical Equipment Sector (Including Software & Electronics)

The Electrical industry, constituting Electrical Equipment, Computer Software Industry, Electronics, Computer Hardware, and others attracted 7.56 percent of the total approved investment in the post-liberalization period since 1991-2004. This sector covers a majority of 5904 approvals with Rs. 187.26 billions during the period under review. The present low level of penetration provides tremendous opportunities for immediate market expansion in almost every segment of electronics.

Prospects and Opportunities

(i) Consumer electronics is a high growth sector, which also has an active replacement market.

(ii) Control and industrial electronics face increasing

demand from projects in power, refineries, petrochemicals, cement etc. Demand for test and measuring instruments will be growing with the rapid development of communications.

(iii) A strong base exists for the manufacture of microcomputers, mini-computers, and mainframe computer system; workstations and other manufactured products like floppy disk drivers, printers, CRT terminals, keyboards and plotters.

(iv) In the software area, India has the third largest pool of software writing talent with world-class skills and at relatively low cost, thus, providing tremendous outsourcing opportunities.

(v) The electronic component sector provides opportunities for joint ventures and contract manufacturing activities in areas like semi-conductors, ICs, chip capacitors, PCBs, etc.

(vi) The policy provides foreign equity participation up to 100 percent and several incentives for EOUs, EHTPs, and STPs.

(vii) A high-powered National Task Force on IT and Software Development were set up by the Prime Minister's Office on May 22, 1998, under the Chairmanship of the Deputy Chairman of Planning Commission. The first report of the task force on IT Action Plan has brought about a new paradigm in setting up IT software and hardware manufacturing units for making them viable for meeting the local demands as well as exports by creating a policy ambience and investment climate in the country comparable to those in Taiwan, Malaysia, and Singapore.

(viii) The Indian IT and Electronics industry recorded a

robust growth of 21.6 percent during 2003-04. In absolute terms, production has increased to Rs. 97,000 crore and 1,14,650 crore during the year 2002-03 and 2003-04 respectively, as compared with Rs. 80,124 crore during 2000-01. In spite of global difficulties in the Information, Communication, and Technology (ICT) Sector, the export of Indian software and services, being estimated to have increased to Rs. 55,500 crores in 2003-04, a growth rate of about 20.4 percent in rupee terms and 28 percent in dollar terms.[13]

5. *Service Sector*

During the post-liberalization period 1991-2004, this sector gained 1378 proposals for FDI approvals with Rs. 165.82 billion, accounting for 6.70 percent of the total amount of FDI approved during the period. The Service sector comprises of Financial/Non-Financial/ Banking Services, Insurance, Hospital & Diagnostic Centers, Research & Development, Education, and other Services.

Prospects and Opportunities

(i) Considerable scope exists for providing modern and innovative service packages in the financial sector. The most promising, sub-sectors of the financial services market are capital markets, venture banking, consumer financing, mutual funds, and infrastructure financing.

(ii) Local financial institutions such as the Industrial Development Bank of India (IDBI), Industrial Credit, and Investment Corporation of India (ICICI), Industrial Finance Corporation of India (IFCI), Unit Trust of India (UTI), and the Shipping Credit and Investment Corporation of India (SCICI) have raised billions through the most sophisticated financial instruments including Deep Discount Bonds.

(iii) The Insurance sector nationalized since 1971, and opened up to private and foreign investors. Foreign investment and access to foreign capital by domestic companies has been progressively liberalized in India.

5.4. Inflows of FDI: Sector-wise Analysis

Table 5.3 presents the sector-wise break-up of inflows of Foreign Direct Investment (FDI) in India during the period January 1991 to March 2004. The study of the sector-wise analysis of inflow of FDI is taken up with a view to identify the prominent industrial sector, which has attracted highest/lowest amount of inflow of FDI during the period under review.

TABLE 5.3

Sector-wise Total Inflows of FDI
(During January 1991 to March 2004)

(Amount Rupees in Crore (US $ in billion)

Rank	*Sector*	*Amount of FDI Inflows*	*Percentage of Total FDI Inflows (in rupees terms)*
1.	Electrical Equipment (including computer software & electronics)	13,930(3.32)	14.50
2.	Transportation	11,517(2.78)	11.99
3.	Telecommunications	10,725(2.56)	11.17
4.	Energy – of which Power, Oil Refining	9,802(2.32)	10.21
5.	Services Sector	8,134(2.04)	8.47
6.	Chemicals (other than Fertilizers)	5,692(1.49)	5.93
7.	Food & Food Processing	4,346(1.09)	4.53
8.	Metallurgical Industries	1,254(0.31)	1.31
9.	Textiles	1,163(0.31)	1.21
10.	Hotels & Tourism	899(0.14)	0.87

Source: Compiled from Economic Survey 2003-04, Government of India, p. 146.Figures in brackets indicate amount in billion dollars.

Table 5.3 indicates that the majority of the inflows during the period of January 1991 to August 2004, had been in Electrical Equipments sector, which has attracted Rs. 13,930 crores (US $3.32 billion) of total inflow of FDI forming 14.5 percent. The Transportation sector is the next priority sector, which has attracted Rs. 11,517 crore (US $ 2.78 billion) accounting for 11.99 percent. On the other hand the Telecommunications sector attracted Rs. 10,725 crore (US $2.56 billion) sharing 11.17 percent of total FDI inflows during the period under review. The Metallurgical Industrial sector, followed by Textiles Industry and Hotels & Tourism sectors are the least attractive sectors for Foreign Direct Investment, since they have attracted only Rs. 1,254 crore (US $ 0.31 billion), Rs. 1,163 crore (US $ 0.31 billion) and Rs. 899 crore (US $ 0.14 billion): accounting for 1.31 percent, 1.21 percent and 0.87 percent respectively of total inflows of FDI. Thus, the analysis highlights that the Electrical Equipment sector is the most priority sector for FDI, which claimed maximum number of FDI approvals. Accordingly, it must be noted that the investment in this sector is likely to shoot up in coming years and this sector will further dominate the Foreign Direct Investments.

REFERENCES

1. Investing in India, FDI Policy and Procedures, September 2004, Published by Secretariat for Industrial Assistance, Department of Industrial Policy & Promotion, Ministry of Commerce & Industry, Government of India, New Delhi. Annex. I.
2. Government of India, Ministry of Finance & Company Affairs, Economic Division, *Economic Survey 2002-03*, p. 186.
3. Government of India, Ministry of Finance & Company Affairs, *Economic Survey 2002-03*, p. 181.
4. Government of India, Planning Commission, *Ninth Five Year Plan (1997-2002)*, Volume II, p. 869.
5. Government of India, Ministry of Finance & Company Affairs, Economic Division, *Economic Survey 2002-03*, p. 187.
6. *Ibid.*, p. 189.

7. Government of India, Ministry of Finance & Company Affairs, *Economic Survey 2003-04*, p. 134.
8. *Ibid.*, Table 7.5, p. 134.
9. Ninth Five Year Plan (1997-2002), *op cit.*, Volume II, p. 801.
10. *Ibid.*, pp. 816-817.
11. Government of India, *Economic Survey 2002-03*, p.196.
12. *Ibid.*, 'Institutional innovations at Jawaharlal Nehru Port Trust', Box 9.10, p. 197.
13. Government of India, Ministry of Finance, *Economic Survey 2003-04*, tables 7.12 & 7.13, p. 140.

6

Prospects and Opportunities of FDI

6.1. Introduction

Foreign Direct Investment (FDI) in India has grown substantially in the last decade following the liberalization of Indian economy in 1991. FDI gives opportunities to Indian Industry for technological upgradation, gaining access to global managerial skills and practices, optimizing utilization of human, and natural resources and competing internationally with higher efficiency. Most importantly, FDI is central for India's integration into global production chains, which involve production by multinational corporations spread across locations all over the world.

India has one of the most liberal policy frameworks for FDI and foreign technology transfer. FDI up to 100 per cent is permitted under the automatic route in the most sectors. Entry under automatic route only requires post-entry notification and no prior approval.

In line with its mission of formulating a transparent investor friendly environment, economic reforms programme; policy and procedures governing foreign investment; and technology transfer have been significantly simplified and streamlined. Today, Foreign Direct Investment (FDI) is freely allowed in all sectors of the country including the services sector through automatic route except a few sensitive sectors like defence, atomic energy, real estate, etc. Under this, the companies need only to inform the Reserve Bank of India within 30 days of receipt of funds and issuance of shares to the foreign investors. Proposals not falling on the automatic route are considered by the Foreign Investment Promotion Board (FIPB) in a time-bound and transparent manner.

6.2. Incentives for Foreign Direct Investment

A series of incentives have been announced to promote investments in India. These include import of capital goods of concessional customs duty (subject to fulfillment of certain export obligations), liberalization of external commercial borrowing norms, tax holiday, and concessional tax treatment for certain sectors. In addition, several State Governments offer incentives, such as subsidy on fixed capital, loans of concessional rates of interest, and attractive power rates. While several incentives are project specific, a number of firms have been successful in negotiating favourable investment terms with the State Governments concerned.

Since the initiation of the economic liberalization process in 1991, sectors such as automobiles, chemicals, food processing, oil and natural gas, petrochemicals, electronics, power, services and telecommunications have attracted considerable investments. Today, in the changed investment climate, India offers exciting business opportunities in virtually every sector of the economy.

6.3. Industrial Growth During 2003-04

Growth in the industrial sector in 2003-04 continued to be healthy. The Index of Industrial Production (IIP) grew by 6.9 per cent. The major element of the buoyancy in industrial growth was the manufacturing sector with 80 per cent weight in IIP. Manufacturing sector witnessed growth of 7.2 per cent, while mining and electricity grew by 5.1 per cent, and 5.0 per cent, respectively.

The consumer durables sector (refrigerators, electric fans, television, motor cycles and cars) witnessed a complete turnaround. It grew by 11.6 per cent during 2003-04 compared with a decline of 6.3 per cent during the previous year. Lower interest rates, the availability of retail finance, and the strong monsoon are among the influencing factors for this sharp growth in this sector.

Growth in the capital goods sector was significant. Production in this sector increased by 12.7 per cent. In this, use-based category, both components-transport equipment & Parts and machinery and equipment other than transport equipment – witnessed high growth. The former grew at 17.0 per cent, while the latter grew at 15.2 per cent in 2003-04.

At a two digit level classification, as many as 12 out 17 industry groups have showed positive growth during 2003-04. Transport equipment and parts grew at 17.0 per cent; followed by paper & paper products, printing, publishing and allied industries (15.9 per cent); machinery and equipment other than transport equipments (15.2 per cent); beverages, tobacco and related products (9.4 per cent); basic metals and alloy industries (9.1 per cent); basic chemicals and chemical products except products of petroleum & coal products (8.2 per cent); wood & wood products, and furniture and fixtures (6.8 per cent). The industry groups that witnessed negative growth are leather and leather & fur products (-4.3 per cent), jute and other vegetable fiber textiles (except cotton) (-4.2 per cent), followed by textile products including wearing apparel (-3.8 per cent) and cotton textiles (-3.3 per cent). However, the key industries of construction sector – both steel and cement registered a positive growth of 6.9 per cent and 6.1 per cent respectively during 2003-04.[41]

6.4. Sector-wise Prospects and Opportunities

As the Foreign Direct Investment influences the Industrial

Production as well as industrial development, it is significant to study in detail the most sought after sectors of Indian Economy where huge potential for foreign investment policy to invite huge investments as also the special promotion drives are discussed.

1. The Power Sector

1.1. Investment Policy

The Government's power sector policy seeks to attract significant private sector investment in the Indian power sector. The key initiatives include:

- Private sector permitted to set up coal, gas or liquid based thermal projects, hydel projects and wind or solar projects of any size.
- Foreign equity participation up to 100 per cent in the power sector has been brought under automatic route (RBI route) approval for generation, transmission, and distribution of power generated in hydro-electric, oil gas based and coal/lignite based power projects.
- Role of the Central Government is minimized and the State Government and State Electricity Boards (SEBs) are empowered to negotiate directly with developers, facilitating speedy clearances for the investors.
- Ancillary sectors such as coal have been significantly deregulated.
- Enactment of Energy Conservation Act, 2001.
- Electricity Act notified on June 2, 2003.

1.2. Reforms and Restructuring of Power Sector

- Twenty one states namely, Orissa, Haryana, Andhra Pradesh, Uttar Pradesh, Karnataka, West Bengal, Tamil Nadu, Punjab, Delhi, Gujarat, Madhya Pradesh, Arunachal Pradesh, Maharashtra, Rajasthan, Himachal

Pradesh, Assam, Chhattisgarh, Uttaranchal, Goa, Bihar and Jharkhand have either constituted or notified the constitution of SERC, SERCs of Orissa, Andhra Pradesh, Uttar Pradesh, Maharashtra, Gujarat, Haryana, Karnataka, Rajasthan, Delhi, Madhya Pradesh, Himachal Pradesh, West Bengal and Punjab have issued tariff orders.

- The State Electricity Boards of Orissa, Haryana, Andhra Pradesh, Uttar Pradesh, Karnataka, Rajasthan, Madhya Pradesh, and Delhi have enacted their State Electricity Reforms Acts which provide, inter-alia, for unbundling, corporatisation of SEBs, setting up of SERCs etc. The SEBs of Orissa, Haryana, Andhra Pradesh, Karnataka, Uttar Pradesh, Rajasthan, Uttaranchal, Delhi and Madhya Pradesh have been unbundled/corporatised. Distribution has been privatized in Orissa and recently in Delhi.

1.3. Potential

Demand is expected to grow to 782 billion KwH by 2006-07. During 10th Five Year Plan (2002-2007) & 11th Five Year Plan (2007-2012), a total capacity addition of 1,13,000 MW is envisaged, entailing an investment of Rs. 5,750 billion in power generation, transmission and distribution. The installed capacity of power generation in the country as on December 2002 is 1,06,812 MW. Another initiative has been taken to develop 50,000 MW of hydro-electric power.

The other specific project opportunities expected in the near future include:

- Power Trading Corporation (PTC) has been incorporated, for the purpose of buying power from mega power projects under long-term Power Purchase Agreements (PPAs) and selling the power to the beneficiary states also under long-term PPAs.

- Transmission projects for power transfer area available for competitive bidding by the Central Transmission Utility (Power Grid) and State Transmission Utilities (SEBs/Grid Corporations). The transmission system projects are being identified for competitive bidding by the Central and State Transmission Utilities.
- Liquid Fuel Based Projects using Low Sulphur Heavy Stock (LSHS), Furnace Oil (FO), Heavy Petroleum Stock (HPS), Naphtha, Vacuum Residue, Condensate and Orimulsion are permitted by the Government. Import of Liquefied Natural Gas (LNG) is also being considered for setting up large capacity combined cycle power plants.
- Attracting investment opportunities are likely to develop in distribution of power as several State Governments have agreed to allow the energy of the private Sector in distribution.

2. *Non-Conventional Energy Sources*

Foreign Investors can enter joint venture with an Indian Partner for financial and technical collaboration and also for setting up of renewable energy based power generation projects. The liberalized foreign investment approval regime is aimed at facilitating foreign investment and transfer of technology through joint ventures. 100 per cent foreign investment as equity is permissible. Government of India is encouraging foreign investors to set up renewable energy based power generation projects on Build-Own-Operate basis.

Potential

In India, investment opportunities are available for the following types of investors and users:

- Investment by foreign investors for manufacturing of renewable energy systems and devices based on: Wind, Solar Photo-Voltaic, Solar Thermal, Small

Hydro, Biomass, Co-generation, Geothermal, Tidal and Urban and Industrial Wastes for their utilization in India and also for exports to developing and Third World countries.

- Investors can participate in Generation, Transmission and Distribution; 78 per cent Hydro potential to be harnessed; Shelf generation projects identified; Convergence of Transmission, Telecom and Information Technology; Renovation and Modernization; Cross Country Grids; Efficiency improvement in generation; Reduction of T&D losses: Energy Audit/Metering; and Energy Conservation and Demand Side Management.

3. *Oil and Natural Gas*

3.1. Investment Policy

The Indian Government has announced significant policy initiatives to attract foreign investment:

- Indian Oil and Gas fields are open for investment by the domestic private and foreign entrepreneurs under the framework of the New Exploration Licensing Policy (NELP) set out by Government of India in 1998.
- FDI is permitted up to 100 per cent in discovered small and medium sized fields through competitive bidding.
- Refining Industry has been delicensed. The demand for petroleum products is estimated to grow at annual rate of around 6 per cent to reach the level of 370 million tones per annum in 2025. The total investment in refining is estimated at around US $ 60 billion by 2025. The investment in marketing infrastructure during the above period is estimated to be around US $ 32 billion. Tremendous opportunity for investment exists in these sectors in the years to come

in which the private sector including the foreign companies can set up their own projects or through joint ventures with public sector companies.

- For petroleum products and pipeline sector, FDI is permitted up to 100 per cent through automatic route.
- FDI up to 100 per cent permitted for natural gas/ LNG pipeline with prior Government approval.
- Subject to the policy laid down by Government, marketing of transportation fuels (viz. MS, HSD, AT) can be permitted to a company investing or proposing to invest at least Rs. 2000 crore in exploration, refining, pipelines or terminals in the oil and gas sector of India.
- FDI is permitted up to 100 per cent on automatic route in infrastructure related to marketing and marketing of petroleum products.
- FDI up to 100 per cent is permitted for purpose of market study and formulation, and for investment or financing.
- For actual trading and marketing, minimum 26 per cent Indian equity is required over 5 years.

3.2. *Potential*

Total sedimentary basins, including deep water 3.14 million sq.kms. (41 per cent of this is still unexplored).

Large Demand for Natural Gas

Year	*Demand (MSCMD)*
2002	151
2007	231
2012	313
2025	391

MSCMD: Million Standard Cubic Meters per Day

Development of Infrastructure

	1998-99	*2024-25*
Product Pipelines Capacity (MMT)	28.55	166
Port Capacity (MMT)	111	361

The present domestic gas supply is only 65 MSCMD. The increasing demand-supply gap is expected to be met by imports of LNG and pipeline gas.

In the refining sector, opportunities exist for investment in public sector oil companies that are divesting their equity to the public. Additional refining capacity of over 40 million tonnes per annum has been installed in the last year, there is scope for further installation of 40 million tonnes per annum to meet India's estimated domestic petroleum products demand of 148.9 million tonnes per annum in 2010.

However, the foreign investors can participate in LNG production and marketing/import terminals; Regional Gas trade from West, North & South/South-East Asia; Development of non-conventional sources like Shale oil, Coal bed methane, Gas hydrates; Refineries; and Pipeline network.

4. Coal and Lignite Sector

The impact of Indian Government's Investment Policy in the Coal and Lignite Sector is presented below:

- Private Indian Companies setting up or operating power projects as well as coal or lignite mines for captive consumption are allowed FDI up to 100 per cent.
- 100 per cent FDI is allowed for setting up coal processing plants subject to the condition that the company shall not do coal mining and shall not sell washed coal or sized coal from its coal processing plants in the open market and shall supply the washed

or sized coal to those parties who are supplying raw coal to coal processing plants for washing or sizing.

- FDI up to 74 per cent is allowed for exploration or mining of coal or lignite for captive consumption.

In all the above cases, FDI is allowed up to 50 per cent under the automatic route subject to the condition that such investment shall not exceed 49 per cent of the equity of a PSU.

5. *Telecommunications*

5.1. *Investment Policy*

Incentives for foreign collaborations coupled with an attractive trade and investment policy have made India an attractive market for telecom equipment suppliers and service providers.

- No industrial license required for setting up manufacturing units for telecom equipment.
- In Basic, Cellular, value added services and global mobile personal communications by satellite, FDI is limited to 49 per cent subject to licensing and security requirements and adherence by the companies (who are investing and the companies in which the investment is being made) to the license conditions for foreign equity cap and lock-in period for transfer and addition of equity and other license provisions.
- The Central Finance Minister has proposed in the Budget 2004-05 for enhancement of FDI sectoral caps in Telecommunication from 49 per cent to 74 per cent.
- In ISPs with gateways, ratio-paging and end-to-end bandwidth, FDI is permitted up to 74 per cent with FDI, beyond 49 per cent requiring Government

approval. These services would be subject to licensing and security requirements.

- No equity cap is applicable to manufacturing activities.
- FDI up to 100 per cent is allowed for the following activities in the telecom sector:
  - (a) ISPs not providing gateways (both for satellite and submarine cables);
  - (b) Infrastructure Providers providing dark fibre (IP Category I);
  - (c) Electronic Mail; and
  - (d) Voice Mail.

The above would be subject to the following conditions:

(a) FDI up to 100 per cent is allowed subject to the condition that such companies would divest 26 per cent of their equity in favour of Indian public in 5 years, if these companies are listed in other parts of the world.

(b) The above services would be subject to licensing and security requirements, wherever required.

(c) Proposals for FDI beyond 49 per cent shall be considered by Foreign Investment Promotion Board (FIPB) on case to case basis.

- Unified license for telecommunication services permitting licenses to provide all telecommunication/telegraph services covering various geographical areas using any technologies and unified access (basic & cellular) services permitted. Licenses to provide basic and cellular service use any technology in a defined area also introduced.

5.2. *Potential*

5.2.1. Cellular Mobile Services

The country is divided into 23 service areas consisting of 19 telecom circle service areas the 4 Metro Service Areas for providing Cellular Mobile Telephone Services (CMTSs). 78 licenses have been issued to 25 companies to provide Cellular Mobile Telephone Service.

India is witnessing the fastest growth in cellular subscribers with addition to over 10 million cellular subscribers during the period of 6 months between April-September, 2003. The cellular subscribers are increased by 20 million during the year 2003-04. The cellular subscribers are expected to increase by 100 million in the next 3-4 years.

5.2.2. Basic Telephone Services

As per NTP 99, Basic Telephone Service license has been opened to private sector without any restriction on the number of players. The Basic service license is issued telecom circle-wise. Basic service providers are permitted to establish last mile linkages, carry their own long distance traffic (within their service area), provide direct interconnectivity and share infrastructure with other basic service providers. There exists large potential for providing telephone connections (estimated at 75 million by 2005 and 175 million by 2010). Till date 33 Basic service license has been issued.

5.2.3. National Long Distance Services (NLDs)

NLDs has been opened to the private sector without any restrictions on the number of operators. The license for NLDO is issued on non-exclusion basis, for a period of 20 years, extendable by 10 years at one time, for inter-circle long distance operation within the territorial jurisdiction of India.

The applicant must be an Indian company registered under the Indian Companies Act, 1956 with a minimum paid up equity capital of Rs. 250 crores. The promoters of the applicant company shall have a combined net worth of Rs. 2500 crores.

5.2.4. International Long Distance Services (ILDs)

International Long Distance Service has been opened to private operator's w.e.f. 1.4.2002 without any restriction on the number of operators. The license for ILD Services shall be issued on a non-exclusion basis, initially for a period of 20 years, with automatic extension by a period of 5 years subject to satisfactory performance in accordance with the terms and conditions of the license particularly in regard to Quality of Service. The applicant company must have a network of Rs. 25 crores.

5.2.5. Internet Services

There is no restriction on the number of Internet Service Providers (ISPs). No license fee is payable up to October 31, 2003; thereafter a token license fee of Re. 1 per annum is payable. ISPs are free to fix their own tariff. ISPs have been permitted to establish their own international gateways for carrying internet traffic. Internet Service Provider's (ISPs) licenses have been granted to about 555 licenses, out of which about 200 licensees are already providing internet services. The number of internet connections in the country is estimated at 4 million.

5.2.6. Global Mobile Personal Communication by Satellite (GMPCS)

There is no restriction on the number of GMPCS licenses and licenses are issued on first-cum-first-served basis. Gateways for GMPCS are to be located in India and operation and maintenance of the same is to be with an organization designated by the Government.

5.2.7. Other Value Added Services

As the telecommunications and Information Technology

(IT) infrastructure in the country is expanding, there is a surge in demand for a range of value added services. The scheme for value added services have been considerably liberalized. These services include ratio paging, public mobile radio trunking, and domestic data using VSATs. Evolving of new services – Tele-education, Tele-medicine, Tele-banking, Call Centre – is catching up with the Indian industry and has recently witnessed significant investments from domestic and foreign investors.

6. *Information Technology*

The Government on October 15, 1999 has established a separate Ministry of Information Technology. The IT Ministry will be primarily responsible for all policy legislation relating to information technology, knowledge based industries, internet, e-commerce, and IT education and IT-based education and development of electronics, computers and creation of Silicon valleys in India.

Information Technology Act, 2000 has been enacted. This Act provides a legal framework for recognition of electronic contracts, prevention of computer crimes, electronic filling of documents etc. It also amends certain related laws to provide a fully sufficient legal environment for conduct of business in cyberspace. A Cyber Controller would control the digital signature mechanism and the entire law implementation.

6.1. Investment Policy

- Automatic route for foreign equity up to 100 per cent in software and electronics. Automatic approval accorded for foreign technology agreements in all areas of electronics except aerospace and defence.
- 100 per cent foreign investment permitted in units set up exclusively for exports. Such units can be set up under any one of the schemes, namely Electronic Hardware Technology Parks (EHTPs), Software

Technology Parks (STPs), Free-Trade Zones (FTZs) and 100 per cent Export Oriented Units (EOUs).

- A number of states have developed their own IT policy to promote the development of software sector.
- Tax holiday up to 2010 for IT units to be set up in Software Technology Parks.
- Tax holiday to R&D for up to 10 years with 125 per cent tax concession.
- Simplification and liberalization of Export & Import Policy.

6.2. Potential

India is the preferred location for software vendors for its quality and cost. India has strong UNIX base which provides opportunity for the development of products for internal based applications. Further, India has global connectivity with international dialing facility from over 13,220 locations. Leased/Switched high-speed data links from major centers through STPs and VSNL for point-to-point communication are also available. Internet connectivity is provided through several networks. Abundant investment opportunities exist in the following thrust areas in India:

(i) Communication infrastructure;

(ii) Optic Fibre Cable;

(iii) Gateways;

(iv) Satellite based Communication;

(v) Wireless;

(vi) Software Development;

(vii) IT-enabled Services;

(viii) IT-enabled Education;

(ix) Data Centers and Server Farms.

7. Pharma and Chemicals

7.1. Investment Policy

The Pharmaceutical Policy-2002 is aimed at the ensuring abundant availability at reasonable prices within the country of good quality essential pharmaceutical of mass consumption, in addition to strengthening the indigenous capability for cost effective quality production. Drug policy is aimed at ensuring abundant availability of essential and life saving drugs of quality at reasonable prices, in addition to strengthening the indigenous production base:

- Control of prices is achieved through the Drugs (Price Control) Order, 1995 wherein 74 bulk drugs are presently price controlled. The number of drugs under price control will be reduced under the new Drugs (Price Control) Orders to be issued in accordance with the Pharmaceutical Policy-2002.
- Industrial licensing has been abolished except for production of products of recombinant DNA technology, bulk drugs requiring in-vivo use of nucleic acids as active principal and specific cell/tissue targeted drug formulations.
- FDI up to 100 per cent is permitted on the automatic route for manufacture of drugs and pharmaceuticals, provided the activity does not attract compulsory licensing or involve use of recombinant DNA technology and specific cell/tissue targeted formulations. FDI proposals for the manufacture of licensable drugs and pharmaceuticals and bulk drugs produced by recombinant DNA technology, and specific cell/tissue targeted formulations will require prior Government approval.

7.2. Potential in Pharma Sector

Indian Pharmaceutical industry has shown tremendous

progress in terms of infrastructure development, technology base and range of production. The industry's strength lies in world class technology, cost effective production of 90 per cent of bulk drugs and all required formulation, rich bio-diversity, competitive R&D costs and over 20 per cent growth rate in exports. With an increasing number of bulk drugs going off patent, and the capability of Indian scientists in process technology, the share of Indian pharma products in world market is expected to rise further.

India derives its technological strengths in pharmaceutical sector on the following bases:

- Self reliance displayed by the production of 90 per cent of bulk drugs and almost the entire range of formulations within the country.
- Low R&D costs.
- Low cost drug formulations for national health progress.
- Strength of National Laboratories.
- Innovative Scientific Manpower.
- Several MNCs conducting clinical trials in India.
- Increasing balance of trade in Pharma Sector.

7.3. Potential in Chemical Sector

The Chemical industry in India, has well established and recorded a steady growth in the overall industrial scenario. The chemical and allied industries have been amongst the faster growing segments of the Indian Industry, producing a wide range of products including organic and inorganic chemicals, dyestuffs, paints, pesticides and specially chemicals. The industry has withstood the challenges from the international market and has seen continued growth in its exports.

The chemical sector together, accounts for over 11 per cent of the total Indian exports. With its established expertise in the IT sector, with focused attention on R&D and its ability to produce high quality products at globally competitive prices, India will play a crucial role in the knowledge-based industries in the coming years.

The Petrochemical sector has been witnessing a growth of over 12 per cent in the last decade, which is about twice the growth rate of Gross Domestic Product. Significant capacity additions during 1990s have reduced import dependency. The total consumption of major petrochemicals (including polymers, elastomers, synthetic fibres and surfactants) during 2001-02 was about 6 million tones. However, the per capita consumption of commodity polymers and synthetic fibres has been 3.8 kgs and 1.7 kg respectively, which is much below the world average of 19.7 kgs and 3.7 kgs.

It is envisaged that the demand of polymers would grow at the rate of about 12-13 per cent and synthetic fibres at about 6 per cent in the current decade. To meet the growing demand, additional capacity of about 10 million tones of synthetic fibre would have to be created. The rapidly growing demand and huge captive domestic market gives an opportunity for investment of over Rs. 70,000 crores.

8. Biotechnology

The setting up of a separate Department of Biotechnology (DBT) under the Ministry of Science and Technology in 1986 has given a new impetus to the development of modern biology and biotechnology in India. In more than a decade of its existence, the department has promoted a accelerated pace of development of biotechnology in the country.

In India, concerted efforts for over a decade in R&D in the identified areas of modern biology and biotechnology have paid rich dividends. The proven technologies at the laboratory level have been scaled up and demonstrated in field. Patenting of innovations, technology transfer to industries and close interaction with them have given a new direction to biotechnology research.

Necessary guidelines for transgenic plants, recombinant vaccines and drugs have also been evolved. A strong base of indigenous capabilities has been created. India's inherent strengths are:

- Rich Biodiversity;
- Large reservoirs of valuable diagnostic and clinical data;
- Vibrant and inventive pharmaceutical industry;
- World class network of educational and research institutions;
- Known strengths in mathematics, logic and computational skills; and
- Super Computing and Software strengths enable extensive use of bio-informatics in new drug discovery.

Potential

- Biotechnology industry serves as a research arm to Agritech, and Pharma industry which increases potential for strategic alliances.
- Joint Ventures in Biotechnology industry based new drugs/pharmaceuticals.
- Global trends show that all large pharmaceutical players are putting their money in healthcare for long term benefits. It is expected that nearly half the drugs in the next decade would be biotech products.
- Tremendous potential in agri-business exists in Indian economy.

- There is a potential for transgenic seeds, bio-fertilizers, etc.
- Number of small firms is high, knowledge based, research intensive industry, with low capital requirements.
- Bilateral and Multilateral International collaboration in R&D specially for knowledge base and product and process development.

Past Consumption of Biotech Products in India and Future Consumption Estimates

(US $ million)

Sl. No.	*Particulars of Biotech Sub-sectors*	*Annual Consumption 1999*	*Future Consumption Estimate 2005*	*Future Consumption Estimate 2010*
1.	Human & Animal Health Care Products	670.41	821.40	1708.49
2.	Agriculture (including seeds)	533.79	671.62	1437.80
3.	Industrial Products	563.32	662.79	978.81
4.	Other Biotech products	21.62	30.23	145.02
	Total	1789.14	2186.04	4270.12

Source: Confederation of Indian Industry, New Delhi.

The field of biotechnology both for new innovations and applications would form a major research and commercial endeavor for socio-economic development in this decade.

9. Roads

9.1. Investment Policy

Government initiatives for promotion of this key infrastructure sector include:

- FDI up to 100 per cent under automatic route is permitted in projects for construction and maintenance of roads, highways, vehicular bridges, toll roads, vehicular tunnels, ports and harbours.

- Private parties allowed to develop service and rest areas along the roads entrusted to them.
- The National Highways Authority of India (NHAI) is permitted to participate in equity in Build Own Transfer (BOT) projects up to 30 per cent.
- Investors in identified highway projects permitted to recover investment by way of collection of tolls for specified sections and periods.
- 10 years of Corporate Tax Holiday can be availed within 20 years of commission of the project.

9.2. Potential

The Government of India has taken up Highways Development Programme to develop world's largest ever highways project. However, investments worth an estimated US $ 34 billion needed till 2005-06 for the development of National and State Highways. Of this figure, the requirement of private sector investment is US $ 8.3 billion.

9.3. Opportunities Exist in

- Construction of highways, bridges, railway-over-bridge, elevated section in urban areas, interchanges, bypasses, etc.
- Highway related en route activities like restaurants, motels, and rest/parking areas as many be decided by the implementing agency.
- Consulting firms: feasibility studies, detailed project preparation & construction supervision.
- Construction Industry: Contracts range up to US $ 50 million.
- Investors: BOT projects on BOT and Annuity basis, participation in bonds and direct borrowings.
- Equipment manufacturers: State-of-the-art technology

development, construction equipment exempted from import duties.

10. Ports

The principal legislations governing Indian Ports are the Indian Ports Act, 1908, and The Major Ports Trust Act, 1963. The Indian Government has announced the following measures to promote foreign investment in the Ports Sector:

- Foreign equity up to 100 per cent is now permissible in construction and maintenance of ports and harbours and in projects providing support services to water transport, such as operation and maintenance of piers, loading and discharging of vehicles, under the automatic route.
- Open tenders will be invited for private sector participation on a BOT basis.
- Major ports have been permitted to form joint ventures with foreign ports, minor ports and other companies to attract new technology, better management practices, implementation of development schemes, and creation of optional port infrastructure.
- Ten year tax holiday to be availed of during the initial fifteen years has been provided under section 80 IA of the Income Tax Act, 1961.

The measures are aimed at attracting new technology, fostering strategic alliances with minor ports to create an optimal port infrastructure and enhancing private sector confidence in the funding of ports.

Potential

The areas identified for privatization or investments by the private sector include:

(i) Leasing out of existing port assets;

(ii) Creation of additional assets;
(iii) Construction or operation of container terminals;
(iv) Construction or operation of bulk, breck-bulk;
(v) Multipurpose and specialized cargo berths;
(vi) Warehousing;
(vii) Container freight stations;
(viii) Storage;
(ix) Facilities and tank farms carnage and handling;
(x) Equipment setting up captive power plants;
(xi) Dry docking and ship repair facilities;
(xii) Leasing of equipment and floating craft from the private sector;
(xiii) Pilotages; and
(xiv) Captive facilities for port based industries.

11. Civil Aviation

The monopoly of public sector air carriers ended with the repealing of the Air Corporation Act, 1953 on March 1, 1994. The Government of India initiated the following investment policy:

- Foreign equity participation in airport infrastructure is permitted up to 74 per cent with automatic approvals and up to 100 per cent with special permission. Such participation could also be by foreign airports authorities.
- FDI up to 40 per cent and NRIs/OCBs investment up to 100 per cent is permitted in domestic air-transport services.
- The Budget 2004-05 increased the sectoral caps for FDI in Civil Aviation from 40 per cent to 49 per cent.
- 100 per cent FDI allowed in Airports; beyond 74 per cent requiring Government approval.

- No direct and indirect equity participation by foreign airlines allowed in domestic air-transport services.
- Foreign Financial Institutions allowed to hold equity in the domestic air transport sector provided they do not have foreign airlines as their shareholders.
- Foreign investors allowed having representation (up to 33 per cent of total) on Board of Directors of a domestic airline company.
- Minimum fleet size for a scheduled operator rose from the existing 3 aircraft to 5.
- Management contract with a foreign airline is not permitted.

Potential

- Modernization and restructure of international Airports at Delhi and Mumbai through formation of joint venture between the Airport Authority of India and private player, to be selected through an international competitive bidding process.
- Important private sector aided projects: New airport near Kochi (US $ 85.7 million), projects for development of new airports at Bangalore and Mumbai with private sector participation.
- Restructuring & Privatization through long term lease. Other airports aided under private sector are: Ahmedabad airport, Amritsar airport upgradation, Chennai cargo-complex, new international terminal and a second runway for Delhi airport, runway extension and international block for Jaipur airport.

12. Food Processing

12.1. Investment Policy

The Government of India's major policy initiations regarding investment in Food Processing sector is analyzed below:

- Automatic approval (including foreign technology agreements within specified norms) is permitted for FDI up to 100 per cent equity of Indian companies, for all food and beverages except for alcoholic beverages and items reserved for small scale sector.
- Foreign equity ownership of up to 24 per cent is allowed even in items reserved for small scale sector. An industrial license carrying a mandatory export obligation of 50 per cent would be required for equity beyond 24 per cent equity.
- No industrial license required for food and agro processing industries except for alcoholic beverages and items reserved for small scale sector, which are: Pickles & Chutneys, Bread, Pasty, Hard boiled sugar candy, Rapeseed Oil, Mustard Oil, Sesame Oil, Ground nut Oil, Sweetened Cashew nut products, Ground and processed spices other than spice oil and Oleoresin spices, Tapioca sago and flour.
- Food processing industry declared a priority sector. New Exim Policy places greater thrust on Agro based Industries.
- Exclusive Agri Export Zones set up for end to end development for export of specific products from geographically contiguous areas.
- Setting up of food parks to enable food and beverage units to use capital intensive facilities, such as cold storage, warehouse, quality control labs, effluent treatment plant etc.
- Agro based 100 per cent Export Oriented Units allowed sales up to 50 per cent in Domestic Tariff Area.
- Imports of capital goods and raw materials permitted at zero per cent import duty for 100 per cent Export Oriented Units.

- Import of food processing machinery allowed freely with low level of duties (25-30 per cent). Custom duty under Export Promotion Capital Goods (EPCG) scheme with specific export commitments is only 5 per cent.
- Corporate tax policy for export earnings as well as for domestic sale has been liberalized. Corporate tax reduced from 50 per cent to 35 per cent.
- Fruits and vegetables products completely exempted from Central Excise Duty.
- 10 year tax holiday for Industrial Parks having food processing activities during initial 15 years.
- Quantitative Restrictions on all food products removed. Customs duty on majority of the products fixed at 35 per cent.
- Presence of virtually all major multi-national companies like Coca-Cola, Pepsi, Britannia, Danone, Nestle, Cadbury, Lever's Kelloggs, Heinz, International Best Foods, Walls, Perfetti, Van Melle, etc.

12.2. Potential

Food processing industry in India has been growing at a rapid speed. Foreign investment in this industry finds place as it is influenced by the following Opportunities:

- India is world's third largest producer of food due to diverse agro-climatic conditions and large trait of arable and irrigated land.
- Presently, a small percentage of farm produces processed into value added products. India need US $ 28 billion of investment to raise food processing levels by 8-10 per cent.
- Food Processing Industry is expected to grow at the rate of 16-20 per cent.

- Largely untapped domestic market of 1000 million consumers: 300 million upper middle class consumers consume processed & Packaged food; and 200 million more consumers expected to shift to processed packaged food by 2010.
- An average Indian spends about 50 per cent of household expenditure on food items.
- Demand for processed food has been rising with because of development in income levels and urbanization.
- Bilateral co-operation in the areas of Investment, Technology Transfer, and International Trade with India as base in: Fruits and Vegetables Products, Animal products, fisheries, Consumer Industry, Wine Manufacturing, Dairy Products, Food Packaging, Cold chain infrastructure, Food Processing Machinery, Food Parks and Agri Exports Processing Zone, Total Quality Management System, and Human Resource Development.

13. *Insurance, Banking and Financial Markets*

This section analyze the impact of Foreign Direct Investment initiation regarding prospects and opportunities in Insurance, Banking and Financial Market sectors in India.

13.1. Investment Policy

Insurance Sector

- FDI up to 26 per cent in the Insurance sector is allowed on the automatic route subject to obtaining license from Insurance Regulatory & Development Authority (IRDA).
- The Government had announced the raising of the FDI cap in Insurance sector to 49 per cent in the Budget 2004-05, but it is yet to get parliamentary approval.

Banking Sector

- FDI up to 74 per cent from all sources on the automatic route will be allowed in private sector banking subject to guidelines issued from RBI from time to time.
- There are 186 branches of Foreign Banks operating in India and control 5 per cent of the Market.

Non-Banking Financial Companies

- FDI in the NBFC sector is put on automatic route subject to compliance with guidelines of the Reserve Bank of India. RBI would issue appropriate guidelines in this regard from time to time.
- Foreign investors can set up 100 per cent operating subsidiaries without the condition to disinvest a minimum of 25 per cent of its equity to Indian entities, subject to bringing in US $ 50 million out of which US $ 7.5 million to be brought upfront and the balance in 2 years.
- Minimum Capitalization Norms for fund based NBFCs:
  - (a) For FDI up to 51 per cent – US $ 0.5 million to be brought upfront
  - (b) For FDI above 51 per cent and up to 75 per cent – US $ 5 million to be brought upfront
  - (c) For FDI above 75 per cent and up to 100 per cent – US $ 50 million, out of which, US $ 7.5 million to be brought upfront and the balance in 24 months.
- FDI allowed in 19 NBFC activities such as Merchant Banking, Underwriting, Portfolio Management Services, Financial Consultancy, Venture Capital, Leasing & Finance, Housing Finance, etc.

13.2. Opportunities in Insurance, Banking & Financial Market

- The Government is encouraging private sector

participation including foreign equity participation up to 26 per cent of the paid up capital in the insurance industry with the passage of Insurance Regulatory and Development Authority (IRDA) Act, 1999. The opening up of this industry offers tremendous opportunities for insurers, insurance intermediaries and other organizations connected with the industry.

- As part of the integration of financial services world over, new opportunities have emerged for banks to enter into the area of insurance, thus opening up viable opportunities to enhance their non-interest income and improve their performance.
- The Insurance sector may be hotting up for new players. A handful of foreign insurance companies – Samsung of Korea, Principal, AXA of Australia and a Japanese insurance major – are quite keen on entering India. Prudential, AIG, Old Mutual, Royal Sun Alliance and Amp operating in India through Joint Ventures with local majors.
- Since the opening up of the Insurance sector, nearly 23 private players have entered the segment in India.
- The Insurance sector in India currently allows the foreign partner to hold only 26 per cent stake in joint venture. The remaining capital has to be pumped in by a local partner. The insurance sector has been lobbying hard for opening up the FDI limits further (proposed to rise to 49 per cent in Budget 2004-05) as the sector requires huge investments to take off.
- India has moved in a major way towards financial groups by offering various financial services through separate arms. This is close to concept of universal banking. ICICI's proposed merger with ICICI Bank has marked a beginning of the trend.

- Retail Banking is another sunrise sector and holds a promising future in India. The market is growing upwards of 50 per cent every year. The major cause of the hope on retail banking is that the penetration level hitherto is about only two per cent. Thus, the actual market potential is tremendous.
- The plastic card market is growing at a healthy rate of 20 per cent. According to an estimate based on the research done by Credit Card and Management Consultancy, the Indian credit card market was expected to grow by a whopping 400 per cent, which touched to 15 million in 2001, up from only 3.1 million in 1997.
- broad investor base and a vibrant primary and secondary market provide opportunities for financial intermediaries and service providers.
- Increasing globalization combined with domestic deregulation will create a demand for sophisticated financial products as well as innovative financing techniques.

14. Retail Sector

In recent budget 2004-05, the Government of India was planning to allow Foreign Investment in Retail Sector of the Economy as FDI in retail sector will boost investments in technology.

When the Government allows foreign direct investment (FDI) in the retail sector, it should be granted in stages, with 26 per cent allowed in the initial stage, followed by 49 per cent in the establishment phase, and 100 per cent when the industry achieves maturity. Inflows of FDI in retail sector would not only boost the sector, but also have a positive impact on the economy as well as food processing technology.

Further, FDI could see an improvement in the lifestyle of the middle-income group, as the entry of international players would lift the wage structure in the industry, besides introducing a wide variety of products to the market.

REFERENCE

1. Central Statistical Organization, & *Economic Survey 2003-04*, Government of India.

7

Impact of FDI on Industrial Development

7.1. Introduction

Foreign capital and technology have been playing a vital role in India's Industrial Development. At the time of Independence, India inherited an industrial structure restricted to a few industries like textiles and sugar. There were only two steel plants and some limited development of engineering in railway workshops and assembly plants. Today, the industrial structure has been widely diversified covering broadly the entire range of consumer, intermediate and capital goods. In most of the manufactured products, the country has achieved a self-sufficiency with foreign collaboration but primarily through domestic efforts. This is indicated by the decline in relative share in industrial production of the traditional manufacturing sectors like food and textiles and the substantial increase in the production of new sectors like engineering and chemicals. The diversification of industrial structure is further reflected in the commodity composition of our foreign trade in which the share of imports of manufactured products has steadily declined and that of engineering products has become a growing component of exports. The rapid stride in industrialization has been accompanied by corresponding growth in technological and managerial skills obtained from abroad, not only for efficient operation of highly complex and sophisticated industrial enterprises but also for their planning, design and construction.

Foreign capital has also been instrumental in filling the gap between domestic saving and the capital needed for development. Further, foreign capital has helped the country in supplying the much needed foreign exchange thereby filling the foreign exchange gap to a considerable extent. The foreign exchange gap equals the difference between imports and exports which can be filled by net capital inflow.

Foreign capital has been a major factor in India's drive towards self-reliance and import substitution in critical areas. Import substitution has led to diversification of domestic production and consequent reduction in imports for certain critical areas like machinery manufacture, crude oil and petroleum products, infrastructural development, etc. The country has been able to export services such as project consultancy, design engineering and project implementation, etc. This has been made possible through the development of indigenous expertise with the help of foreign assistance.

Besides, foreign capital has helped in boosting our exports by modernizing and diversifying India's industrial structure.

The purpose of this study is to point out the impact of foreign direct investment (FDI) on various facets of Indian Industry/Economic System.

In the previous section, we analyzed sector-wise liberalized policy of the Government, Prospects and opportunities. As FDI brings with it the crucial managerial skills, technology, brand names and the experience of a global player, the Government of India has been liberalizing the FDI policy as to integrate the Indian economy with International economic system. Significantly, India has become a safe avenue for Foreign Investment in almost all the sectors of the economy.

Further, it is significant to say that India is now in good potential with regard to employment generation, investment performance, stimulating economic growth, development of infrastructure, equilibrium in Balance of Payments by accelerating its export performance, etc.

Hence, this section is devoted to analyze the impact of foreign investment on the following segments in India.

7.2. Impact of FDI on Competition and Economic Growth

The impact study of the influence of Foreign Direct Investment on the competition and Economic Growth of the Indian Economy assumes significance as the ongoing liberalization policy. Economic theory explains that the efficient functioning of markets depends on an adequate level of competition between producers. When FDI takes the form of a green-field investment, the result is to establish a new enterprise, increasing the number of players in a market and thus consumer choice. In turn, this can increase competition in a national market, thereby driving down prices and increasing the economic welfare of consumers. Increased competition tends to stimulate capital investments by firms in plant, equipment, and R&D as they struggle to gain an edge over their rivals. The long-term results may include increased productivity growth, product and process innovations, and greater economic growth. Such beneficial effects seem to have increase Gross Domestic Product (GDP) in India. Apart from other factors the inflows of Foreign Capital played an important role in accelerating economic growth also in this country.

As the flow of FDI has been liberalized and various sectors such as Atomic, Minerals, Agriculture (including plantation), Coal & Lignite, Defence & Strategic Industries, Drugs & Pharmaceuticals, Housing & Real Estate (development of integrated townships), Insurance, Mining, Petroleum, Power,

Telecommunications, Trading, etc. have been opened up for FDI, the important changes that have been occurred in the industrial pattern during the post-liberalization period are as under:

7.2.1. Industrial Growth During the Post-Liberalisation Era

The industrial sector registered impressive growth in 1995-96 during whole of the 1990s. The economic reforms had begun in 1991-92 and it was hoped that industrial growth would pick-up in response to them. However, three years from 1991-92 to 1993-94 industrial growth remained rather low. In 1994-95 industrial sector showed a sign of recovery as overall industrial growth was 8.4 per cent. In 1995-96 when rate of industrial growth rose further to 13.0 per cent, both the government and the industrialists attributed the excellent performance of the industrial sector to economic reforms. The post-reform boom petered out in 1996-97. The industrial growth in this year was as low as 6.1 per cent. The three years that followed did not show much promise as in these years the average rate of industrial growth was 5.8 per cent per annum.

During 1999-2000, Indian industry appeared to return to a higher growth rate of 8.0 per cent. There were buoyant expectations in the corporate sector. A survey of 'business confidence' conducted by the FICCI indicated that about 70 per cent of the 424 respondents expected industrial growth to rise 10 per cent in 2000-01. Capacity utilization was also expected to rise to 83 per cent, putting an end to the period of slow industrial growth.

However, industrial growth in 1999-2000 and 2000-01 turned out to be only modest. Industrial production registered a growth rate of 6.7 per cent in 1999-2000 which was distinctly lower than the expected rate of industrial growth. During 2000-01 industrial production registered a modest growth rate of 5.0 per cent, contributed by 5.3 per cent in manufacturing, 4.0 per cent in electricity and 3.7 per cent in mining. The manufacturing sector grew by only 2.9 per cent. Industrial sector registered a modest 5.8 per cent growth in 2002-03.[1]

According to Report on Currency and Finance, 2002-03, the industrial performance improved in 2002-03. This recovery is likely to be sustained in 2003-04 as well due to various industry-specific factors besides an overall rising business confidence, improvement in corporate profitability, corporate restructuring-induced productivity gains, better monsoon and softening of interest rates.[2]

The government expects the Indian industry to be an efficient and competitive one and able to stand on its own in the face of foreign competition. "In order to ensure this, Government on its part is committed to remove all obstacles and bottlenecks for efficient functioning of the industry. This would entail removal of infrastructural constraints in power, transport and telecommunications; reducing bureaucratic controls in as many spheres as possible and ensure that financial markets are competitive and capital is available at competitive rates."[3]

7.2.2. Savings and Investment Growth

The gross domestic savings rate has failed to increase during the 1990s. It was 24.3 per cent in 1990-91. Thereafter, the recovery started in 1994-95 and for two years the gross domestic savings rate fluctuated around 25.0 per cent. It declined again and remained at 24.0 per cent in 2001-02.

In India, major share of the savings are coming from the household sector. In recent years, more than three-quarters of the total savings in India were generated in the household sector. The peak in the savings are of 25.1 per cent in 1995-96 is being attributed to a significant increase in the net financial savings of the household sector. For a long period since Independence the private corporate sector did not generate significant share of savings. However, its savings had increased from below 3 per cent of GDP in 1990-91 to about 4.9 per cent in 1995-96 which subsequently declined and were at 4 per cent of GDP in 2001-02. Public sector savings have failed to increase during the post-economic reform period despite the government's pronouncements to improve the profitability of State enterprises. Since 1998-99 savings of the public sector have been negative.

Gross domestic capital formation has been generally higher than gross domestic savings by 1-2 per cent of GDP. Foreign capital inflows bridged this investment-savings gap. Domestic capital formation which was estimated to be 24.6 per cent of GDP in 1997-98 declined to 23.7 per cent of GDP in 2001-02. This level is around 2.5 per cent lower than the average for 1994-95 to 1996-97 which was definitely a substantial step up from the level of the early 1990s.

Prior to the 1990s the government relied completely on foreign borrowings to bridge investment-savings gap. Foreign Direct Investment which was virtually non-existent until 1990-91, rose during the 1990s and amounted to $3,557 million in 1997-98. It is by no means an impressive performance. Moreover, it is rather disappointing that foreign direct investment declined for two years in succession after 1997-98. Foreign Direct Investment inflows in India for the year 2000-01 were $2,339 million. These were marginally larger than the foreign direct investment inflows in the previous year when they had amounted to $2,155 million. Inflows in 2001-02, however, showed signs of improvement, which aggregate of $3,904 million.

7.2.3. *Growth of Infrastructure Industries*

Modern industrial development is not possible without a

substantial expansion of the infrastructure industries. The latter include Electricity, Coal, Steel, Crude Petroleum, Petroleum Refinery, and Cement. These infrastructure industries have a weight of 26.7 in total industrial output (1993-94=0). Electricity is one of the major sources of commercial energy and plays a vital role in industrial development of India. On account of this reason, it has been developed on a considerable scale in India during the last five decades. From 5.1 billion KWH in 1950-51, electricity generation rose to 534.3 billion KWH in 2002-03. The production of coal rose from 32.3 million tones in 1950-51 to 341.3 million tones in 2002-03. The production of Crude petroleum which was only 0.3 million tones in 1950-51 rose to 33.1 million tones in 2002-03. The production of finished steel rose from 1.04 million in 1950-51 to 6.82 million tones in 1980-81 and further to 33.0 million tones in 2002-03. The production of Cement which was only 2.7 million tones in 1950-51 rose to 116.4 million tones in 2002-03.[4]

7.2.4 FDI Inflows vs. Gross Fixed Capital Formation

Another way of examining the impact of FDI inflows is to express their share as a percentage of gross fixed capital formation. Gross fixed capital formation summarizes the total amount of capital invested in factories, stores, office buildings, and the like. Other things being equal the greater the capital investment in an economy, the more favorable its future growth prospects are likely to be viewed this way, FDI can be seen as an important source of capital investment and a determinant of the future growth rate of an economy. Figure 3.1 summarizes inward flows of FDI as a percentage of gross fixed capital formation by region for 1999. In general, FDI now accounts for about 16 per cent of worldwide gross fixed capital formation and 27 per cent in Latin America and 27 per cent in Western Europe. In the early 1990s, the figure was only around 4 per cent worldwide. It has been moving upward since; suggesting that FDI is becoming an increasingly important source of investment in the world's economies.

Gross Fixed Capital Formation as a proportion of GDP is not usually expected to rise immediately after the structural reform process begins. However, in India, it rose from 20 per cent in 1989-90 to 23 per cent in 1995-96. The growth rate of gross fixed capital formation in the post-reform period was 1 per cent lower than before.

Since, Indian Government liberalized FDI policy regime, the share of private sector in gross fixed capital formation rose from 18.7 per cent to 32.0 per cent over the period 1985-86 to 1995-96. If we consider GFCF in machinery and equipment, we note that the private corporate sector is now the leading sector accounting for merely 45 per cent of it. Further, a change in the composition of gross fixed capital formation away from infrastructure and unregistered manufacturing has been observed. This is likely to adversely

Table 7.1

GROSS DOMESTIC PRODUCT AT FACTOR COST BY INDUSTRY ORIGIN

(Rs. in crore)

Year	FDI	Agriculture, forestry, fishing, mining and quarrying	Manufacturing construction, electricity, gas and water supply	Trade, transport, storage & communication	Financing, Insurance, real estate and business services	Public Administration, defence and other services
1991-92	376	239253	167967	133080	75027	86536
1992-93	1051	252205	175175	140487	79430	90494
1993-94	2042	262059	185070	150500	90084	93632
1994-95	4241	276049	204092	166131	95085	96674
1995-96	7316	275153	229098	188167	102847	104298
1996-97	10171	299461	246848	202396	109995	110843
1997-98	13317	295050	256121	218822	122784	123817
1998-99	10550	312485	265956	235757	131892	136658
1999-2000	9409	314253	279130	255817	145863	153379
2000-01	18513	313806	298689	273380	150910	161900
2001-02	29212	333808	308935	296905	157733	170452
2002-03	22853	320433	328169	317788	174645	180286

Source: Government of India, Economic Survey 2003-04.

affect potential output and export growth in coming years. Investments by Non-Resident Indians and foreign institutional investors have largely gone to the corporate sector.

7.2.5. Increase in the Share of Industrial Sector to GDP

The share of the Industrial sector in Gross Domestic Product (GDP) has slowly but consistently increased over the pre-liberalization period. For instance, the share of industry (including manufacturing, electricity, gas and water supply, trade, communications, and other sectors) in GDP at factor cost increased from 13.3 per cent in 1950-51 to 21.6 per cent in 1980-81 and further to 24.4 per cent in 2001-02 (at 1993-94=0).

Empirical Analysis

In order to measure the impact of FDI on the industrial share to Gross Domestic Product (GDP), multiple correlation technique has been applied where; the share of industrial sector to GDP for a period of 12 years has been classified as under:

- Agriculture, forestry, fishing, mining and quarrying
- Manufacturing, construction, electricity, gas & water supply
- Trade, transport, storage & communications

TABLE 7.2

Correlation Result of FDI and the GDP at Factor Cost by Industry of Origin

Technique	*Agriculture, Forestry and logging, fishing, Mining and quarrying*	*Manufacturing, construction, electricity, gas and water supply*	*Transport, communication and trade*	*Financing, insurance, real estate & business services*	*Public administration and defence and other services*
Correlation co-efficient	0.88	0.92	0.93	0.90	0.91
Co-efficient of Determination (RSQ)	0.78	0.85	0.86	0.81	0.82
Probable Error (Limits of the Correlation)	0.88+/- 0.04	0.92+/- 0.03	0.93+/- 0.03	0.9+/- 0.04	0.91+/- 0.03

- Financing, insurance, real estate and business services
- Public Administration & defence and other services.

The results of Multiple Correlation, Correlation Coefficient of Determination and Probable Error (P.E.) have been presented in the above table.

The above results disclose that the Correlation (r) between FDI and Trade, communication sector is found to be high as 0.93 and its co-efficient determination (r^2) is 0.86, which represents a positive high significant correlation and the dependent variable (i.e. GDP of trade, communication sector) shall be expected to have influenced to the extent of 86 per cent in response to the change in the independent variable (i.e. FDI). Correlation coefficient between FDI and manufacturing, communication, electricity sector found at 0.92 with r^2 of 0.85, also observed as positive high significant. However, correlation between FDI and other sectors being 0.88, 0.90, and 0.91 respectively in case of Agriculture, mining; Financing, Insurance; and Public Administration, defence services.

Majority of the inflow of FDI is being attracted by high priority sectors, i.e. Power & Oil with 28.2 per cent of the total FDI approved in India during 1991 to 2004, 16.7 per cent telecommunications, 8.4 per cent Transportation, 7.6 per cent electrical equipment.[5] Thus, it can be concluded that these sectors have been contributing high share of production to the GDP in India.

7.3. Impact of FDI on the Export Performance of Indian Industry

The impact of Foreign Direct Investment (FDI) on the Export performance of Indian Industry has been significant to analyze, as the various policy pronouncements of the Government in recent years based on the belief that FDI helps in technological upgradation of the industrial sector and resolving foreign exchange constraints to develop by its contribution to increased exports apart from bringing in net resource, inflows on the capital account of the Balance of Payments. To quote from the Government's Industrial Policy Statement of 1991, "Foreign Investment would bring advantages of technology transfer, marketing expertise, introduction of modern managerial techniques and new possibilities for promotion of exports".

The Government of India has opted for a policy of trade liberalization in recent years. Massive trade policy reforms were announced in 1991 to open up the economy to foreign trade and to integrate the Indian economy with the global economy in the new international economic order that is taking shape with the setting up of the World Trade Organization (WTO) in 1995. All these measures to promote Foreign Investment inflows contained in the new Industrial Policy and the various concessions to such investments have provided opportunities to MNCs to penetrate the Industrial productivity in excess of domestic consumption, which resulted in export promotion.

Hence, this study has been conducted to analyze the effect of FDI on exports of Indian industry. Amount of Foreign Capital Inflows as well as the value of Exports by the Indian Industry during the period 1991-04 has been presented in Table 7.3.

As it is clear from the Table 7.3, the Foreign Investment inflows and Indian Exports have been increased considerably over the period 1991-2004 under review. From $ 24,579 million in 1991-92, Foreign Investment inflows rose to $ 50,143 million in 2002-03 and further to $ 83,030 million in 2003-04. Exports during this period also rose from $ 17,865 million to $ 61,718 million in 2003-04.

TABLE 7.3

FOREIGN CAPITAL INFLOWS AND EXPORTS DURING 1991-04

(US $ millions)

Year	Foreign Capital Inflows	Exports by Indian Industry
1991-92	24579	17865
1992-93	24240	18537
1993-94	29276	22238
1994-95	25914	26330
1995-96	24176	31797
1996-97	36191	33470
1997-98	39292	35006
1998-99	34170	33218
1999-2000	40531	36822
2000-01	55542	44560
2001-02	47108	43827
2002-03	50143	52719
2003-04	83030	61718

Source: Government of India, Economic Survey 2003-04.

Rapid increase in exports in 1999-2000 and 2000-01 is explained by recovery in world demand after the Asian crisis and the adoption of various export facilitating measures. The year 2001-02 was bad for exports as well as inflow of foreign capital as they registered decline due to weakening of global demand, poor supply response of exports due to various domestic impediments to export growth, appreciation of the rupee, etc. During 2002-03 exports registered an impressive increase of 19.2 per cent. Main reasons for this recovery have been identified as under:

- World wide economic recovery;
- Rise in Foreign Capital inflows from $ 47,108 million in 2001-02 to $ 83,030 million in 2003-04;
- Hike in international prices in 2002;

- Recovery of the domestic manufacturing sector; and
- Introduction of various export promotion measures by the Government of India.

Apart from the other factors, the inflows of foreign capital played an important role in accelerating export growth in India.

Empirical Analysis

The analysis is based on assumption that the other factors being constant, export performance of the Indian industry is due to liberalization of foreign capital regime. It can be inferred that the foreign capital has an impact on the export promotion by the Indian industry. Whether the impact is significant or not is tested by using the Regression Technique.

The result of correlation between foreign investment and exports is presented below:

TABLE 7.4

Relationship between Foreign Capital and Exports of Indian Industry

Technique	
Correlation (r)	0.921
Co-efficient of Determination (r^2)	0.852

The result in Table 7.4 shows that the Correlation coefficient between the selected variables i.e. foreign capital and exports is 0.921, indicates positive high significant correlation and its coefficient of Determination is 0.852 which indicates that the independent variable (foreign investment) shall influence the dependent variable (exports) to the extent of 85.2 per cent.

However, this impact has been further tested through Analysis of Variance (ANOVA) by using Two-way Classification Model.

Let us take the hypothesis that there is no significant difference between FDI and Exports. Applying the Analysis of Variance technique, we get the following result:

TABLE 7.5

ANOVA Table Foreign – Capital Vs. Exports

Source of Variation	*Sum of Squares*	*Degree of freedom (v)*	*Mean Square*	*F Value*
Between Variables	64.31	1	64.31	0.35
Between years	577.00	12	48.08	0.26
Residual	2200.69	12	183.39	
Total	2842.00	25		

F value (between FDI and Exports) = 64.31/183.39 = 0.35

The table value of F at 5% level of significance for $V_{1=}1$ and V_2=12 is 4.73. Since the calculated value between FDI and Exports, i.e. 0.35 is less than the table value, the hypothesis holds true. Hence, the Foreign Investment inflows and Exports do not differ significantly. Consequently, the exports may certainly be influenced by foreign investment inflows.

F (between years) = 48.08/183.39 = 0.26

The table value of F for V_1=12 and V_2=12 at 5% level of is 2.69. The calculated value i.e. 0.26 is less than the table value. Hence, the flow of Foreign Capital during the years of post-liberalisation does not differ significantly.

Hence, the analysis discloses that the export performance of the Indian industry certainly influenced by the flow of foreign investment in India.

7.4. Impact of FDI on Foreign Exchange Reserves

India has come a long way since the onset of economic reforms in 1991, which was largely triggered by serious difficulties on the external front. In over a decade of economic reforms, the level of Foreign Exchange Reserves has steadily increased from US $ 5.8 billion at the end of March 1991 to US $ 75.4 billion by end of March 2003 and further to US $ 119.5 billion by end-June 2004.

The increase in Foreign Exchange Reserves in the recent period has been on account of Capital and Other Inflows. The following are the major sources of accretion to the FOREX reserves:

- Foreign Investment;
- Banking Capital;
- Increase in other types of Capital Inflows;
- Short-term credit; and
- Valuation changes in reserves.

TABLE 7.6

Sources of Accretion to Foreign Exchange Reserves: 1991-2004

(US $ billion)

	Items/categories	*1991- 04*
A.	Reserve outstanding as on March 1991	5.8
B.I.	Current Account Balance	-28.4
B.II.	Capital Account (net) (a to e)	119.0
	(a) Foreign Investment	60.3
	(b) NRI deposits	23.3
	c) External Assistance	11.8
	(d) External Commercial Borrowings	12.1
	(e) Other items in Capital Account	11.5
B.III.	Valuation change	4.4
B.IV.	Gold Valuation	1.0
	Total (A+B.I+B.II+B.III+B.IV)	96.0

Source: RBI Annual Report 2003-04.

An analysis of the source of reserves accretion in Table

7.6 during the entire post-reform period reveals that the increase in FOREX reserves has been facilitated by an increase in the annual quantum of Foreign Direct Investment (FDI) from US $ 133 million in 1991-92 to US $ 4.7 billion in 2003-04.

TABLE 7.7

Foreign Investment Inflows and Foreign Exchange Reserves: 1991-2004

FOREIGN INVESTMENT INFLOWS AND FOREX RESERVES

(In US $ million)

Year	Foreign Investment	FOREX Reserves
1991-92	151	9,220
1992-93	589	9,832
1993-94	4,611	19,254
1994-95	5,753	25,186
1995-96	5,629	21,687
1996-97	7,816	26,423
1997-98	9,169	29,367
1998-99	5,743	32,490
1999-2000	12,121	38,036
2000-01	15,911	42,281
2001-02	14,351	54,106
2002-03	12,252	76,100
2003-04	32,603	112,959

Source: RBI Annual Report 2003-04.

The data in Table 7.7 shows that the Foreign Exchange Reserves have been increasing gradually on par with hike in Foreign Investment inflows in India during 1991-2004. As Foreign Investment is the major source of accretion to FOREX Reserves, Government of India has been liberalizing its policy regime with regard to foreign investment.

Empirical Analysis

Hence, an attempt has been made to analyse the impact of Foreign Investment on FOREX Reserves during the period 1991-2004. To calculate this, Regression technique/Correlation has been applied where the Foreign Exchange Reserves for a period of 13 years have been taken into consideration. The values are divided into two stages, i.e. the pre and post revision of FDI. The years from 1991-92 to 1998-99 considered as stage one where there is no inclusion of Re-invested earnings and other Capital flows in FDI. However, the year 1999-2000 is taken as a cut off point as FDI has been revised by including Re-invested earnings on par with the international best practices. After the revision of FDI i.e. since 1999-2000 to 2003-04, FOREX Reserves have been significantly increased due to fast growing inflow of Foreign Investment.

TABLE 7.8

Relation Between FDI and Forex Reserves

Results of Correlation Coefficient

Model	*r*	r^2
Between FDI and FOREX Reserves	0.93	0.86

From the correlation co-efficient results in Table 7.8, it can be inferred that the significance impact of FDI on FOREX Reserves is observed to the extent of 86 per cent. The value has been further tested through the Analysis of Variance (ANOVA) technique.

Let us take the hypothesis that there is no significance difference between FDI and FOREX Reserves. Applying the ANOVA technique, gives the following result:

The calculated value between the two variables 14.89 is greater than the table value; hence the hypothesis is inferred that the FDI may not significantly impact the FOREX Reserves. A slight increase in Foreign Investment cannot be attributed to Foreign Exchange Reserves, but the increase in FOREX Reserves could be due to other reasons like growth of exports, surplus on Current Account balance, strong positive earnings from invisibles. However, there is an indirect impact of FDI on FOREX Reserves as surplus found on Current Account due to high share of accretion of Foreign Investment (Table 7.6).

TABLE 7.9

ANOVA Table – FDI Vs. Forex Reserves

Source of Variation	*Sum of Squares*	*Degree of freedom*	*Mean Square*	*F Variance Ratio*
Between FDI and FOREX	5,180	1	5,180	14.89 (4.73)
Between years	6,686	12	557.13	1.60 (2.69)
Residual	4,175	12	347.92	
Total	16,041	25		

Note: Figures in brackets indicate Table values at 5% level, For V_1=1 and V_2=12, $F_{0.05}$=4.73 and For V_1=12 and V_2=12, $F_{0.05}$=2.69.

The calculated value within the years 1.60 is less than the table value, hence the hypothesis is hold accepted. Therefore, it is inferred that the growth in inflows of foreign capital during the second stage of the study period i.e., since 1999-2000 (post-period of FDI revision by including Re-invested earnings) has played a significant impact in acceleration of high FOREX Reserves which have been increased to US $ 129.55 billion by January 31, 2005.

7.5. Impact of FDI on Balance of Payments

FDI's effect on a country's Balance-of-Payments Account is an important policy issue for most of the host governments.

The Balance of Payments is a statistical statement that systematically summarizes, for a specific time period, the economic transactions of a country with the rest of the world. Transactions consist of *Merchandise, services, income, transfers* and *financial claims on, and liabilities to, the rest of the world.* To understand the concept of balance of payments the study first familiarizes with its accounting. Then it will examine the link between FDI and the balance-of-payments.

Balance-Of-Payments Accounts

A country's balance-of-payments accounts keep track of both its payments to and its receipts from other countries. Any transaction resulting in a payment to other countries is entered in the balance-of-payments accounts as a debit and given a negative (-) sign. Any transaction resulting in a receipt from other countries is entered as a credit and given a positive (+) sign. Balance-of-payments accounts are divided into two main sections: the *current account* and the *capital account*.

The Current Account transactions are grouped in to three categories. The first category, merchandise, refers to the export or import of physical goods (e.g., autos, computers, chemicals). The second category is the export or import of services (e.g., intangible products such as banking and insurance services). The third category, investment income, refers to income from foreign investments and payments that have to be made to foreigners investing in a country. A current account deficit occurs when a country imports more goods, services, and income than it exports. A current account surplus occurs when a country exports more goods, services, and income than it imports.

The Capital Account transactions involve the purchase or sale of assets. When the capital is flowing into the country at the time of sale of assets is entered as a credit on the capital account. When capital flows out of the country, enters the capital account as a debit. A basic principle of balance-of-payments accounting is double-entry bookkeeping. Every international transaction automatically enters the balance of payments twice—once as a credit and once as a debit.

Governments normally are concerned when their country

is running a deficit on the current account of their balance of payments. When a country runs a current account deficit, the money that flows to other countries is then used by those countries to purchase assets in the deficit country. A deficit on the current account is financed by selling assets to other countries; that is, by a surplus on the capital account. Countries that run current account deficits become net debtors.

Capital Account in India is classified into three major categories viz., Private Capital; Banking Capital; and Official Capital.

Private Capital is sub-divided into a) long-term and b) short-term, with loans of an original maturity of one year or less constituting the relevant dividing line. Long-term private capital covers Foreign Investments (both Direct and Portfolio), long-term loans, Foreign Currency Deposits, and an estimated portion of the unclassified receipts allocated to the capital account.

Since the Balance of Payment accounts are prepared on the double-entry system of accounting, sum of all debits equals the sum of all credits and the accounts are always in balance.

FDI and the Balance of Payments

Given the concern about current account deficits, the balance-of-payments effects of FDI can be an important consideration for a host government. There are three potential balance-of-payments consequences of FDI.

First, when a Multi-National Enterprise (MNE) establishes a foreign subsidiary, the capital account of the host country benefits from the initial capital inflow. (A debit will be recorded in the capital account of the MNE's home country, since capital is flowing out of the home country.) However, this is a one-time-only effect. Set against this must be the outflow of earnings to the foreign parent company, which will be recorded as a debit on the current account of the host country.

Second, if the FDI is a substitute for imports of goods and services, it can improve the current account of the host country's balance of payments. Much of the FDI by Japanese automobile companies in the United States and United Kingdom can be seen as substituting for imports from Japan. Thus, the current account of the U.S. balance of payments has improved somewhat because many Japanese companies are now supplying the U.S. market from production facilities in the United States, as opposed to facilities in Japan. Insofar as this has reduced the need to finance a current account deficit by asset sales to foreigners, the United States has clearly benefited from this.

A third potential impact to the host country's balance-of-payments position arises when the MNE uses a foreign subsidiary to export goods and services to other countries. There are some striking examples of this phenomenon. In the Czech Republic, Skoda, the national automobile company, was a well-established producer and exporter. After its sale to Volkswagen in 1992, however, exports boomed as the new owners redirected the company's sales efforts toward the European Union. The share of exports in Skoda's sales increased from 34 per cent in 1990 to 52 per cent in 1995 and 80 per cent in 1999.

Important measures for maintaining Balance of Payments in order are as follows:

(i) Foreign Assistance;

(ii) Private remittances from abroad;

(iii) External Commercial Borrowings and NRI Deposits;

(iv) Foreign Direct Investment; and

(v) Trade Policy comprising Export and Import Policy.

In the immediate post-Independence period, the Government of India used the sterling balances to cover the deficit in balance of payments. However, since 1991, the Government has been offering various concessions, facilities and incentives to the foreign investors with a view to encouraging foreign investment inflows into the country. The measures have helped in increasing foreign investment substantially from US $ 151 million in 1991-92 to US $ 32,603 million in 2003-04 and also increasing the share of foreign investment in the total capital inflows (net) above 54 per cent during the period of study under review. Accordingly, the balance of payments, Capital account position shall be greatly influenced by the foreign investment flows into the country, as well the balance of payment Current Account position shall be influenced by rapid growth in exports which have been increased to US $ 61,718 million in 2003-04 over US $ 17,865 million in 1991-92, and also the FOREX Reserves have been reached US $ 119.5 billion by June 2004. Hence, presently the balance of payments situation is found satisfactory.

Of all the above factors that influence the Balance of Payments position, inflow of Foreign Investment may certainly have impact. The data regarding Overall Balance of Payments during 1996-2003 is presented in Table 7.10.

It is observed from the Table 7.10 that the position of Balance of Payments (overall balance) has been increased from the year 1996-97 to 2002-03 as against negative balance of US $ -1,221 millions in 1995-96. However, the Foreign Investment inflows have been increased till 2000-01 and gradually declined during the subsequent years. In such a situation, it is difficult to study the impact of Foreign Direct Investment on the position of Balance of Payments directly. Hence, a statistical tool needs to be applied to study the impact.

TABLE 7.10

FOREIGN INVESTMENT INFLOWS AND BALANCE OF PAYMENTS (Overall Balance) IN INDIA 1996-2003

(In US $ million)

year	Foreign Investment	BOP (Overall Balance)
1995-96	5629	-1221
1996-97	7816	6793
1997-98	9169	4511
1998-99	5743	4222
1999-2000	12121	6402
2000-01	15911	5856
2001-02	14351	11757
2002-03	12252	16980

Source: Govt. of India, Economic Survey 2003-04.

Empirical Results

TABLE 7.11

Relation Between FDI and BOP

Technique: Co-efficient of Correlation, Coefficient of Determination
From 1996-97 to 2002-03

Model	*r*	r^2
Between FDI and Balance of Payments	0.41	0.17

From the result of Correlation Analysis in Table 7.11 shows that value of r=0.41 indicates a positive low correlation between the two variables (FDI and BOP). Its Co-efficient of Determinant (r^2) =0.17 indicating 17 per cent of variation in the dependent variable are caused by independent variable i.e. Balance of Payments are effected by the change in independent variable i.e. Foreign Investment.

The value has been further tested through the Analysis of Variance (ANOVA) technique to study the significant impact.

Let us take the hypothesis that there is no significant difference between the two variables as such the Foreign Investment may certainly influence the Balance of Payments position in India. ANOVA technique applied and the following result has been found:

TABLE 7.12

ANOVA Table – FDI Vs. BoP

Source of Variation	*Sum of Squares*	*Degree of freedom*	*Mean Square*	*F*	*Table value $F_{0.05}$ level*
Between Variables	28.14	1	28.14	2.60	5.99
Between Years	140.00	6	23.33	2.16	4.26
Residual	64.86	6	10.81		
Total	233.00	13			

The results in Table 7.12 show that:

For (1,6) d.f. $F_{(0.05)}$=5.99; and for (6,6) d.f. $F_{(0.05)}$=4.26.

The calculated values of F 2.60 and 2.16 are less than the table values at 5 % level of significance. As such, the hypothesis is accepted. Hence, there is no significant difference between the variables, as such it can be inferred that the inflows of Foreign Investment have shown positive impact on Balance of Payments position.

7.6. Impact of FDI on Employment

Another beneficial employment effect claimed for FDI is that it brings jobs to a host country that would otherwise not be created there. The effects of FDI on employment are both direct and indirect. Direct effects arise when a foreign MNE employs a number of host-country citizens. Indirect effects arise when jobs are created in local suppliers as a result of the investment and when jobs are created because of increased local spending by employees of the MNE. The indirect employment effects are often as large as, if not larger than, the direct effects. For example, when Toyota opened a new auto plant in France in 1997, estimates suggested the plant would create 2,000 direct jobs and perhaps another 2,000 jobs in support industries.

When FDI takes the form of an acquisition of an established enterprise in the host economy, as opposed to a green-field investment, the immediate effect may be to reduce employment as the multinational tries to restructure the operations of the acquired unit to improve its operating efficiency. However, even in such cases, research suggests that after the initial restructuring, enterprises acquired by foreign firms tend to grow their employment base at a faster rate than domestic rivals do. For example, an OECD study found that between 1989 and 1996 foreign firms created new jobs at a faster rate than their domestic counterparts. In the United States, the work force of foreign firms grew by 1.4 per cent per year, compared to 0.8 per cent per year for domestic firms. In Great Britain and France, the workforce of foreign firms grew at 1.7 per cent per year, while employment at domestic firms fell by 2.7 per cent per year. The same study found that foreign firms tended to pay higher wage rates than domestic firms, suggesting that the quality of employment was better. Another study looking at FDI in Eastern European transition economies found that although employment fell following the acquisition of an enterprise by a foreign firm, often those enterprises were in competitive difficulties and would not have survived if they had not been acquired. After an initial period of adjustment and retrenchment, new investments and employment either remained stable or increased often followed employment downsizing.

In India, during the past three decades or so, production

has been expanded in all the sectors of the economy due to liberalized policy towards Foreign Direct Investment, removing barriers to enter the MNCs in India. In response to these developments the absolute level of employment has also grown.

In the recent past, there has been deceleration in the growth of employment in spite of accelerated economic growth. The employment elasticity in major sectors of the economy has been presented in Table 7.13.

TABLE 7.13

Employment Elasticities in Major Sectors in India

Sector	*1983 to 1987-88*	*1993 to 1993-94*	*1993-94 to 1999-2000*
Agriculture	0.87	0.70	0.01
Mining and Quarrying	1.25	0.59	-0.41
Manufacturing	0.59	0.38	0.33
Construction	2.81	0.86	0.82
Electricity, Gas & Water supply	0.30	0.63	-0.52
Trade, Hotels and Restaurant	0.87	0.68	0.62
Transport, Storage and Communications	0.47	0.55	0.63
Financing, Real Estate, Insurance and Business Services	0.49	0.45	0.64
Community, Social and Personal services	0.52	0.68	-0.25
All Sectors Total	0.68	0.52	0.16

Source: Government of India, Planning Commission, *Tenth Five Year Plan 2002-07*, Volume I, Annexure 5.6, p. 163.

The data in Table 7.13 reveals that the employment elasticity in all the major sectors has been towards declining trend except in construction. Overall employment elasticity declined from 0.52 during 1983 to 1993-94 to 0.16 during 1993-94 to 1999-2000. The fast decline was found in agriculture as it declined from 0.70 during 1983 to 1993-94 to 0.01 during 1993-94 to 1999-2000.

As all the sectors of the Indian economy have been opened up for Foreign Direct Investment, it is significant to study the employment by sectors in India. The sector-wise distribution of employment is presented in Table 7.14.

From the Table 7.14, it is clear that there are four major sectors viz., Agriculture, Manufacturing, Trade, and Community, social & personal services, combinely accounted for 89.7 per cent of the total employment in 1999-2000. Mining and Quarrying, Electricity, Gas and Water supply, Construction, Transport, Storage and Communications, and Financial Sectors do not absorb much labour force. These industries together accounted for a mere 10.3 per cent of total employment in 1999-2000.

TABLE 7.14

Employment by Sectors

Industry	*Employed workers (in millions)*			*Percent distribution*		
	1983	*1993-94*	*1999-2000*	*1983*	*1993-94*	*1999-2000*
Agriculture	207.23	242.26	237.56	68.4	64.2	59.8
Mining & Quarrying	1.76	2.70	2.27	0.6	0.7	0.6
Manufacturing	34.03	42.50	48.01	11.3	11.3	12.1
Electricity, Gas & Water supply	0.85	1.35	1.28	0.3	0.4	0.3
Construction	6.78	11.68	17.62	2.2	3.1	4.4
Trade	19.22	27.78	37.32	6.3	7.4	9.4
Transport, Storage and Communications	7.39	10.33	14.64	2.4	2.8	3.7
Financial Services	1.70	3.52	5.05	0.6	0.7	1.3
Community, Social and Personal services	23.80	35.13	33.20	7.9	9.4	8.4
Total Employment	302.76	374.45	397.00	100.0	100.0	100.0

Source: Planning commission, Government of India, *Economic Survey 2001-02*, Table 10.9, p. 241.

From employment data by sectors, it is clear that since 1983, there has been decline in employment in agriculture as percentage terms. In fact, even the absolute number of employed workers declined in this sector over the six year period 1993-94 to 1999-2000. However, agriculture has retained its predominant position as a provider of employment. In 1999-2000, agriculture had accounted for 59.8 per cent of the total employment.

The number of workers employed in manufacture rose from 34.03 million in 1983 to 42.50 million in 1993-94 and further to 48.01 million in 1999-2000. There is only a marginal improvement, as the percentage of employed workers in manufacturing rose to 12.1 per cent in 1999-2000.

Next, the importance sector for employment generation is Trade, which is accounted for 9.4 per cent of the employed workers in 1999-2000 as against 6.3 per cent in 1983.

Community, Social and Personal Services accounted for 8.4 per cent of the employed workers in 1999-2000, and employment in this sector declined at -0.55 per cent in the same period. Reduction of employment may be due to discouraging fresh appointments and encouraging VRS by the Government of India.

However, Transport, Storage and Communications are important segments of the infrastructure which attracts majority of the Foreign Direct Investment, but their employment potential is rather limited. In 1999-2000, this sector accounted for a mere 3.7 per cent of the employment. Likewise, Financial Services despite their strategic role in the economy accounted for only 1.3 per cent of the employment in 1999-2000. Over the period in absolute terms, employment in this sector has rapidly grown. The number of employed workers increased from 1.7 million in 1983 to 3.52 million in 1993-34 and further to 5.05 million in 1999-2000.

Finally it is concluded that the overall employment has been increased to 340.82 million in 2001 and further to 343.36 million in 2002[6] due to the sectoral growth of Foreign Direct Investment (FDI) and sectoral liberalization of Government Policies. Hence, it can be inferred that the FDI and the entry of MNCs in the Indian Economy may certainly put in shoot up the employment opportunities.

REFERENCES

1. Data compiled from Reserve Bank of India, Report on Currency and Finance, 2002-03, (Mumbai, 2004), Table 2.15, p. 13. And Government of India, *Economic Survey, 2002-03,* Table 7.3, p. 131.
2. Reserve Bank of India, *Report on Currency and Finance,* 2002-03 (Mumbai, 2004), p. 13.
3. Government of India, Ministry of Finance & Company Affairs, Economic Division, *Economic Survey 2002-03.*
4. Reserve Bank of India, Report on Currency and Finance, 2002-03; S.K. Misra & V.K. *Puri, Indian Economy – Its Development Experience,* (New Delhi, 2004), p. 418.
5. Figure 5.2: Sector-wise share in FDI Approvals during 1991-2004, were shown in Chapter V of this Thesis.
6. Planning Commission, Government of India, Tenth Five Year Plan 2002-07, Volume I.

8

Summary of Findings and Suggestions

The present study has been broadly divided into four major parts. The first part of the study deals with the analysis of scenario of global FDI flows by selecting various regions of Developed, Developing, and Central & Eastern European Countries. The second part covers approvals and actual inflows of FDI in Indian context, which also analyses country-wise inflows of FDI into India. The third part examines sector-wise analysis of FDI as to find out the sector which attracts huge amount of FDI. The fourth part evaluates the impact of FDI flows on various facets of Indian Economy and finally presents major findings and suggestions.

Major findings from all parts of the study along with important suggestions have been presented in the following paragraphs.

Government Policy on FDI

Although the Economic liberalization has increased the inflow of foreign capital to India, it has been much lower than several other developing countries in the Asia. After reaching a highest amount of $3.57 billion in 1997, FDI inflow to India dropped to $2.16 billion in 1997 and marginally increased to $2.63 billion in 2000. India's share of global FDI flows declined from 0.75 in 1997 to 0.24 in 2000. The FDI inflow is far below the annual target of $10 billion set by the

Government. This is because of poor infrastructural facilities, lack of encouragement, etc. Not only the foreign capital is shying away from India but also it is feared that there are signs of capital flight for India.

There are many ardent critics of foreign investment and technology, and its related problems. However, the opening up of the economies of a number of nations for foreign companies and the several measures they have taken to woo foreign capitals are clear indicators of the positive contribution of foreign capital and technology.

Government of India had been considering only equity investments by excluding factors like reinvested capital in the computation of FDI. However, in 2003 Government aligned the methodology with the internationally accepted practice. As per the revised data, FDI inflow in 2000-01 is reckoned at $4.03 billion against $2.34 billion earlier, while $6.13 billion in 2001-02, $4.67 billion in 2002-03, and $4.68 billion in 2003-04.

One important criticism of the liberalization of foreign investment has been that it would take place mostly in non-priority sectors. However, about 80 per cent of the foreign investment in India since the liberalization has gone to priority sectors. Now several of the priority sectors/industries, including the infrastructural sector, which were earlier exclusively reserved for the public sector, are opened for foreign investment.

Global Foreign Direct Investment Flows

The past 20 years have seen a marked increase in both the *flow* and *stock* of FDI in the world economy. The average yearly inflow of FDI increased from about $254 billion in 1991-96 to a record high of $ 1.39 trillion in 2000, with a growth rate of 29.1 per cent over the last year.

There was a steady rise in the global FDI flows in the

Nineties. This rise was more marked during the period 1998, which was $691 billion, rose to $1087 billion in 1999 with a growth rate of 57.3 per cent. However, this growth rate has been declined to 27.7 per cent during 2000, in spite of the global FDI inflows increased from $1087 billion in 1999 to $1388 billion in the year 2000.

Global inflows of foreign direct investment (FDI) declined in 2003 for the third year in a row, by 18% to $560 billion. This follows a massive fall of 41% in 2001 (from $1.4 trillion in 2000 to $818 billion) and another 17% in 2002 (to $679 billion). This was prompted again by a fall in FDI flows to developed countries at $367 billion; they were 25 per cent lower than in 2002. Worldwide, 111 countries saw a rise in flows, and 82 countries observed a decline. It was only developing countries as a group that experienced a recovery, with FDI inflows rising by 9 per cent, to $172 billion overall.

As for as percentage distribution of Global FDI inflows is concerned, the developed countries attracted 74 per cent on an average during 1998-2003 as compared to 61 per cent during 1991-96. The share of developing countries being declined to 24 per cent during the period of study (1998-2003) as it was 36 per cent in 1991-96; and the CEE attracted just 3 per cent of the total global inflows.

The world wide FDI outflows have been increased from $597 billions in 2002 to $612 billions in 2003 with an annual growth rate of 2.6 per cent. The average global outflows of FDI during 1998-2003 found at $816 billion, out of which, Developed countries dominated with outflow of $751 billion (i.e. 92 per cent of total world FDI outflows). Developing countries shared $61 billion and the CEE $7 billion, which could be just 7.5 per cent and 0.5 per cent respectively of the total world FDI outflows.

India's Position in the Global FDI Flows

In 2002, of the total FDI flows to the developing world, India received just 2.9 per cent whereas China got 32.5 per cent, Brazil 10.2 per cent, Mexico 8.4 per cent, Hong Kong 8.5 per cent and Singapore 4.7 per cent. These economies with higher level of FDI have achieved higher level of development, and higher per capita income.

Component-wise Approvals of FDI

The amount of Foreign Direct Investment in India has been approved by various agencies such as Secretariat for Industrial Assistance (SIA), Reserve Bank of India (RBI) and Foreign Investment Promotion Board (FIPB).

It is observed that Rs. 2476.9 billions of total Foreign Direct Investment was approved through all the three agencies during the period from 1991 to 31st August 2004 under review. Out of the total approvals, FIPB accounted for Rs. 2170.4 billions, forming 87.8 per cent of total investment and claiming a gaint share. The SIA and RBI route accounted for 2.5 per cent 9.7 per cent respectively. However, the share of SIA route in total investment was 67.9 per cent in 1991, leaving 32.1 per cent to RBI and FIPB route.

Among the three agencies, FIPB route of approvals has gained a lot of significance for approvals of Foreign Direct Investment, since it has accounted for 69 per cent to 96 per cent of the total amount of investment approved from 1991 to 2004. Thus, we conclude that the amount of investment approved by SIA route was prominent in 1991, the first year of liberalization, but then onwards the FIPB route has claimed almost 80-90 per cent of total Foreign Direct Investment approvals.

Hence, the empirical analysis also strongly supports that the FIPB route plays a significant role in the process of approving the FDI inflows in the country.

Country-wise Approvals of FDI

The analysis of country-wise approval of Foreign Direct Investment in India indicates that during 1991-2004 total amount of Rs. 2476.9 billions of FDI approved from 113 countries including NRI investments.

India's perception abroad has been changing steadily over the years. This is reflected in the ever growing list of countries which are showing interest to invest in India. And as a result, India's over dependence on the US for foreign funds too has declined over the years.

However, among the top 10 investors in India, Mauritius only found increasing trend at 56.9 per cent during the period January-August 2004, as compared to 2003, which placed 2nd position by contributing 15.2 per cent of total approvals during the period under review. U.K. occupied 3rd position with 9.6 per cent, followed by Japan with 4.8 per cent, Korea (South) 4 per cent, Netherlands with 3.9 per cent, Germany 3.8 per cent, Australia (2.8 per cent), France (2.7 per cent), and Malaysia with 2.5 per cent respectively.

Approvals Vs. Actual Inflows of FDI

Analysis of FDI approvals and actual inflows discloses that the approvals of foreign investment increased from Rs. 5.30 billions in 1991 to Rs. 59.90 billions in 2004. These have increased significantly from 1992 onwards, the second year of economic reforms, and reached to Rs. 38.90 billion, which accounts for 633.9 per cent increase over 1991. They aggregated to a total of Rs. 2476.90 billions (US $ 66.73 billions) in the post-liberalization period, i.e. 1991 to 2004.

A close observation of actual inflow of Foreign Direct Investment reveals that they increased from Rs. 3.51 billion in 1991 to Rs. 120.95 billion in 2004. Cumulative inflows during 1991 to August 2004 amounted to Rs. 1283.74 billions (US $ 31.45 billions).

However, by comparing the actual inflows of FDI to that of the approved amount, we find that a significant increase in the ratio was at 66.1 per cent in 1991 due to implementation of reforms in foreign investment. Further, an interesting aspect is that, there was an increasing trend in the ratio of inflows to approvals from 1995, which found at 164.5 per cent in 2002. As the coverage of FDI revised by the Government during 2000-01 on par with the international best practices, by including Re-invested Earnings and Other capital flows, 214.7 percentage of approved FDI realized in 2003. Similarly, a steep increase in the ratio at 201.9 percentage of actual inflows of approvals observed during the period January-August, 2004.

FDI approvals over the period January 1991 to August 2004 amounted to Rs.2476.90 billions, while actual FDI inflow was only Rs.1283.74 billions. Thus, the aggregated actual FDI inflows were only about 51.83 per cent of FDI approvals during the period under review. In other words, almost 48.17 per cent of FDI approved has not been materialized.

State-wise Analysis FDI

A close examination of the State-wise approvals of Foreign Direct Investments reveals that about half of the total FDI approved, aggregating 48.5 per cent of total FDI approved, concentrated in top five States, namely, Maharashtra (14.78 per cent), Delhi (12.24 per cent), Tamil Nadu (9.2 per cent), Karnataka (7.6 per cent), and Andhra Pradesh (4.69 per cent). However, the other states in the country covered remaining 51.5 per cent of the total amount of FDI approved.

Andhra Pradesh state, where 70-80 per cent of population depends upon Agriculture Sector and recently marching towards industrialization, stood at 5th position with 1,276 numbers of approvals equal to 4.9 per cent of the total, and in terms of investment of FDI approved, was at Rs. 1,16,091 million. This is about 4.7 per cent of the total amount of FDI approved to the States. Gujarat, Madhya Pradesh, Orissa, and West Bengal positioned at 6th, 7th, 8th, and 9th respectively followed by Andhra Pradesh.

Sectoral Analysis of FDI

In terms of the industries, where amount of FDI approvals has come to India, Table 5.2 shows that the most important top 5 sectors are Fuels (Power & Oil) (28.2 per cent), Telecommunications (16.7 per cent), Transportation (8.4 per cent), Electrical Equipments (7.6 per cent), and Service Sector (6.7 per cent). These sectors have combinely accounted for 67.6 per cent of the total amount of FDI approved (i.e., more than half of the total FDI approved), whereas the other sectors attracted remaining 32.4 per cent during the period under review.

However, as for as the actual inflow of FDI is concerned, the top five sectors receiving FDI in India are Electrical Equipment $ 373 million (accounting for 18 per cent inflow), Drugs and Pharmaceuticals $ 286 million (14.43 per cent), Consultancy Services $ 214 million (10.76 per cent), Fuel including Power and Oil $ 190 million (9.55 per cent), and Metallurgy $ 164 million dollar (8.27 per cent) respectively.

Thus, the analysis highlights that the Electrical Equipment sector is the most priority sector for FDI, which claimed maximum number of FDI approvals. Accordingly, it must be noted that the investment in this sector is likely to shoot up in coming years and this sector will further dominate the Foreign Direct Investments.

The initial policy stimulus to foreign direct investment in India came in July 1991 when the new industrial policy provided, inter alia, automatic approval for projects with foreign equity participation up to 51 per cent in high priority areas. In recent years, the Government has initiated the second-generation reforms under which measures have been taken to further facilitate and broaden the base of foreign direct investment in India. The policy for FDI allows freedom of location, choice of technology, repatriation of capital and dividends. As a result of these measures, there has been a strong surge of international interest in the Indian economy. The rate at which foreign direct investment inflow has grown during the post-liberalization period is a clear indication that India is fast emerging as an attractive destination for overseas investors.

During 2003-04, Electronics and Electrical Equipment Industry attracted the largest volume of FDI Inflows US $ 3.32 billion. Transportation industry is the second largest recipient of FDI inflows, followed by Telecommunications, Energy, Service Sector, etc.

With a huge demand-supply gap still existing in the infrastructure sector, there seems ample scope for more foreign investments in this region. A more simplistic, investor-friendly and committed policies by the Government will definitely attract the attention of world economy. Hence, foreign investment is required to fill this huge gap as the Indian economy is already reeling under resource crunch.

Prospects and Opportunities for FDI

India has undertaken several concrete measures in recent years, to attract Foreign Direct Investment in the country. At present, FDI is permitted under the automatic approval route, almost all sectors except for a small negative list. FDI under the automatic route has been permitted up to 100 per cent for all manufacturing activities (with certain exceptions) in Special Economic Zones (SEZs). Foreign equity participation of up to 26 per cent has been allowed in the insurance sector (recently increased up to 49 per cent), subject to the issue of necessary license by the Insurance Regulatory and Development Authority (IRDA). 100 per cent FDI has also been allowed in telecom sector.

The ongoing economic reforms in the area of foreign investment in various sectors of Indian Industry have improved India's attraction as a foreign destination in the perception of international community.

The advantages of India as an investment destination rest on strong fundamentals which include a large and growing market; world-class scientific, technical and managerial manpower; cheap labour; abundance of natural resources; a large English speaking population; independent judiciary, etc. This is now recognized by a number of global investors who have either already established a base in India or is in the process of doing so. Ongoing initiatives such as further simplification of legislation, de-licensing, setting up a regulatory authorities at Central/State level, etc. is expected to provide the necessary impetus to increase FDI inflows in future.

The large volume inflows of FDI would depend on domestic economic conditions and the FDI policy, world economic trends, and strategies of global investors. Government, on its part is fully committed to creating strong economic fundamentals and an increasingly proactive FDI policy regime.

The positive efforts of the Government to improve the investment climate, including sustained improvement on infrastructure front, have led to renewed optimism about India as an emerging investment destination. Some of the independent assessments in this regard include:

- Findings of a joint UNCTAD Corporate Location Survey in April 2004 has shown that top three investment hot spots for the next four years are *China, India,* and *the United States.*

- The Goldman Sachs Global Economic Paper of October 2003 "Dreaming with BRICS: The Path to 2050" has predicted that over the next 50 years, *Brazil, Russia, India,* and *China* could become a much larger force in the world economy.
- The A.T. Kearney Report, September 2003, on FDI Confidence Index has ranked India sixth in the confidence Index and rated India as one of the top 10 most preferred investment locations.
- The Deutsche Bank Report, December 2002 has predicted positive growth of largely export-oriented investments in India.
- Given its growing competitive edge in the knowledge based industry, India has emerged as one of the favorite investment destinations for Foreign Venture Capital Funds (*Far Eastern Economic Review,* December 2002).

Impact of FDI on Industrial Development

1. FDI on GDP by the Industry

The Correlation result of FDI and share of GDP by the Industry disclose that the Correlation (r) between FDI and Trade, communication sector is found to be high as 0.93 and its Coefficient determination (r^2) is 0.86, which represents a positive high significant correlation and the dependent variable (i.e. GDP of trade, communication sector) shall be expected to have influenced to the extent of 86 per cent in response to the change in the independent variable (i.e. FDI). Correlation Coefficient between FDI and Manufacturing, Communication, Electricity sectors found at 0.92 with r^2 of 0.85, also observed as positive high degree relationship. However, Correlation between FDI and other sectors was at 0.88, 0.90, and 0.91 respectively in case of Agriculture-Mining; Financing-Insurance; and Public-Administration-Defence Services.

2. FDI on Export Performance

The impact of Foreign Direct Investment (FDI) on the Export performance of Indian Industry has been significant to analyze, as the various policy pronouncements of the Government in recent years based on the belief that FDI helps in technological up-gradation of the industrial sector and resolving foreign exchange constraints to develop by its contribution to increased exports apart from bringing in net resource, inflows on the capital account of the Balance of Payments.

The result shows that the Correlation coefficient between the selected variables i.e. foreign capital and exports is 0.921, indicates positive high significant correlation and its coefficient of Determination is 0.852 which indicates that the independent variable (foreign investment) shall influence the dependent variable (exports) to the extent of 85.2 per cent.

The analysis of ANOVA also discloses that the export performance of the Indian industry certainly influenced by the flow of foreign investment in India.

3. FDI on Foreign Exchange Reserves

The Foreign Exchange Reserves have been increasing gradually on par with hike in Foreign Investment inflows in India during 1991-2004. As Foreign Investment is the major source of accretion to FOREX Reserves, Government of India has been liberalizing its policy regime with regard to foreign investment.

The calculated value (ANOVA) within the years 1.60 is less than the table value, hence the hypothesis is accepted. Therefore, it is inferred that the growth in inflows of foreign capital during the second stage of the study period i.e., since 1999-2000 (post-period of FDI revision by including Re-invested earnings) has played a significant impact in acceleration of high FOREX Reserves which have been increased to US $ 129.55 billion by January 31, 2005.

4. FDI on the Balance of Payments

FDI's effect on a country's Balance-of-Payments Account is an important policy issue for most of the host governments.

From the result of Correlation Analysis in Table 7.11 shows that value of r=0.41 which indicates a positive low correlation between the two variables (FDI and BOP). Its Co-efficient of Determinant (r^2) =0.17 indicating 17 per cent of variation in the dependent variable are caused by independent variable i.e. Balance of Payments are effected by the change in independent variable i.e. Foreign Investment.

The value has been further tested through the Analysis of Variance (ANOVA) technique to study the significant impact.

The calculated values of F 2.60 and 2.16 are less than the table values at 5 % level of significance. As such, the hypothesis is accepted. Hence, there is no significant difference between the variables, as such it can be inferred that the inflows of Foreign Investment have shown positive impact on Balance of Payments position.

5. FDI on Employment Effect

Another beneficial employment effect claimed for FDI is that it brings jobs to a host country that would otherwise not be created there. The effects of FDI on employment are both direct and indirect. Direct effects arise when a foreign MNE employs a number of host-country citizens. Indirect effects arise when jobs are created in local suppliers as a result of the investment and when jobs are created because of increased local spending by employees of the MNE. The indirect employment effects are often as large as, if not larger than, the direct effects.

However, it has been observed that the overall employment

has been increased to 340.82 million in 2001 and further to 343.36 million in 2002 due to the sectoral growth of Foreign Direct Investment (FDI) and sectoral liberalization of Government Policies. Hence, it can be inferred that the FDI and the entry of MNCs in the Indian Economy may certainly put in shoot up the employment opportunities.

Suggestions

Keeping in view the findings of the study the following suggestions have been made.

1. The economic benefits of FDI, which were not appreciated by developing countries like India till recently, are too overwhelming to be ignored. Today, FDI is considered a complimentary capital that brings know-how and technology to strengthen the host country's production capacities and competitiveness. This in the long run generates surplus in the economy for use in other sectors.
2. The Government of India need to further liberalise its FDI policy as to increase the share of FDI inflows in the global context so that the country can attain high development and increase the per capita income.
3. An investment friendly environment is a pre-requisite for any deficit State with scarcity of capital resources. At this juncture when the country like India requires large infusions of funds, the Government should further open up the economy for FDI flows. Take the example of China which has attracted FDI into exporting industries.
4. The Government must also take bold steps to globalize industry by eliminating the various roadblocks. For example, the Government should crackdown the corruption. According to a World Bank study, 55 per

cent of Indian companies regularly make illegal payments to get things done. FDI investor reportedly pays 6-10 per cent of the contract value. But in countries like Singapore only 2 per cent companies faced this problem.

5. The other major barriers to FDI projects are poor infrastructure including power, roads, ports, airports and communication. Policy instability and poor corporate governance practices also hurt. Regardless of the political set up, the country's policy on foreign trade, fund flows and trade in services should always be stable and conform to global best practices. In fact, FDI should be permitted in the small-scale sector also.
6. The Government should set up a single-window facility for FDI promotion that would take care of all formalities. Cap on FDI may be kept, though at low levels, in the consumer goods industries. Indeed, FDI would promote investments, raise national output and generate employment.
7. Empirical results disclose that the ratio of Actual Inflows of FDI as to the Approved amount is very poor, which accounted for just 48.5 per cent. Hence, the Government has to take necessary steps to increase the same. Accordingly, the gap between Approvals and Actuals is ought to be reduced.
8. As various sectors have been opened for FDI, the benefits are being enjoyed by only the large scale industries as well as persons/companies having political influence. But, such benefits of FDI shall be extended to even small-scale and cottage industrial units with a view to develop the backward regions in the country.

Practical Utility of the Study

The present exercise as a whole is a fact-finding research work to predict and monitor the position of India in the Global scenario. The study has been carried out to judge the inflows of FDI into India from various countries; state, industry-wise analysis as to point out those sectors which attract high share of FDI; and ultimately to ascertain whether the Industrial Development in India is being influenced by the inflows of FDI or not. For this purpose, different statistical techniques have been applied as to derive at the empirical results.

Since the topic itself is a contemporarily relevant, the findings of this study assume a greater significance and are quite useful to various organizations and institutions.

This study has been potentially relevant to a number of authorities such as Banks, Financial Institutions, Investors, Government, Public and Private Industrial Corporations, and Research Organizations. The Government can use the findings of the study for taking major policy initiations like Foreign Collaborations, Foreign Investment Policies, Foreign Trade Policies, Mergers and Acquisitions, etc. The scholars who are presently working in this area, it will be an ideal reference to them. On the whole, the findings of this study if properly considered by the concerned authorities can go a long way in bringing a fruitful results and high degree of industrial development in India.

Further Extension of the Study

Every attempt has been made to make the study more intensive. Still there are some limitations in this study due to lack of time and coverage of data. To over come these limitations and to enhance the scope of the study, further research work may be undertaken in the following areas:

- Study of Foreign Institutional Investors – their role in the economic development;

- Impact of Foreign Portfolio Investment on the Industrial performance;
- Role of Foreign Trade – in Imports and Exports;
- Foreign Currency Reserves Position in India;
- Balance of Payments Position in India; etc.

Annexures

ANNEXURE–I

LIBERALIZATION IN THE FDI SECTOR AND CEILINGS ON FOREIGN INVESTMENT

Sector	*Ceiling (%)*	*Riders*
Advertising & Film Production	100	Automatic
Agriculture (including plantations)	0	No FDI is allowed in agriculture
Airports	100	Automatic, but beyond 74 percent government approval is a must
Banking	74	Automatic but subject to RBI guidelines
Broadcasting	20-49	Up to 20 percent in direct-to-home broadcasting and 49 percent in an uplinking hub that leases out facilities
Coal & Lignite	74-100	100 percent in coal processing points; 74 percent in exploration and mining
Defence	26	Prior approval of government required
Domestic Airlines	40	No equity participation allowed by private airlines; 100 percent investment allowed by NRIs and OCBs
Drugs and pharmaceuticals	100	Caveat: drugs manufactured fall outside compulsory licensing
E-commerce	100	26 percent needs to be eventually divested to Indian public
Hotels	100	What holds true for infrastructure goes so for hotels too
Housing and Real Estate	100	Entry allowed only in development of integrated townships and commercial premises
Insurance	26	Automatic but license from IRDA is a must
Mass Rapid Transport System	100	No qualifications
Non-Banking Financial Institutions	51-75	For up to 51 percent $0.5 million to be invested upfront; For up to 75 per cent, $5 million. 100

		percent for NBFCs if there are holding companies
Petroleum	51-100	51 per cent in petro products and joint ventures in other areas; 100 percent in exploration
Pipelines	51	FDI up to 51 per cent is allowed in the pipeline sector
Postal Services	100	Excludes distribution of letters
Power	100	FDI allowed in generation, transmission and distribution
Print Media	26	FDI up to 26 percent of paid-up capital of Indian entities publishing periodicals and newspapers dealing with news and current affairs.
Refining	26-100	26 percent in case of PSUs; 100 percent in private companies
Roads & Ports	100	No caveats; no riders. FDI in infrastructure is welcome
SEZs	100	All manufacturing activities excepting (a) arms and ammunition, defence equipment, etc.; (b)narcotics, hazardous chemicals, etc.; (c) distillation and brewing of alcoholic drinks; and (d) cigarettes/Cigars, tobacco substitutes
Tea Sector	100	FDI up to 100 percent allowed in tea sector, including tea plantations. However, compulsory disinvestment of 26 percent equity in favour of the Indian partner within 5 years required.
Telecommunications	49	100 percent investment allowed in ISPs not providing gateways
Trading	100	Only in facilities targeting export markets

Source: (i) Ashish Gupta, "Primer: Know your FDI", *Business Today,* February 3, 2002, p. 15, and
(ii) Government of India, *Economic Survey,* 2002-03 (Delhi, 2003), Box 7.2, p. 146.

ANNEXURE–II

STATEMENT OF ACTUAL INFLOW OF FOREIGN DIRECT INVESTMENT INLCUDING NRI INVESTMENT

(Rs. Billion)

Actual inflow of FDI	*1991*	*1992*	*1993*	*1994*	*1995*	*1996*	*1997*	*1998*	*1999*	*2000*	*2001*	*2002 (May)*
Government's Approval	1.9	4.8	9.9	15.0	38.7	57.6	101.3	82.4	61.9	63.4	96.4	43.3
RBI Automatic Approval	-	0.5	2.4	3.6	5.3	6.2	8.7	6.1	7.[illegible]	17.0	32.4	25.3
NRI Schemes	1.6	1.5	5.6	11.1	19.7	20.6	10.4	3.6	3.5	3.5	2.3	0.1
Total	**3.5**	**6.8**	**17.9**	**29.7**	**63.7**	**84.4**	**120.4**	**92.1**	**73.0**	**83.9**	**131.1**	**68.7**

Source: SIA News Letter, Ministry of Commerce and Industry, Government of India.

Bibliography

Books

Agarwal A.N., *Indian Economy: Current Developments,* Willey Eastern Limited, New Delhi.

Agarwal, Jamuna P., *Determinants of Foreign Direct Investment: A Survey,* Weltwirtschaftliches Archiv.

Aggarwal & Chowdhary, *Indian Economy: Crisis and Reforms,* Shipra Publications.

Ahluwalia. Isher, *Industrial Growth in India – Stagnation since the Mid-Sixties,* Oxford University Press, Delhi.

Ajit Kumar Sinha, *New Economic Policy of India,* Deep & Deep Publications, New Delhi.

Bhata, *Indian Economy: Issues and Policies,* Vikas Publishing House, New Delhi.

Bhuleshkar & Desai, *Indian Economy Under Liberalised System: Issues and Problems,* Himalaya Publishing House

Francis Cherunilam, *Global Economy and Business Environment,* Himalaya Publishing House.

Francis Cherunilam, *International Business Environment,* Himalaya Publishing House.

Gangadhar V., *Financial Trends in the Indian Corporate Sector* (Thesis Publication), Ajanta Publications (India).

Gupta. K.R., *Liberalization and Globalisation of Indian Economy,* Atlantic Publishers and Distributors, New Delhi.

Gupta. S.P., *Liberalisation: Its Impact on the Indian Economy,* Macmillan India, Delhi.

Harishankar Singhnia, *Economic Issues Global & National*, Vikas Publishing House Pvt. Ltd. Delhi.

M.L. Jhingan, *The Economics of Development and Planning*, Vrinda Publications (P) Ltd.

Manab Adhikary, Global Business Management – In an International Economic Environment, Macmillan India Limited.

Rajwade. A.V., Foreign Exchange International Finance & Risk Management, Academy of Business Studies, New Delhi.

Reuber, G.L., H. Crookell, M. Emerson and G. Gallais-HamonnoPrivate Foreign Investment in Development, London and New York: Routledge.

Ruddar Datta and Sundaram, Indian Economy, Sultan Chand & Sons Company Ltd., New Delhi.

S.K. Misra & V.K. Puri, Indian Economy – Its Development Experience, Himalaya Publishing House.

S.P. Gupta, Statistical Methods, Sultan Chand & Sons.

Sinha N.K.P. & Singh, Industrial Development in India, Rawat Publications, New Delhi.

Uma Kapila, Understanding the Problems of Indian Economy, 3rd Edition 2002-03, Academic Foundation.

Uma Kapila, *Indian Economy Since Independence: The Ongoing Economic Reforms*, Delhi Academic Foundation.

Varghese, *Indian Economy Problems & Prospects*, Ashish Publishing House, New Delhi.

Venkata Subramanian. K, *Policy and Performance of Indian Economy*, Manoj Prakasham Publications, Bangalore.

Vibha Mathur, *Trade Liberalization & Foreign Investment in India 1991-2001*, New Century Publications, Delhi.

Vinod Vyasulu Hemalata Rao, *Indian Economy: Emerging Challenges*, Printwell, Jaipur.

Articles

Brewer. Thomas, Government Policies, Market Imperfections and Foreign Direct Investment, Journal of International Business Studies.

Caves. Richard E., *Multinational Enterprise and Economic Analysis,* Cambridge University Press, Cambridge.

Chanchal Chopra, Foreign Direct Investment, Technological Build-up and Export Performance: An Indian Case, Review of Commerce Studies, University of Delhi.

Duttaray, Mukhopadhyay, *The Relation between Foreign Direct Investment and Growth: Causality and Mechanisms,* Indian Journal of Economics, Volume LXXXII, January 2003.

Firoz Rezvani, Wagdy Abdallah, *Investing in China's Economic Development Zones: A Managerial Guide,* International Journal of Management, Volume 20, June 2003.

Gangadhar V. Prof. & Yadagiri, *Trends of Foreign Direct Investment in India,* The Chartered Accountant, December 1995.

Kumar, T. Krishna, *Economic Growth, Productivity gains and Foreign Capital: A Comment,* Journal of Quantitative Economics, July 2003.

Lucas. Robert E.B., *On the Determinants of Direct Foreign Investment: Evidence from East and South East Asia,* World Development.

M.Y. Khan, *Promote FDI for higher growth,* The Hindu Business Line, December 27, 2004.

Marwah, Lawrence R. Klein, *Economic Growth and Productivity Gains from Capital Inflow: A Rejoinder,* Journal of Quantitative Economics, January 2004.

Moran. Theodore, *Foreign Direct Investment and Development,* Institute of International Economics, Washington, D.C.

Nagesh Kumar, *Economic Reforms and their Macro-Economic Impact,* Economic and Political Weekly, March 2000.

Neetu Prakash, *Foreign Direct Investment in India,* The Management Accountant, Vol. 39, ICWAI, April, 2004.

Nirupam Bajpai & Jeffrey D. Sachs, *Foreign Direct Investment in India – I,* The Hindu, June 30, 2000.

S.K. Khaitik, *Globalization and Post Reforms Scenario of Global Economy: Some Issues,* The Indian Journal of Commerce, Volume 56, December, 04.

Sadhana Srivastava, *What is the True Level of FDI Flows to India?* Economic and Political Weekly, Volume XXXVIII, No. 7, February 15, 2003.

Surendra Pradhan, *Foreign Direct Investment: Risk, Return and Host Country's Strategy,* Journal of Management Research, December 2000.

Tushar K. Mahanti, *FDI approvals rise in 2004 following improved investment scenario,* The Economic Times, November 24, 2004.

Reports and Official Publications

Asian Development Outlook 2002, 2003, 2004.

Budgets, the Government of India: 2000-01 to 2004-05.

Centre for Monitoring Indian Economy (CMIE) Reports.

DESTINATION INDIA, Issue No. 2, 2003, Secretariat for Industrial Assistance, Ministry of Commerce & Industry, Government of India.

Economic Development and Chance – South Asia and the Third World, New Age International Ltd.

Foreign Capital and Economic Growth World Development.

Finance India, Volume XVII, December 2003, 2004.

Global Development Finance 2003, 2004.

Government of India, Ministry of Finance & Company Affairs, Economic Division, ECONOMIC SURVEY, 2003-04 and previous reports.

Government of India, Planning Commission, Tenth Five Year Plan, 2002-07, Volume I, (Delhi, 2003).

Global Financial Stability Report, International Monetary Fund (IMF), 2003, 2004.

Indian Foreign Policy – Agenda for the 21st Century, Volume I – Foreign Service Institute, New Delhi, in Association with Konark Publishers Pvt. Ltd.

International Monetary Fund, Balance of Payments Manual, Washington, D.C.

Organization for Economic Co-operation and Development (OECD), Working Papers.

Publications of Government of India, Planning Commission, Ninth Five Year Plan, 1997-2002, Volume I, (Delhi, 1999).

Presidential Comments by Dr. Y.V. Reddy, Governor, Reserve Bank of India on the speech "Intolerable Surge? International Capital Flows and the Indian Policy Response" delivered by Ms. Anne O. Krueger, First Deputy Managing Director, IMF at National Institute of Bank Management (NIBM), Pune on January 21, 2004.

Press Releases, Ministry of Commerce & Industry, Government of India, August 2004.

Reserve Bank of India Reports – www.rbi.org.in

Reports Published by Secretariat for Industrial Assistance, Department of Industrial Policy & Promotion, Ministry of Commerce and Industry, Government of India, New Delhi.

Report on Currency and Finances, Reserve Bank of India.

The Economic Challenger – A Forum for Economic Thinking in the 21st Century, No. 6, Issue 23, April-June 2004.

United Nations Conference on Trade and Development, (UNCTAD), World Investment Report – FDI Policies for Development: National and International Perspectives, United Nations, New York and Geneva, 2003. (www.unctad.org).

World Bank, World Development Reports, 2002, 2003, 2004.

Index

A

Accession Eight-Czech-Slovakia, 123
Africa, 123, 132, 142
Africa and Asia, 115, 154
African Countries, 156
American Depository Receipts (ADRs), 175, 181
Andean Countries (Colombia, Ecuador and Venezuela), 165
Andean Pact, 77
Andhra Pradesh, 218, 219
Andhra Pradesh-Delhi, 232
Andhra Pradesh-West Bengal, 215
Anti-FDI Lobby, 212
Argentina, 138
Argentina-Africa, 56
ASEAN Countries, 158, 160
Asia Pacific Region, 123, 132, 160
Asia, East Europe, 113
Asian
    Countries, 209, 210
    Society, 10
    Tigers, 55, 144, 145
Australia, 193
Automatic Route (RBI), 29, 37, 39, 177
Automobile Component Manufacturer Association (ACMA), 233
Automobile Industry, 72, 233

B

Bharati Telenet, (Madhya Pradesh), 231
Bihar, 219
Bilateral Investment Treaties (BITs), 73-75
Biotech Products in India, 264
Biotechnology, 262, 263
Border Crossings, 81
BOT (Build, Operate and Transfer), 235, 237, 238
Brazil, 144, 165
British Rule, 209
Burundi, 156

C

Cabinet Committee on Economic Affairs, (CCEA), 36, 97
Canada, 116
Canada-US Auto Pact, 77
Capital
    Account Categories, 295
    Markets, 7
    Movement-Liberalization, 79

CCEA, 49
Cellular Mobile Services, 256
Central and East European Countries, (CEE), 111, 115, 116, 121, 123-125, 132, 135, 140, 165, 168, 305
Central Asia, 141
Cheap Labor, 73
Chemicals, 103
Chidambaram, P, 49
China, 57-60, 72, 116, 124, 128, 132, 135, 143, 145, 149, 194, 211, 212, 213
 and Eat Asian Countries, 55
 and India, 128, 160
 and Singapore, 55
China's
 FDI Level, 60
 Resources, 58
  Cheap Labor, 58
  Large Market, 58
China-Australia, 116
China-Korea, 158
China-Mexico, 55
Civil Aviation, 267
Coastal Open Cities, 57
Code of Liberalization of Capital Movement, 79
Compulsory Licensing, 30
Confederation of Indian Industry (CII), 10, 52
Consumer Finance, 234
Convention on Recognition-Arbitral Awards, 164
Corporate Taxation, 16
Cross Border Mergers, 111, 132
Custom Clearance Procedure, 81
Czech Republic, 168

D

Debt Securities, 15
Defence Industry Sector, 39, 41
Delphi (USA), 235
Department of
 Company Affairs, 14, 48
 Economic Affairs, 14
 Industrial Policy and Promotion (DIPP), 13-15
Developed Countries, 2, 7, 8, 20, 41, 52, 54-57, 71, 72, 77, 108, 110, 115, 116, 119, 122, 123, 125, 126, 128, 150, 153, 154, 161, 162, 173
Developing Economy, 143, 147, 209
DG Civil Aviation, 239

E

East Asia, 214
Economic
 and Industrial Development, 173
 Development, 1, 2, 3, 54, 59, 173, 174
 Development Zones (EDZ), 57
 Development Zones in China, 57
 Globalization, 54
 Growth, 2, 3, 9, 10, 11, 25, 72, 110, 113, 122, 158, 173, 174
 Liberalization, 92, 305
 Policy Reforms, 2, 214
 Reforms, 156, 279
Economy, 25, 30, 56, 66, 72, 92, 209, 214

Developing, 1
Global, 111, 113
India, 2, 25, 92, 96, 102, 214, 220
International, 65
Market Based, 9

Educational and Health Policy, 70
Electronic
and Computer Industries, 55
Registration System, 164

Employment, 8, 10, 59
Energy Conservation Act, 248
Entrepreneurship, 1
Equity Capital, 14
European Union (EU), 76, 80, 81, 124, 138, 139
Exchange Rate Policy, 69
Export, 51, 56, 296
Incentives, 92
Performance of Indian Industry, 285

External Commercial Borrowings, (ECBs), 181

F

Fast Trade Committees, 45
FDI (Foreign Direct Investment), 4-11, 12-15, 17, 21, 22, 25, 36, 37, 39-42, 46-56, 57, 59-64, 65, 69-7-75, 78-82, 93, 99, 100, 110, 111, 113, 115, 232-234, 245, 246, 251-255, 272-279, 286, 292, 293, 296, 300, 301, 305-317
Approvals-Country-wise Analysis, 185, 198
Barriers, 77
Characteristics, 7
Components, 12
Determinants, 64, 70, 73, 75-81
Economic Determinants, 81
Financing, 137
Flow, 29
Flows
in Central East Europe, 165
in Latin America and Caribbean, 162
Routes, 177
to Financial Services, 165
Growth, 75
Impact of
Regional Integration Framework on-, 78
Balance of Payment, 293, 316
Competition and Economic Growth, 278
Employment, 299, 316
Foreign Exchange Reserves, 289
Industrial Development, 276
in all Minerals, 37
in All Sectors, 61
in Diamonds and Precious Stones, 37
in India, 15, 60
in Petroleum, 37
Incentives for-, 246
Industry-wise Analysis, 219
Inflows, 202, 208, 215
Decline, 131
Salient Features, 158-160

Liberalization, 68, 70
Locational Determinants, 81
On all Automatic Routes, 38
Outflows, 150
Performance, 140
Performance Index, 142
Policies, 66, 67, 70, 79, 80, 156
Policy, 37, 54
Framework, 74
Regime, 283
Potential
Index, 144, 145
Ranking, 145
Proposals, 218
Reforms, 30
Sectoral
Analysis, 311
Distribution, 168
Pattern, 164
Sector-wise Analysis, 220, 226, 242
State-wise Analysis, 310
FERA (Foreign Exchange Regulation Act), 16, 27, 28, 45, 86, 92, 97, 207
FIIA (Foreign Investment Implementation Act), 54, 62, 207
FIIs (Foreign Institutional Investors), 35, 39
Film Industry, 37
Finland, 1'48
FIPB/SIA Routes, 206, 207, 209
FIPC (Foreign Investment Promotion Council), 207
Five-Year Plan (10th), 237
Food Processing Investment Policy, 268-269
Food Processing, 268-269
Foreign Capital, 2, 3
Foreign Capital Movement, 22
Foreign Collaboration, 94-97, 99, 101, 102, 103, 105, 106, 276
and Multinational Corporations, 103
Approval, Industry-wise Distribution, 102
in India, 107
Foreign Currency Convertible Bonds, (FCCB), 175
Foreign Equity, 231
Foreign Exchange, 25
Control, 23
Rates, 22
Reserves, 86, 290-293
Foreign Institution Investors (FII), 175
Foreign Investment Promotion Board (FIPB), 34, 43-45, 61, 97, 100, 101, 179, 180, 182, 184, 231, 238, 255
Foreign Investment, 2, 4, 7, 8, 17, 18, 20, 25, 28-30, 42, 43, 86, 214, 215, 218-227, 241
Appropriate Theory, 19
Boost Measures, 32-34
Capital Movement Theory, 16
Eclectic Theory, 21
Imperfection Theory, 17, 18
Implementation Authority, (FIIA), 46
In India, 4
International Theory, 18
Location Specific Theory, 19, 20
Monopolistic Advantages Theory, 17

Policy, 86
Promotion Council, (FIPC), 47
Promotional Law, 61
Sector Reform Program, 174
Foreign Investment,
ICICI, 241, 273
IDBI, 241
SCICI, 241
UTI, 241
Foreign Investment, Policy, 26
Foreign Private Capital, 93
Foreign Technology Collaboration, 99, 101
FPI (Foreign Portfolio Investment), 4
France, 116, 300
Free Trade Agreements-USA and Canada, 77
FTZ (Foreign Trade Zone), 57
FTZ (Free Trade Zone), 57-59

G

General Elections, 214
Germany, 193, 122, 124, 143, 147
Global FDI Flows, 115, 126, 305-307
Global FDI Flows India's Position, 308
Globalization, 9, 67, 113
Government Securities and Treasury Bills, 34
Great Britain, 300
Gross Fixed Capital Formation (GFCF), 10, 282, 283
Gujarat Earthquake, 208
Gujarat, Madhy Pradhya, Orissa, West Bengal, 218

H

High Income Economies, 147
Hughes Ispat (Maharashtra), 231
Hungary, 168
Hungary-Peru, 194

I

Immigration and Employment, 24
Imperial (now Indian) Tobacco Company, 108
Import Liberalization Program, 92
India and China, 59
India's
Financial Investment Policy, 85
Industrial Development, 28, 276
Macro-Economic Policies, 52
Share in FDI Flows, 211
Indian
Industry, 28, 92, 103, 245, 277
Market, 53
Oil and Gas Fields, 251
Stock Exchange, 32
India-Turkey, 160
Indonesia, 138, 144
Industrial
and Economic Cooperation, 28
Development, 28, 173, 281
Growth, 246
Licensing, 174
Policies, 67

Policies and Promotion Committee Report, 47
Policy, 1948, 25
Policy Resolution, 1956, 27, 93
Policy Statement, 27
Structure, 56
Industrialization, 1, 2, 29, 30, 32, 59, 72, 142, 173, 218
and Economy, 27
Industrialized Countries, 21
Industries, 28, 43, 68, 100, 107, 137
Chemical, 108
Industries/Sectors, 178, 180
Industry Ministry, 97
Information Technology, 61, 258
Action Plan, 240
Software, 240
Infrastructure Service, 215
Insurance Act, 1999, 40
Insurance Regulatory and Development Act, (IRDA), 36, 40, 46, 273
International
Capital Market, 175
Centre for Settlement of Investment Disputes (ICSID), 164
Commerce, 4
Financial Institutions (FIIs), 1
Long Distance Services, (ILDS), 257
Monetary Fund (IMF), 5, 7
Production, 111
Internet
Service Providers (ISP), 232, 257
Services, 257
Investment
Commission, 49, 50
Opportunities, 259
Inward FDI, 154
Ireland and Qatar, 145
Israel-Oman, 194

J

Japan, 66, 142, 147
Japanese
Companies, 296
Investment in USA, 72
Jawahar Lal Nehru Port (JLPT), 238

K

Kargil War, 214
Karnataka, 218, 219
Kenya, 156
Korea, 212

L

Latin America, 113, 115, 123, 125, 132, 135, 140, 165
Least Developed Countries (LDCs), 8, 115
Least Development Countries, 56
Liberalization, 41, 43, 52, 79, 80, 156, 206, 208, 246
and Globalization, 70
Economic, 101, 126
of FDI, 110
Trend of-, 97

Licensing Provisions Liberalization of-, 95
Literacy Level, 59
Local Capital Market, 176
Luxumberg, 116, 124

M

Macro/Micro Effects, 11
Macro-Economic Policies, 69
Magna International (Canada), 235
Maharashtra-Andhra Pradesh, 215
Maharashtra-Gujarat, 50
Malaysia, 212, 240
  Bahrain, Bahamas, 149
  FDI Performance, 144
Manmohan Singh, 49
Marketing (Markets), 3, 17, 18, 20-33, 56, 70, 72, 77-79, 81, 107, 110, 286
  and Management Skills, 44
  Development, 20
  Domestic, 11
  External, 11
  Foreign, 11, 63, 72
  Potential, 23
Mass Rapid Transit System (MRTS), 39, 209
Mauritius, 193, 198
Mexico, 79, 80, 164, 165
MIGA, 156, 164, 211
Ministry of
  Commerce and Industry, 13, 47, 52
  Industry, 43, 45, 46, 207
  Science and Technology, 262
MNCs (Multinational Corporations), 19, 52, 71, 92, 96, 97, 100, 103, 123, 174, 286, 301
Modernization and Restructure of International Airports (Delhi), 268
Monetary and Fiscal Policies, 69
Multinational Enterprises (MNEs), 18
Multinationals, (MNs), 12, 19, 22, 42

N

NAFTA, 76, 77, 79, 80
National
  FDI Policy Framework, 66
  Highway Authority of India (NHAI), 235
  Long Distance Services (NLDS), 256
  Statistical Commission, 60
Natural Resources, 1, 71, 73
New Economic Policy, 93, 94
New Industrial Policy, 28, 206
Non-Conventional Energy Sources, 250
Non-Conventional Energy, 229
NRI's Investment, 32, 180, 208
NSICT, 238
Nuclear
  Explosion, 214
  Test Pokhran, 208

O

OECD Countries, 79
Oil and Natural Gas Investment Policy, 251

Oil Exporting Countries, 94
Oil Exporting Developing Countries, 94
Oil Refinery, 103
Organizational and Technical Skills, 7
Orissa-Jharkhand, 249
Orissa-Punjab, 249
Outward FDI Performance, 146, 147
Overseas Corporate Bodies (OCBs), 31, 32, 34, 220

P

Panama and Singapore, 149
Patents and Copyrights, 18
People's Republic of China, 58
Peru, 164
Pharma and Chemical Investment Policy, 260
Philippines, 212
Planning Commission, 60, 240
Planning Era, 93
Poland, 168
Ports, 266
Ports and Shipping, 236
Ports Reforms Period, 99
Power Sector
  Investment Policy, 248
  Reforms and Restructure, 248
Power Trading Corporation, 249
Print and Broadcast Media, 37
Private Capital Movement, 23
Private Foreign Investment, 174
Privatization, 113, 140, 156, 175, 176, 229, 233, 268
  Policies, 67
  Program, 175, 176
Protectionist Measures, 72
Punjab-Bihar, 219

R

Refinery Industry, 251
Reforms, 2, 214
Republic of Korea, 66, 144
Russian Federation, 123, 168
Rwanda, 156
  SEBI, 35

S

Second World War, 18
Sector,
  Agriculture, 218
  Banking, 39
  Coal and Lignite, 253
  Electrical Equipment, 239
  Financial, 174
  Financial Investment, 54
  Indian Industrial, 107
  Industrial, 227
  Industries, 279, 286
  Information, Communication and Technology (ICT), 241
  Infrastructure, 43, 236
  Insurance, 40, 273
  Power, 248
  Priority, 103
  Print Media, 41
  Private, 46, 58, 174
  Public, 16, 43
  Telecommunication, 230

Traditional, 51
Textile and Tea, 51
Sectoral Distribution of FDI Flows, 153, 156
Security, 24
Sedimentary Basins, 252
Service Sectors, 30
SIA (Secretariat for Assistance), 100, 101, 179, 180, 184
Singapore, 10, 211, 240
Singapore-Germany, 198
Society, Indian, 95
South East Asia, 141
South East Asian
Countries, 61
Region, 144
Special
Composite Committee, 35
Economic Zones (SEZs), 37, 55, 57, 58, 62
State Electricity Boards Details, 249
Structural Reform Policies, 174
Sweden, 138
Switzerland, 138

T

Taiwan, Botswana and South Africa, 149
Taiwan, Province of China, 66, 144, 240
Takeovers buy TNCs, 106
Tamil Nadu, 219
Tariffs, 57, 76, 234
Tax Incentives, 97
Technical
Collaboration, 97
Monitoring Groups, 48
Technological Monitoring Group, (TMG), 14, 15
Technology, 2, 3, 5, 19, 28, 30, 31, 42, 55, 105, 173, 174, 220, 232, 306
Foreign, 2
Importing of-, 3
Policy Statements, (TPS), 94, 95
Transfer, 10, 56, 286
Telecom Investment Policy, 254
Telecom Policy, 232
Telecommunication and Finance, 165
Terrorist Attack on Indian Parliament, 208
Textile and Sugar Industries, 276
Thailand, 212
TNCs (Transnational Corporations), 11, 18, 62-64, 65, 67, 68, 70, 76, 79, 81-83, 103, 106, 108-111, 116, 122, 123, 128, 140, 147, 164
Trade Barriers, 79
Trade Liberalization, 76
Trademarks, 32, 40
Transfer of Superior Technology, 106
Transport and Communication, 103
Transport Industry, 233
TRIMS (Trade Related Investment Measures), 208

U

UK, 58, 72, 122, 124, 126, 132, 193, 194
UK, Germany, Malaysia and Denmark, 211

UK-Germany, 50
UN Commission for Asia and Far East, 23
UN Conference on Trade & Development (UNCTAD), 6
Underdeveloped Countries, 2-4, 23, 96
Universal Social Obligation (USO), 232
USA, 20, 50, 58, 77, 81, 116, 122, 124, 126, 132, 135, 138, 139, 143, 145, 147, 150, 153, 193
  Companies details, 230
  Investment in Europe, 72
  Markets, 296
  Sanctions, 214
USA and UK, 296
US-Canada, 122
Uttar Pradesh, 108, 218, 219, 229

V

Value Added Services, 230
VSNL, 232

W

World
  Bank, 164, 229
  Development Report, 54
  Economy System, 92
  Groups, 156
  Investment Report, 6, 9
  Trade Centre, 208, 286

❑❑❑